# JUST A *Little* GIRL

God shows up in the laboratory of human experience and the divine evidence radiates through the lives of those who encounter Him. Be prepared to meet Him through the profound and authentic life of Dr. Victoria Sarvadi. Far more than "just a little girl," she is a mighty woman who walks with God.

—**Bron Barkley**, M.A., D. Min.

Skillfully written, a book of personal monumental life changing testimonials! Heartwarming, encouraging, inspirational and hard to put down. A very personal and uplifting book filled with life as it is. Dr. Sarvadi's life story is a testament of God, His love, and faith in answered prayers. *Just a Little Girl* invites you, the reader into her dilemmas and glorious triumphs, and will take you thru life-changing events. A spiritual journey that is sure to edify and encourage the reader!

—**Dr. Chris and Sasha Holloway**, Ministers and Recording Artists

In *Just A Little Girl* you will see the fingerprints of God in Victoria Sarvadi's life. Her love for Jesus was evident since the time she met Him in the spirit realm as a teenager. With total dependence on God and a childlike faith, her testimony will ignite the flame of faith in many. She has experienced pain and trials—however, it was how she chose to face them that made her who she is today...a strong woman of God who found her purpose.

—**Susie Jennings**, Author, *31 Days of Mountaintop Miracles*,
Director, Operation Care International, Dallas

Tears fill my eyes as I read how Victoria Sarvadi's life has been formed by an insatiable desire for spiritual truth. My heart melts by the love and passion Vicki has beautifully expressed in the pages of her book. Each page, for me, was a feast! A feast of truth bound up in the life of an amazing and tenacious woman of God, with revelation and wisdom that few carry and exemplify these days. Her simple, yet deep way of bringing others along with her on a journey of exploration, development and growth etched in *Just a Little Girl* is truly surprising, faith producing and exhilarating. This is a book I want everyone to read!

—**Jody Ryabinov**, Co-Founder and Minister,
Songs of Israel, Zicron Yacov, Israel

Victoria's amazing story shows her heart for God and her desire to bring unconditional love to her family, friends and those around her. It isn't often we see this level of transparency in someone like Victoria—a woman who has lived a life full of challenges and blessings. Most of us worry what people might think about us—but not this courageous author. Because she opens her heart to share her struggles, experiences, and hopes—openly and without fear, we can relate to her life in a transforming way. May Victoria's accomplishments lead to victories in your life.

—**Barry and Batya Segal**, Recording Artists and
Co-Founders, Vision for Israel

*Just a Little Girl*, is a word painting on the canvas of life. Victoria Sarvadi tells a riveting story of her personal journey combined with her faith in the Almighty Creator. Through her moving narrative, our faith in G-d is fortified. This is a must read for believers and non-believers alike. You will not be able to put it down!

—**Jonathan Settel**, Messianic Recording Artist

Dr. Victoria Sarvadi is a storyteller unlike none other and her story is so unique and special that it moved me to tears, laughter and mostly to give thanksgiving to our G-D. This book is a MUST READ!

—**Rabbi Itzhak Shapira**, Author, *The Return of the Kosher Pig*,
Founder, Ahavat Ammi Ministries

# JUST A
# *Little* GIRL

*How a Clinical Death Brought a
Teenage Girl Face-to-Face With An Angel
and Head-to-Head with Her Faith*

## VICTORIA SARVADI
*with* ALLISON BOTTKE

NEW YORK

NASHVILLE   MELBOURNE

# JUST A *Little* GIRL

*How a Clinical Death Brought a Teenage Girl Face-to-Face*
*With An Angel and Head-to-Head with Her Faith*

Published in New York, New York, by Morgan James Publishing. Morgan James and The Entrepreneurial Publisher are trademarks of Morgan James, LLC. www.MorganJamesPublishing.com

The Morgan James Speakers Group can bring authors to your live event. For more information or to book an event visit The Morgan James Speakers Group at www.TheMorganJamesSpeakersGroup.com.

ISBN 978-1-63047-883-4 paperback
ISBN 978-1-63047-885-8 eBook
ISBN 978-1-63047-884-1 hardcover
Library of Congress Control Number:
2015919316

## Shelfie

A **free** eBook edition is available
with the purchase of this print book.

CLEARLY PRINT YOUR NAME ABOVE IN UPPER CASE

**Instructions to claim your free eBook edition:**
1. Download the Shelfie app for Android or iOS
2. Write your name in **UPPER CASE** above
3. Use the Shelfie app to submit a photo
4. Download your eBook to any device

**Cover Design by:**
Rachel Lopez
www.r2cdesign.com

In an effort to support local communities, raise awareness and funds, Morgan James Publishing donates a percentage of all book sales for the life of each book to Habitat for Humanity Peninsula and Greater Williamsburg.

Get involved today! Visit
www.MorganJamesBuilds.com

**A legend continues—Kate Alexander, grandchild number six.**

*TG Burnett Photography*

# DEDICATION

This book is dedicated to my husband Paul for his patient endurance during all of my late nights of typing in bed with the lights on, closed doors indicating I needed some "Do Not Disturb" time and my absence during dinners and movies that would have been ordinarily spent together as I labored to get this book written. You have been a true source of encouragement and I love you for it.

Also, to my adult children Shannon, Cynthia, Diana, Kristen, Wes and Brittany, and my four sons in law, Mark, David, Zack and John Paul, a family that truly is a reality of love and relationship and a huge source of inspiration to me. I appreciate and love you all. Thank you for loving me back.

Blessings to my precious infant and late son, little George. Mommy loves you and will never forget you. You were truly a gift from God.

To my special friends Richard and Dawn Rawson, Steve and Charissa Arizpe and Jay and Sally Mincks, all who have walked with Paul and me through lack and plenty, joy and sadness and true friendship. Our friendship is no doubt a testimony of true covenant.

To my covenant friends and now family members through marriage, Dr. Bron and Darlene Barkley who were beacons of light that guided me and my family to many truths in God and who support me in ministry even to this day.

I also would like to dedicate this book to the late Patty Medhurst Fedor, a friend who was an anchor during my times of seeking the truth of the Holy Spirit and illumination of His Word. Rest in Peace Patty.

And to my friends and Bible students of the Nathaniel Fellowship. Your incessant hunger for the knowledge of God continues to give me compounded reasons to study His Word. Thank you for all that you give back to me.

# TABLE OF CONTENTS

# Acknowledgements and Thanks

I owe a debt of gratitude to some of the most impactful teachers in the world. I wish to thank Dr. John Garr, Dr. Richard Booker, Dr. Brad Young, and the late Dr. Dwight Pryor for their friendship and for pouring their scholarly wisdom into my life. I owe a special thanks to the late Dr. William Bean who went beyond protocol to help me in establishing my graduate education through very creative means. I'll see you later Bill!

There is no way I could have organized my life story or arranged the unique presentation of my life events without my talented editor Allison Bottke. Allison was forced to deal with my menopause Swiss cheese memory and yet still create an accurate and interesting read of my life story. Thank you for your many hours and exhaustive efforts.

Thanks to Eva Marie Everson for her copy-editing. I found we had so much in common. Her margin comments were very helpful and so entertaining.

Thank you to the publishing team at Morgan James Publishing Inc. Working with you has been a pleasure and a privilege.

Hugs and kisses to my granddaughters Kate Alexander and Ashtyn Barkley for agreeing to be models for the cover of this book.

Kudos to John Paul Barkley and Travis Burnett and their company Re-raise the Bar for creating my logo, website, the Precious Gems teaching pages, and KALEIDOSCOPE, our bi-monthly newsletter. And last but not least, to TG Burnett Photography for the front cover.

# FOREWORD

By Dr. Richard Booker

It was a joy to read Dr. Victoria Sarvadi's manuscript (although she will always be Vicki to me). It is an honor that she asked me to write this foreword. In reading so many books, you learn to read paragraphs at a time. However, because of my friendship with Vicki and Paul, I read every sentence.

*Just a Little Girl* is a wonderful and compelling read. I laughed and cried from beginning to end. My wife, Peggy and I have lived through much of Vicki's story with her and Paul. As a result, I read the book from a personal standpoint as well as from the standpoint of a Bible teacher and author.

It is always inspiring to read someone's personal journey in life and Vicki's story is certainly inspiring. I appreciate her honesty in sharing the good, the bad and the ugly. We all have issues in life but sometimes writers are reluctant to share their fears and failings. While her story is written from the perspective of a woman, her human experience is just as relevant for men to read—and I hope they will.

Vicki showed great courage and transparency in telling her story. I commend her for showing her humanity, which is a good reminder to all of us that God uses imperfect people who are willing to follow Him no matter the cost. We see this in the Bible where the failings of the chosen people and the prophets, priests and kings are written along with the good they accomplished. Yeshua/Jesus is the only perfect One.

In addition to her personal life, it was a blessing to read about her spiritual journey. Many of us have followed a similar spiritual path and can certainly relate to this part of her story. Her zeal for God is obvious, and hopefully contagious, as she describes her experiences seeking Him. God is not pleased when we "settle" in a place of spiritual comfort, complacency and convenience. God hates "lukewarm" (Revelation 3:15-16) and so should we. The Bible tells us to seek God with our whole heart and to hunger and thirst after righteousness (Jeremiah 29:13; Matthew 5:6). Vicki has done this and God has rewarded her with new, fresh, and exciting revelations of Himself. I know He has much more for her as she continues her journey.

I am proud to have Vicki as a graduate of my Institute and to call her my spiritual daughter. I am encouraged that she is passing on to others what she has learned and continues to learn. The Bible says that "with what we have learned, find a few faithful who can pass that knowledge and life to others" (2 Timothy 2:2). In other words, make disciples. Vicki is doing this through her life, her teachings, and now through this book. Much more than "just a little girl," she is a woman of God who is making a difference in people's lives. I can't wait to see what else God has for her as she presses towards the mark of her high calling (Philippians 3:14).

Dr. Richard Booker, Author; Founder of Sounds of the Trumpet and The Institute for Hebraic Christian Studies

# *Prologue*
# HOMECOMING

## Yisrael – Israel

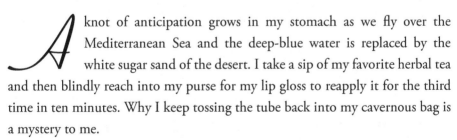

*...I will most certainly bless you; and I will most certainly increase your descendants to as many as there are stars in the sky or grains of sand on the seashore. Your descendants will possess the cities of their enemies, and by your descendants all the nations of the earth will be blessed, because you obeyed my order.*
Genesis 22:17-18 CJB

*A* knot of anticipation grows in my stomach as we fly over the Mediterranean Sea and the deep-blue water is replaced by the white sugar sand of the desert. I take a sip of my favorite herbal tea and then blindly reach into my purse for my lip gloss to reapply it for the third time in ten minutes. Why I keep tossing the tube back into my cavernous bag is a mystery to me.

I can feel the plane descending and notice the subtle shift in the sound of the powerful jets. I've been blessed to gaze out the window on the descent into some of the most renowned airports around the world. However, this approach grips my emotions. The historic and religious significance of where we are heading overwhelms me.

While there is a seemingly never-ending debate over exactly where human history began on the planet, there is no doubt the land we are approaching is where Jewish history began—the land of Israel.

However, Israel began not as a *place*, but as a *person*.

The historical facts of Judaism can all seem very complicated. Especially for non-Jews raised in America under the influence of Hollywood or the umbrella of a Christian denomination, many of which teach little to nothing about Jewish history, tradition or culture. Trust me, I get how confusing it can be. There was a time when my husband Paul and I understood virtually nothing of the Jewish roots of the faith of Jesus. Paul was born in Ohio and raised Catholic and I'm a Texas native who grew up in a Lutheran family.

*Yisrael* is the name given to Jacob in Genesis 32:28 after he wrestled with the Messenger of God who then bestowed upon him the Hebrew name *Yisrael*. Later, the twelve sons of Jacob (aka: *Yisrael*) became the forefathers of the Twelve Tribes of Israel—whose offspring were given a national identity as they became known as the Israelites. Today, ten of Israel's twelve tribes (also known as the Northern Kingdom and as Judah's *brothers*) have lost their documentation (and I believe the memories of their identities as well,) and predominantly exist assimilated in the nations as the Bible clearly states.[2] Judah, which was once a separate kingdom included the tribes of Benjamin and some of the Levites and now make up what is known as the Jewish people of today. This remnant of Jacob's children still maintain their identity and are called "the children of Israel."[3]

For many modern-day Christians weaned on Cecile B. DeMille epic films, the story of Judaism and of Israel began with the Ten Commandments and with Charlton Heston as Moses, the mass exodus of the Hebrew people from Egypt and the wrath of Yul Brenner who played Ramses, the Pharaoh.

Jewish history actually starts with the story of Abraham, his son Isaac, and his grandson Jacob. Known as the Patriarchs, Abraham, Isaac and Jacob are often referred to as the physical and spiritual ancestors of Judaism.

Some would argue whether Judaism is, in fact, a religion, an ethnicity, a culture, or a heritage. I would suggest it is all that, and more.

Understanding the Judaism that Jesus obediently observed has shaped how I see Christianity. It shapes the way I now read the Bible, and the way I approach my Messiah. It has helped to lift the fog of spiritual amnesia that for years kept me from experiencing a deeper relationship with God.

As a Christian, the more I learn about the Jewish faith of Jesus the more I want to know. And the more I know, the more I want to share this knowledge with others. This desire to teach—to share God's truth as it's revealed to me— runs through my blood like oxygenating cells. In fact, I have been given this prophetic mandate.

The truth is, after years of seeking and study, I find familiarity and comfort in the land of the people who gave us the Bible, in the prophets whose words are still being fulfilled today, and in the celebrations and traditions of the faith *of* Christ that bring balance and meaning to life. I find purpose in my love of the Messiah Yeshua—who many call Jesus—and who has ushered in the way to stand before the God of the universe.

## An Unexpected Path

I've lived a banquet style life – filled with a feast of blessings one can only describe as supernaturally miraculous. I didn't initially set out to write a memoir, and I'm pretty certain most folks who know me won't expect this. What those who know me will expect to read is something about my passion for the Jewish *Mashiach* (Messiah). With a Doctorate in Hebraic Studies, a book that speaks to my inclination to teach about the toxic changes made by the Greco-Roman church of the fourth century seems more likely. As co-founder and former associate minister of Shalom Hebraic Christian Congregation and currently the spiritual leader of a home fellowship, maybe a book on Christian Jewish roots history would make sense. Then again, I suspect some people may anticipate I would write something about parenting – seeing as I've raised six children—five of who are now parents to our nineteen grandchildren. Or perhaps something on marriage, since I've managed to have only one husband for almost four decades—a young man I married when I was a child of fifteen myself. Or maybe I would write something performing arts related, since my husband and I co-founded (through our Foundation,) The Nathaniel Center, a performing arts center in Houston.

But instead, it was the Spirit of God convicting me to write the story of how *we* met—the personal story of my journey to meet the Messiah—the Jewish Lord. This relationship—this love story—is really the foundation of my life and purpose.

I devote so much time to my Bible studies and teaching, I sometimes forget the mandate I was given to share my testimony. Although testimony is *personal*, it is not intended to be *private*, and sharing with others what God has done in our life is critical. This call is made known throughout scripture, such as in Isaiah 12:4 where it reads, "Give praise to the Lord, proclaim his name; make known among the nations what he has done, and proclaim that his name is exalted." (NIV)

## An Unconventional Warrior

It's sometimes hard to be taken seriously when you're a petite blonde with an affinity for fashion and five-inch Christian Louboutin high heels.

I get that.

I'm constantly in battle with traditional expectations. I'm completely aware I don't look like a typical Bible teacher (if there is such a thing) and certainly not one whose passion is in Hebraic study.

I've been called "over the top," "a fashionista," and I once overheard someone refer to me as a "brilliant blonde Barbie," a description that years ago would have made me bristle, but coming at this season in life made me smile.

However, for every pair of shoes I own, for every bead or gemstone I wear, I'd like to think there exists a far more substantial internal sheen. I love the Lord, my *Yeshua* (Hebrew for Jesus, God's Salvation) with all my heart and soul. And I would like to think it's not the outward bling but the inward brilliance of His love shining through that defines who – and Whose – I am.

I'm really just a little girl who loves her Abba—Father—a King who sits upon a throne of righteousness and grace. And as royalty, I imagine He possesses all the bling in the universe.

## Touchdown

The increased activity of my fellow passengers and the escalation of their volume jolts me from my reverie. I realize I have pressed my nails into the flesh of my fisted palms as I stare out of the jet's small oval window.

It's hard to believe in a few minutes we will be landing on the soil where the patriarchs of our faith lived, and where the Lord once walked.

Often something quite extraordinary happens when the wheels of a commercial airplane hit the Ben Gurion runway in Tel Aviv. Instead of the occasional sigh of relief from harried or white-knuckle travelers, there is often a collective shout of joy and hallelujah that fills the cabin like a celebratory crowd in a sports bar on game day when the winning touchdown occurs.

Applause erupts. Emotions overflow. And grown men weep unashamedly.

For many, Jews and non-Jews alike, landing in Israel is "coming home." In fact, for many Jews with one-way tickets, it actually *is* "coming home" as they emotionally make their "*Aliyah*"[4] to permanently reside in their homeland.

I had experienced this homecoming phenomenon on my first trip to Israel during Passover over a decade ago. No one on that commercial flight really knew one another, but we all shared in the joy of arriving at the most controversial piece of real estate in the world.

This trip is decidedly different, and my heart swells as I look at my fellow sojourners buckled into the plush leather seats around me.

There are only seventeen passengers on board (including three crew members), and fourteen of us are related. The activity and excitement are palpable as our plane continues its descent. I'm filled with maternal pride and joy as I watch two of my adult daughters, their husbands and eight of my grandchildren struggle to catch a glimpse out the windows of the private Legacy Embraer air jet that has been our domicile for the last eighteen hours. The children have behaved like troopers, but their little bodies are anxious to escape the confines.

I can't say I blame them.

The backdrop of the desert sand and rocky terrain give way to the white high-rise buildings of the modern city of Tel Aviv as shouts ring out, and I try to process all the information flooding my brain—and heart.

"We're almost there, babe," my husband says as he leans over the aisle with a grin and gently places his hand over mine. "We're doing it, Victoria Deeson Jackie Gleason. We're bringing all of them home."

Paul's megawatt smile is contagious—that he uses his elaborate nonsensical nickname for me from our teenage dating years makes me smile. I'm filled with such admiration and respect for my husband; we've been through so much together.

As a young girl, I had no idea what I wanted in a husband. Only that he be more sensitive and understanding than my own father. My dad was inherently a good person and a good provider, but he could be a tad discouraging and judgmental. I wanted a husband who wanted more for himself *and* for me—a husband who reached for the stars and would encourage me to do the same.

As far back as I can remember, I wanted to wedge myself deep into the crevices of life. I wanted to sing, dance, and experience everything life had to offer. Mostly, I wanted to be a wife and mother—not because my mom made those roles look all that attractive, but because of something I felt deep within my spirit. There was something inside me that always wanted to learn more, do more, and experience more—and to then share that with others. I wanted to nurture new ideas and support the exploration of possibilities not only in my own life, but in the lives of those close to me. What better way to do that, I thought, than as a mother—and wife?

I look at Paul, my family, and everything we have accomplished and know without a doubt I am exactly where God has called me—us—to be. The blueprint timeline grid of my life is playing out exactly as I saw it thirty-five years earlier in a near-death experience that started this long journey.

"I can't believe it!" I say to Paul. "This is one of the gifts on the grid...I saw all of us here!"[5]

Paul shakes his head knowingly and smiles.

The truth is, I've been "seeing" things for a long time.

Ever since I died on a bed in the ICU at the Houston Medical Center.

## A Supernatural Vision

I can't deny there are times when it's hard to claim (let alone understand) the supernatural gifts of discernment, prophecy, healing, and words of knowledge God seems to have given me. Yet like most gifts, they have come at a price.

It has taken a lot of trial and tribulation to get here, but I've grown to depend on the revelations, prophetic visions, and words from God that have become an integral part of my life. Yet it would be impossible to walk in God's truth and righteousness (and not in my own power or pride) without the leading of the Spirit. I never take for granted the open lines of communication I have with the Holy Spirit.

When this doorway of communication first opened, it confused and frightened me. Prophetic dreams and the impartation of spiritual wisdom were completely foreign to me. Paul was twenty-one; I was almost nineteen (just a little girl in many ways,) and our daughter was only three when our newborn son was called home to Heaven. Ten hours later I died in the ICU.

It was an event that changed the course of our lives.

Over the years, our individual pursuits and collective paths would take us down miraculous and majestic roads. Who knew we would, on numerous occasions, break bread with several presidents of the United States, entertain the queen of Romania in our home, and call as friends some of the most renowned Hebraic scholars in the world? Who knew our business would grow into a major publicly traded corporation with unimagined success? Who knew we would personally be connected to famous athletes, politicians and corporate owners or be co-founders of The Nathaniel Foundation that would give millions of dollars to world-changing ministries around the world? Who knew I would one day get a Th.D. in Hebraic Studies?

Who knew?

The Almighty Creator knew.

He set the plans in motion long before I was given a new life—and new marching orders.

Our Heavenly Father knew the plans He had for me—plans to travel a circuitous spiritual route in order to reach a place where I could share the

Jewish roots of the faith of Jesus—long before I had even an inkling of what those roots were.

## A Strong Pillar

The majority of my adult memories are of being pregnant, giving birth, raising children, taking care of grandchildren, and supporting the career path of my husband. I have little life experience that does not include nurturing the life of another. I have six grown children ranging in age from twenty-three to forty, and nineteen grandchildren—toddlers to teenagers—who are hopeful, talented and intuitive – many possessing wisdom and talent far beyond their years.

Yet in addition to these memories, I've had the opportunity to be involved in the development and support of a great many significant ministries that have touched countless lives all over the world. Lives that I have had a personal interest in.

I've been blessed beyond measure, and little of this would have been possible without God—and Paul Jay Sarvadi.

Paul will tell you he knew we were going to be married the first time we met.

It took a bit more to convince me, but not much.

As a teenager, I loved the usual suspects, the singers, actors, fragrances, and fashions of the time. I had a few boyfriends, but I didn't profess to be "in love" with any of them. I'm not one of those gushy love-talk girls. In retrospect, that may be one of the reasons Paul was attracted to me. For as long as I can remember, I've been somewhat aloof regarding how openly affectionate I am, and Paul has always been open for a challenge, which in retrospect made us a perfect match.

He intrigued me from the start.

"I want to be president," Paul said when we first met.

"Of what?" I asked. He was already the president of the student council; I wasn't exactly sure what was left.

"Of the United States," he said with a grin.

At sixteen and ready to be an adult, he was clearly a leader. He had so many goals, plans and career aspirations. I'd never met a boy so focused—so mature. Teachers loved him and he commanded a lot of respect from fellow students. He was in the Spanish club, the science club, on the school golf team, played second-string quarterback, and worked part-time in his own lawn service business. He didn't have to work to be smart—it came naturally to him. And he had his own car—a Pontiac LeMans handed down from his mother. I was smitten by his drive and determination, but not so much by his car.

Forty years later he still impresses me (and thankfully his cars have gotten so much better)!

As Chairman of the Board, CEO and co-founder of Insperity Inc. (a major publicly traded corporation specializing in human resources and business performance solutions), Paul will tell you he cut his teeth on business in his early twenties by way of Amway. He liked the positive encouragement and motivation that were the cornerstones of the Amway Corporation. He worked hard, and entrepreneurial success came quickly. We bought our first home before Paul turned twenty-one. As we reached the Emerald level, his ability to lead, encourage and motivate our down-line of distributors became the landmark of how he would treat and empower employees in subsequent businesses.

One of the greatest things about Paul is that he is secure enough in himself to let me be me. In other words, whether I'm assured and driven or fearful and confrontational, he is unwavering in his love and acceptance. His steadfast response to the ebb and flow of the emotional tides in my life has allowed for my unfettered growth. He is a man with a passion to follow God's call and encourages me to follow mine.

But that doesn't mean I don't throw him a curve ball every now and then.

For example, there was the time when Paul and I attended an Opera Leggera holiday performance at The Nathaniel Center.[6] Since I often produced the show and was typically in the tech room, he sat with friends.

I wish I could have seen his face when the curtain went up, and I was one of the performers in the production. The cast and crew had kept my participation and rehearsals a secret, and I had studied for six months with opera singer and expert Sasha Holloway. I always loved to sing, but opera was new to me.

That night I overheard someone talking to Paul, "I had no idea Victoria could sing opera!"

"Neither did I." Paul exclaimed with a laugh. "Very little surprises me when it comes to my wife. There is nothing she can't do when she puts her mind to it." he said.

I could also say the same about him. Without a doubt, the Spirit of God is abundantly present in my husband's life. Paul has an amazing and inspiring story of his own to tell, but it's not my place to tell his story here.

What I can tell you is that his spiritual journey and his entrepreneurial vision are truly exceptional. Today he openly gives God all the glory, honor and praise for his success—personally and professionally. A man who deeply loves and cares for his family. A man whose outstanding communication and leadership skills made him the youngest man to ever be inducted into the Texas Business Hall of Fame in 2007. A man who took the vision for a human resources business and turned it into a publicly traded company with annual gross revenues in the billions.

I suppose I could be just a tad biased, but I don't think so.

## A Debt of Gratitude

Paul and I both love Israel. We personally realize that we owe a great deal to our Jewish brothers and sisters who sacrificed so much for the sake of the spiritual condition of the Gentiles of the pagan lands during the first and second centuries.

This grassroots movement of the followers of *Yeshua* was made up of His own countrymen. These Jews, in essence, became the light of the entire Gentile world as they sacrificed their very lives to enlighten the nations to come out of paganism, which at the time included child sacrifices, temple orgies and a serious gluttony of food and wine.[7]

The greatest light to the nations came midway through the first century when a Jewish sect called "The Way of *Yeshua*" broke traditional protocol and began to share the good news of salvation to *all* the nations. In Jewish understanding "The Way" described the manner in which one lived their lives in relation to God and man and is derived or translated from the Hebrew word *hallachah* (walking out or practicing one's faith) from the word *holech* (walks).

Our family is in Israel as foreigners, sojourners from a faraway country. We are seeking truth, peace of mind and to witness the many sights and places the Bible documents as miracles in battle, places where physical and spiritual healings took place, and supernatural interventions occurred.

We are here at The Feast of Tabernacles to follow a time-honored Jewish tradition that Jesus, himself, observed and to make memories that will last a lifetime. We understand "The Way of *Yeshua*," and our desire is to walk in it.

## Appointments with God

Leviticus 23:2 depicts the celebrations that many Christians refer to as "Jewish holidays." Speak unto the children of Israel, and say unto them, Concerning the feasts *of the Lord,* which ye shall proclaim to be holy convocations, even these are *my* feasts (KJV- emphasis added by the author).

These feasts are not so much Israel's festivals, or festivals for the Jews, but rather God's appointments with man. Festivals of the *Lord.* These are God's feasts that He gave to His people.

It was Passover—the feast *Yeshua* so longed to celebrate with His disciples— that the early church fathers and believers kept and honored for centuries until First Testament wisdom began to be replaced by emerging new doctrines. In many ways, true biblical "Christianity," which was the 1ˢᵗ century faith of *Yeshua*, was hijacked. We ventured off from the rich root of *Yeshua's* ways, His lessons with their confounding idioms, His culture and traditions, His Jewish mindset, the feasts He loved, and the Word (or Torah) He embodied.

Today, many Christians are re-examining these rich appointed times of God. They are seeing the value of integrating these celebrations into their lives, and are paying homage to these festivals—these feasts—by returning to the feasts *Yeshua* loved. In so doing, Christians are actually fulfilling prophecy.

*Adonai Tzva'ot* (The Lord of Hosts) says concerning specifically Sukkot, "When that time comes, ten men will take hold — speaking all the languages of the nations — will grab hold of the cloak of a Jew and say, 'We want to go with you, because we have heard that God is with you'" (Zechariah 8:23 CJB).

At the beginning of the movie *Fiddler on the Roof,* Tevya says, "How do we keep our balance in life? We have traditions for everything—how to eat, sleep, dress, worship, celebrate, and live. Because of this, everyone knows who he is and what God expects of him. Without our traditions, life would be as shaky as … a fiddler on the roof!"

Tradition is one of the cornerstones of the Jewish life. I remember watching *Fiddler* as a young girl, and it was Tevya's opening song, *Tradition,* that stood out in my mind. I can hear it now as I think about our decision to make Israel the destination of this year's annual family vacation.

Life is all about the rhythm – the heartbeat – and the balance of tradition and biblical truth.

Today, our Nathaniel Foundation supports numerous worldwide ministries in the nations and in Israel, including Vision for Israel.[8] The founders, Barry and Batya Segal, are hosting us on this trip and will be joining us for dinner this evening at our hotel.

We arrive in Israel just before sundown and there's a tangible excitement in the air as the entire nation prepares for the High Holy Days. To be able to share this special place with our children and grandchildren at an equally special time is a hallmark experience.

People are hungry for knowledge and truth, and God is bringing us together for such a time as this. An estimated six thousand Christians have traveled from all over the world to celebrate this special holiday. It is also the birthday of our oldest daughter, Shannon Michelle, who will be joining us here in Jerusalem with her husband and six children, making the day all the more memorable.

## Safe Landing

The shouts, squeals, and applause when our wheels hit the runway are deafening, but they confirm my expectations. I hope the same experience greets our other children and grandchildren as they arrive on airlines from different locations and make their way to the King David hotel where everyone will stay.

With my feet about to touch Jewish soil, I feel more alive than ever. We are about to embark on a nine-day family vacation unlike anything we have experienced before. In fact, it's a blessing that is really a gift from God—a gift He promised me long ago.

Memories of His prophetic promise flood over me as the jet coasts to a stop on the tarmac where a caravan of vehicles awaits us.

*Thank you, Lord, for giving me this amazing family, for bringing us all here to Your homeland, for giving me the gift of Your Spirit, and for giving me another chance at life.*

I was a teenager when God gave me the mandate that eventually brought Paul and me into a passionate pursuit of the Jewish Jesus...*Yeshua*—a journey that began with my death on a cold hospital bed in the ICU many years ago.

# Chapter 1
## GOING THROUGH THE GRID

**Peretz**: One who breaks through or stands in the gap – Messiah

*Are they not all ministering spirits, sent forth to minister for them who shall be heirs of salvation?*
Hebrews 1:14 KJV

There is little doubt in my mind God has a plan for our life; He will even send angels if necessary. I know this because He sent one to me.

The doctor was concerned throughout my second pregnancy, particularly about my weight.

"Victoria, you must gain more weight. Are you eating?"

"Yes, I'm eating, but I'm just not very hungry with this baby, not like I was with Michelle."

Our three-year-old daughter Michelle (Shannon Michelle on her Birth Certificate) was in perfect health and anxious to meet her sibling. We had been "playing baby" with one of her dolls to prepare her.

The week before I was due, I became unbelievably sick.

Keeping up with an active toddler on the best of days is no easy task; it's almost impossible when you're not feeling well. I couldn't keep any food down, not even the wonderful Romanian delicacies Paul's visiting grandmother made for us. I was incredibly weak and tired all the time, and my sleep was often filled with unsettling dreams. One dream in particular that week was strange and haunting. It would be the first of many prophetic dreams I would have over the course of my life.

I dreamed I sat in a beautiful stream with crystal-clear rippling water in the middle of a dense forest, and I was about to give birth to a son. Without pain, my precious little one arrived quickly. However, when I tried to reach for him, I felt like I was moving in slow motion, almost as though I was paralyzed. Before I could take him in my arms, he was caught up in the swift current, and I watched in horror and anguish as he flowed down the stream, over the rocks and around the bend until he was out of sight.

"No!" I shouted helplessly, frozen and unable to move. Just before he disappeared, I noticed he wasn't crying and that he had brown spots all over his body, similar to freckles.

When I woke up, I immediately shook off the strange sense of foreboding that often follows a bad dream. Everything was going to be fine, I told myself. Our family was growing, and I knew God had a special plan and purpose for this child.

Some people can clearly identify a specific time in their lives when they know they had a life-changing God encounter—a spiritual epiphany. I never thought I would be one of those people, because for as long as I could remember, I was encountering God. I always knew who He was. I was raised in a Christian family and God was always a part of our lives ... Well, at least once a week. My husband was raised in a "good Catholic home," and he revered God with faithful formality. Neither of us ever doubted God's existence.

However, as we prepared for the birth of our second child, we were both about to have spiritual epiphanies and meet a very different God than the one we thought we knew.

## The Appointment

Paul always accompanied me to my doctor's appointments, and I was particularly glad on February 10th, because I didn't have the energy to go alone. This flu bug (or whatever it was) had completely sapped my strength, and I secretly hoped my doctor would admit me to the OB-GYN floor and put me on bed rest until this baby came, or maybe change his mind and conduct the C-section he initially postponed to give our baby more time to grow.

I remember climbing up on the examination table, so glad to be off my feet, and the next thing I knew I was laying on a hospital bed with Paul holding my hand. He was repeating, "Honey, please wake up, please wake up…" Our pastor was standing to Paul's right and a strange woman—a nurse perhaps—was sitting at the end of my bed crying.

I sat up and squeezed Paul's hand, but for some reason, he wasn't acknowledging me. Then, our pastor started to recite the 23rd Psalm: "Yea though I walk through the valley of the shadow of death…" (KJV)

*Who was dying? Me?*

I couldn't figure out what was going on, and because no one seemed to be listening to what I was trying to say I got frustrated and decided to lie back down.

That is how *I* recall it, but I was told later that isn't exactly what happened.

Actually, when the doctor entered the exam room at his office on that dreary February day, I was barely conscious on the examination table, unable to even raise my head. He took one look at me and immediately picked up the phone to call the hospital.

"This is Dr. Holt. I have an emergency admit coming in STAT."

When I arrived at the nearby Spring Branch Community Hospital, I was dehydrated, jaundiced and comatose within a few hours. Two days later when my labor finally started, they say I groaned, but I never woke up.

With the help of general anesthesia and a Caesarean section, our tiny baby boy was born.

I remember none of this.

As resourceful and optimistic as he was, Paul had been on autopilot as I remained unresponsive and doctors were unable to diagnose why. When I went into labor, things quickly went from bad to worse. The obstetrician eventually came out to the waiting room to report on the serious situation going on in the delivery room.

"Mr. Sarvadi, your son has been born, but he is struggling to breathe. Our neo-natal team is doing everything they can."

"A son…" Paul said quietly. "How is Victoria?"

"We're waiting for her to wake up from anesthesia. That young lady is a fighter, let's pray your boy is, too."

Paul left his Catholic roots when we got married, but he automatically prayed the formal "Our Father" after the doctor left the waiting room. However, it was a far less traditional prayer that followed.

*Please God, let my son live, and please take care of my wife.*

Our baby fought hard, but about an hour later, he gently passed from this world into the loving arms of his Heavenly Father. The nurse let Paul hold our son for a few minutes before they took him away and Paul later said the combination of love and grief he felt were unlike anything he had ever experienced. Paul's father George was also able to hold his grandson for a few precious moments, and although my dad looked at our baby and said good-bye, he couldn't bring himself to hold him.

Paul didn't know how he would break the news to me when I woke up, but he believed with every fiber of his being I would wake up. No matter how bad things looked.

## Countdown to Crisis

Ten hours after our newborn son entered Heaven, it appeared I was not far behind him. That's when the doctors decided it was critical to transfer me to the Houston Medical Center for life support.

"We've exhausted all of our efforts, Mr. Sarvadi," one of the doctors told Paul. "Your wife is still not conscious and new symptoms are manifesting rapidly. Her liver and kidneys are beginning to fail. We've given her five units of platelets but her blood still isn't coagulating. Your wife's case is exceptional—beyond anything we are able to handle."

They were going to transport me to Methodist Hospital, one of the many jewels in the crown that made up the renowned Houston Medical Center, with the hope the specialists there could determine why my health was deteriorating.

Our pastor came to Spring Branch Hospital to pray as we were waiting for the ambulance to arrive, and I learned later his recitation of the 23rd Psalm left Paul unsettled. He wasn't ready to entertain the idea I might not make it.

When we discussed this particular time later, Paul assures me his desperate pleas of, "Honey, please wake up, please wake up…" were consistently met with unresponsive silence, although I distinctly recall sitting up in bed and trying to grasp Paul's hand. I know I heard the pastor praying, and I could swear I was aware of everything going on around me.

When they loaded me into the ambulance, I thought the doctors appeared tense. Fear was apparent on their faces. I assumed they were taking me somewhere with an expert neo-natal department to prepare for my child's birth.

I just wished someone would explain things a little more, instead of acting like I wasn't even there.

*Hang on, little one, we'll be there soon,* I said silently to my baby as the vehicle began to move. I patted my bulging belly, certain I felt the baby gently kick.

## A Miraculous Change of Heart

The special circumstances allowed for Paul to ride shotgun in the ambulance during my transport—a forty-five-minute harrowing drive for my young husband. The traffic in Houston was awful, and the roads were rife with detours, potholes and bottlenecks. The frustrated ambulance driver screamed obscenities at other drivers as he made his way to the Med Center.

Paul says he was thankful I was completely unaware of what was happening, but that wasn't the case for him, and knowing the truth was killing him—and changing him.

There was nothing too difficult for Paul Sarvadi to tackle, nothing he couldn't solve, nothing he could fear. Wise beyond his twenty-one years, he was a hard-working and honest young man who deeply loved his family. Raised in a Catholic home by parents of integrity and virtue, Paul was taught great family values and responsibility, and was encouraged to excel in school.

What he wasn't taught was how to approach the God of the Universe by way of His own promise of Messiah *Yeshua*. He didn't really know God. Not personally, not relationally. But God knew him, and He was using all the pain and uncertainty Paul was feeling to change my husband's heart.

This crisis sent him to a place of faith he had never been before.

As the ambulance made its way through the frenetic labyrinth of traffic, praying seemed to be the only thing Paul could do. He says he thought about the events of that morning—our son's birth—and death. He thought about me lying unresponsive on the gurney behind him—oblivious to what was happening—about how unfair he had been to me these past few months as he was caught up in the trappings of his entrepreneurial endeavors. He thought about our young daughter waiting in anticipation at home, and about the plans he would have to make to bury our son. His mind was overwhelmed and his heart heavy. Strangely enough, he wasn't angry at God. In fact, Paul says for the first time, he was actually open to God's divine plan as it dawned on him this wasn't something he could fix on his own—and that was okay—because it wasn't for him to fix. Keeping me alive was God's responsibility—and God could do it.

It took this crisis for him to see no amount of self-discipline, self-motivation or self-confidence was going to miraculously heal me or bring back our son. Only God could do that, if He willed—and the convicting power of this Holy Spirit wisdom caused Paul's heart to change.

Years later he said, "I had become so vested in our Amway business, and financial success had become so important, I lost sight of what really mattered. It took the loss of our baby and the possibility of losing my wife to open my eyes."

As he repented for his self-righteousness, he confessed only Jesus was righteous, and he needed a relationship with Him, even if I didn't pull through.

Paul told me later that almost immediately he felt a warm blanket of forgiveness and love fall upon him, giving him comfort and reassurance of God's faithfulness.

It was then the ears of his heart opened, and he heard the still small Voice of the Spirit speak directly to him. "Have no fear. No matter what the doctors say, no matter how dire the report may be, Victoria is going to live. I have a plan for her—and you."

Paul will tell you to this day that he couldn't explain it, he couldn't quite understand it, but in that harrowing ambulance ride, God gave him a sublime gift of faith and a heartfelt peace he had never known.

While my husband sat up front praying fervently, and while God was transforming his heart and spirit, I could swear I lifted my head up to see what was going on around me. A young paramedic with brown hair steadied what appeared to be IV bags and checked my vital signs. I'd never been at this vantage point in an ambulance, and I marveled at the interesting equipment all around me. The colors were vivid—bright orange in a sea of stark white and the fluorescent light above me cast a blueish shade on the crisp white sheet that covered me. I saw everything going on around me. I remember how bumpy the ride was, and praying the jarring wouldn't hurt my baby.

Suddenly, the vehicle came to an abrupt stop as the doors swung open. Bright light surrounded me as two young men roughly pulled the gurney from the back of the ambulance. As they released the collapsed legs to full position and swiftly wheeled me into the hospital, I felt myself slipping off the stretcher and spinning as if I were inside a kaleidoscope.

"Be careful," I wanted to shout. I prayed they wouldn't drop me. Thankfully, Paul suddenly showed up by my side.

I knew he wouldn't let anything happen to me.

## Code Blue

Once we got inside, things started to happen quickly as they transferred me from the stretcher to a hospital bed and began to systematically connect me to various technical instruments, tubes and monitors. I was still upset no one spoke directly to me—what was it about bedside manner they didn't get?

After an initial examination, I saw one of the doctors walk over to Paul, who stood at the back of the room. I couldn't make out everything he said, but I heard his last sentence, and it made me angry.

"It doesn't look good. You should call your family, if she makes it through the night it will be a miracle."

*How thoughtless to say something negative like that within earshot of a patient!*

That's when I felt the bed moving again. They were taking me somewhere—very quickly—and when Paul bent down to kiss me on the forehead, I tried to scream.

"Don't let them take me, Paul! They don't have me positioned right on this bed—and they're moving way too fast—the baby and I are going to fall off...I can feel us falling..."

I had felt an unsteady floating sensation from the moment they pulled me from the ambulance, as though the gurney was not level or I was hanging off of it somehow. Now, as they hurried me into yet another room with even harsher lights, the fear became reality as the security of the bed vanished, and I felt myself fall—and die.

Suddenly, the equipment around me made loud beeping sounds to alert the hospital staff something was wrong.

"Code Blue, ICU, Code Blue, ICU."

In his book *90 Minutes in Heaven*, Don Piper recalls what it was like when he found himself standing in heaven after dying on the road in a horrific traffic accident.

It wasn't like that for me. I didn't have any sense of myself standing on firm celestial ground when I died, only a profound sense of falling head-first into a void of space and time, with ever-increasing velocity. Like falling off the roof of a very tall building.

I felt like I was free-falling very fast through what I can only describe as a grid of time measurement. A blueprint-like scale of grid lines and I instinctively knew this timeline was personal and uniquely mine. It was my own universe, a divine future plan of time and space calculations—a place I shouldn't be moving through at such a warped speed. It was at that point I realized I was dying. The term, "Life is passing you by," suddenly had new meaning to me, as I felt the sensation of literally passing through my grid of life considerably faster than human time.

Yet, I was unafraid.

What I vividly recall as I fell through my lifetime grid was the awareness of an incredible amount of knowledge available to me at various points along the way. All of this knowledge was like treasure to me, treasure troves of information and keys to hidden secrets that reminded me of gems or golden bars. They glistened and shone and were so beautiful. I knew these treasure boxes contained the mysteries of God's Word, gifts of prophecy, teaching, knowledge and wonderful experiences involving people I loved—and God. I knew these gifts were specifically and irrevocably mine. I wanted these treasures. In fact, I felt like they were *rightfully* mine—after all, this was my life I was passing through! But I had to leave them all behind as my hastened journey through time would not allow me to acquire—experience—any of these gifts.

Suddenly, the space through which I was soaring tunneled and narrowed and when I could go no further I stopped falling—like being stuck in the tip of a funnel. Then, I felt an immediate release from my physical body—like I was being delivered out of myself. I literally felt my life force—my spirit—leave my body.

In this newly birthed "spirit self," I retained all of my mental faculties. I could see, remember and reason. I could feel emotions, and I still had all my memories and my personality. Yet there was a euphoric realization that I felt no pain—I was somehow disconnected from that earthly burden. I felt wonderful freedom, no longer restricted to the limitations of my human body.

I had a clear presence of mind, will and emotions—everything about me was still intact but not in a physical sense. I felt like I could move anywhere, through walls, even the cosmic universe if I wanted to, but then I realized something was holding me back from ultimate freedom. It was as if an invisible tether or umbilical cord connected me to some kind of weight.

Then, from a vantage point high above, I looked down at what was keeping me from experiencing complete freedom and what I saw amazed me. It was my own body. It didn't even look like me. My color looked wrong, sort of a greenish yellow. Severe edema made me look puffy and bloated. My eyes looked swollen shut, like a defeated boxer. There were tubes everywhere. And I instinctively knew the body I was looking at was not pregnant—that my baby was gone.

A deep sadness washed over my spirit as I continued to look down at my body, and that's when I realized I wasn't alone. Hovering to my right was a great and powerful messenger of glowing bronze and amber, clothed in shining white. In a split second, I realized I recognized him and knew him by name.

"*Peretz*," I said in my spirit, and I instinctively knew he had been with me all my life. He had been my protector, my teacher, my guardian angel.

As we watched the doctors and nurses work to revive the body that was not breathing, we began to communicate silently—I guess you could say telepathically—in absolute perfect understanding.

"*Peretz*, where is my baby?" I asked.

"Your son is on the lap of the Father. All is well."

"Please, take me to him, I want to see my son and the Father, please lead me to them."

"This isn't your time to go," he responded. "You need to go back and finish living your life."

"But I can't go back, I can't…please help me, *Peretz*…please cut the cord… untether me…set me free."

I wanted to break through, to move on to the next dimension instead of being stuck in between. I wanted to be with my baby.

"Be patient, child. You will be returning soon, in just a few minutes," he said.

I looked down at my body. I knew it was painful there, and I really didn't want to go back.

"*Peretz*, I don't want to go back."

I distinctly remember actually trying to reason with the powerful messenger, explaining that my husband was perfectly capable of caring for Michelle. They would be fine without me, that my son needed me. *Peretz* assured me my baby was safe—he had passed quickly from his earthly life into his Heavenly one.

It was then I received the prophetic words from *Peretz* that would change my life. Words I sought desperately to understand—words that would only make sense after years of seeking and spiritual growth.

His words were profound, powerful, and voluminous—impossible to repeat verbatim. It was like encyclopedic revelation downloaded instantaneously to my mind. However, the gist of the communication remains crystal clear. He told me the grid of time and space I fell through was God's plan for my future—a plan already in place, calculated and numbered for me to live. He told me I needed to acquire the gifts of knowledge, wisdom, and understanding God irrevocably had gifted to me.

Now, here's the part that amazes me every time I think about it—or share it. Even after everything he told me about the treasures and gifts that were going to be mine, I once again tried to reason with him—to get him to change his mind. I tried to talk my guardian angel out of "making" me go back.

Unbelievable, right?

I told him even though I wanted all the gifts, and everything looked really wonderful, I was willing to let it all go to stay with my baby and go on into the heavenly realm. (I expect when I actually do get to Heaven, and can one-day talk with *Peretz* again, he will tell me what a bobble head I sounded like at this moment.)

"The Father has much for you to do," he said. "You need to go back."

Then, my Angel said something that stopped my arguments.

"The Sovereign One has heard the prayers of the saints and has honored them for His glory."

I now understood this wasn't just about me. It was about the people—the saints—who cared about me—who were fervently praying for me. God was answering—and honoring—their prayers. It was about the Holy One and His Glory. It was about His irrevocable plans, purposes and gifts for my life. He had things He wanted to give me, and important things He wanted me to do.

"Your testimony will create faith in many," *Peretz* said. "You will finish your days, go through your time and space grid as God ordained, and you will acquire special gifts of knowledge God intends you to use for His plans and purposes."

This was so much information to process, yet I understood what a gift it was.

Then, God began to pour out revelation after revelation through my guardian angel, and in my spirit, I began to know things I had never known before. What I was experiencing was spiritual, but it was just as real as a physical experience.

*Peretz* glowed with the revelation he shared, and assured me God's Spirit was going to help me accomplish all He wanted me to do.

"Victoria, all the treasures you saw will be yours!"

Although it would take decades to completely understand and process everything I heard, I would never forget *Peretz's* last words to me as I felt the strong tug on the tether and began to quickly descend toward my body.

"You will acquire all the gifts of knowledge, wisdom, and experience you saw in the grid, and as the Words of God are revealed and imparted, you will teach many others what the Spirit of God reveals to you."

Just before my spirit returned to my physical body, I looked once more at *Peretz* hovering protectively over me, and I suddenly remembered my first vision of him, back when I was just a little girl.

## Chapter 2
# PROVING HIM WRONG

**Avinu**: Our Father—Daddy

*But to as many as did receive him, to those who put their trust in his person and power, he gave the right to become children of God, not because of bloodline, physical impulse or human intention, but because of God.*

John 1:12-13 CJB

*I* didn't have a *conscious* memory of the event when I first met my guardian Angel. I was very young, but nonetheless, seeing *Peretz* jarred a familiar experience firmly imprinted in my spirit.

My mother had an elaborate Singer sewing machine in a heavy wooden cabinet. Growing up, I remember Mom sewing clothes for my younger sister and me on that fancy machine.

I was learning to walk and using everything as a crutch in order to stand. I'm not sure how I did it, but I managed to upset the sewing machine cabinet while trying to pull myself up, and it tipped over on top of me. It happened so fast that my parents thought I was instantly dead because I didn't cry, and I wasn't moving—my eyes fixed and mouth open. As they rushed to lift the cabinet off my tiny chest, I took a big breath. There wasn't a scratch on me—it was as though something—someone—had come between me and the cabinet.

Over the years, when recalling the event, my parents often said, "That cabinet should have crushed you, or cut you in half."

After that, Mom said I often spoke of angels, pointing at things unseen to her.

A classic religious picture hung over my bed as a child. I was awed by it.

The picture showed two barefoot children walking over a perilous bridge with rushing water underneath, one older girl with a little boy I assumed was her brother. She appeared quite protective of him, and because I had a younger sister, I understood this protective nature. She had her right arm around his shoulders and in her left hand, she carried a cute little basket. With her full skirt, white puff-sleeved blouse, black vest and apron, she reminded me of Heidi, the little orphan girl in a Shirley Temple movie I'd seen on television. The two children in the painting had escaped the certain death of falling through a broken slat in the bridge because their (very prominent) guardian angel was hovering above—watching over them.

I was mesmerized by the magnificence of the golden-haired angel with huge white wings. She wore a billowing light pink flowing robe with a sea foam green shawl. Her protective hands were outstretched toward the children. A beatific glow around the crown of her head seemed to emanate from the single star suspended just at the top. The angel was beautiful, and I stared at this painting and prayed and talked to my own guardian angel.

The theology of angels is clearly present in both Testaments. Angels have long held prominent positions in literary and artistic works. Although the artist of this particular painting is unknown, the painting itself is extremely well known (especially by my fellow baby boomers.) I don't know what became of that picture in my room, but I wish I still had it.

The original was painted around 1880, and the first mass reproduction appeared on a 1900 German postcard. It became known as the Heilige Schutzengel painting, which is German for Holy Guardian Angel.

Although my parents raised me in the Lutheran church, Mom (Frances) and Dad (Rodney) were originally Baptist, but at some point early in their marriage, they both adopted the Lutheran doctrine. Becoming Lutheran allowed my father to drink beer, and come 5:00 each evening, he looked forward to "popping a couple flip tops."

You might say we had a faith of "formality," not necessarily a living faith.

My parents were not openly affectionate with one another, the only time I recall them actually touching was when they would occasionally dance the jitterbug in our living room. This was often to a Fats Domino or Everly Brothers tune. I loved to watch them dance.

I was raised by a strict father and an emotionally distant mother. Not so much an unusual combination, especially for someone born and raised in the Bible belt of Texas.

In my early years, we were an active family, always involved in something. We often went to baseball and football games at the Astrodome and every year we attended the livestock show and rodeo. I remember taking vacations to places like Galveston, Corpus Christi, Padre Island, San Marcus, San Antonio, and even Mexico. Creatures of habit, we always stayed in Howard Johnson's and stopped at every Stuckey's along the way for white divinity and pecan rolls.

I have good memories of times with my dog Bruno, a collie that actually allowed me to ride him like a horse. He also growled at my parents if they took a switch or a belt to me. I quickly learned to run and call out to Bruno when I had been reprimanded.

Mom sewed matching dresses for my sister and me. We always looked like two Shirley Temple clones, with can-can dresses over layers of tulle. Gosh, those dresses were itchy! Mom took pride in dressing us in cute clothes and shoes, whether she bought or made them. After all, she had a top of the line Singer and was a great seamstress.

For church, we wore white gloves and patent leather Mary Jane shoes with matching purses. One time I left my little black patent leather purse with baby blue and pink flowers on a city bus we took to the downtown Sears store. I cried and cried for days.

We shopped at Sears often. I loved the smell of fresh popcorn that greeted us as we walked in the door and I remember getting the orange slice jelly candies with sugar crystals at their fabulous candy department.

Every month we went to the Hostess store where Mom bought a lot of cupcakes, Twinkies, Sno Balls, Donettes and fried pies. The freezer was always filled with treats along with Neapolitan ice cream and popsicles. Mom hid Bit-o-Honey candies in an upper kitchen cabinet, but I knew where they were and climbed the counters for them often. She made fruitcakes every Christmas—oh how I hated them! She fried a lot—a Southern cook for sure. We had a huge garden, and Mom canned (and fried) a lot of vegetables.

Mom grew up in the Corpus Christi area. She told me her father was a gambler and because of their precarious finances, she wasn't taken care of very well as a young girl during the Depression. Her parents divorced early, and her grandmother became the most stable person in her life.

Mom loved her grandma.

A petite five-foot-three, my mother wore her short hair in curls and was always stylishly dressed in her young adulthood. Her fashion was classic sixties, tailored pencil skirts with thin belts, knee length of course and pearls. In the later years of her life, she practically lived in shapeless dusters with big pockets that swallowed her up—a far cry from how I remembered her when I was a little girl.

Dad grew up in East Texas, and he had a Texas drawl that got thicker every time we visited our relatives in Shelby County. He grew up on a farm, and his family helped a lot of people during the Depression. He worked from the rising of the sun along with his dad and siblings. He had a powerful work ethic and believed in working with his hands. He was blue collar all the way, and showed disdain for lofty goals of advanced education—especially where women were concerned. Women had a place, and it certainly wasn't in business, education, or anything outside of traditional roles. Some would call him a male chauvinist -all six-foot-four inches of him.

Dad took me to an animal slaughterhouse once when I was seven. He felt it would "toughen me up." He forced me to sit on the bottom of a milk pail and watch as a bull was shot, hoisted up, and its throat cut. I was horrified as blood splattered everywhere. I cried so hard I couldn't catch my breath, and my dad was embarrassed by my reaction. The owner took me up to his house where his wife, who looked a lot like Mrs. Cleaver from *Leave it to Beaver*, gave me a cup of tepid tap water in a scratched-up blue metal cup. I waited on the porch for my dad- trying to recover from the house of horrors. I called a cat over so I could pet him. He slowly came close, then to my shock, began to heave and convulse and then vomit an entire mouse right in front of me. Backing up a few steps on the porch, I covered my face and cried again. At the ripe age of seven I became a vegetarian and I have never owned a cat.

For an allowance, my sister Rhonda and I had daily chores. She pulled weeds in the garden and I cleaned the house. I was obsessed with living in an organized and clean home.

I was involved in lots of extracurricular activities, worked hard for straight A's and the occasional B and graduated high school on the honor roll, albeit in a rather circuitous route.

My parents rarely attended any of my school events, and I always tried to convince myself that was okay, because I didn't want to get discouraged by the cloud of negativity and mental mediocrity that existed in our home.

## Critical Cultivation

A staunch Democrat and Union man, my Dad, who resembled Elvis Presley in his younger years, was a commercial master plumber foreman by trade. He always had a pick-up truck (in addition to our family car) and was an avid deer hunter. But what he really loved to do was garden.

I always felt my father loved the land—the soil—far more than he loved anything else, maybe including me. His huge vegetable garden brought him great joy—unlike me, a child whose drive and ambition seemed to cause him more embarrassment than pride. I was like a wild seed that continued to sprout where least expected (or wanted,) and my father was the self-appointed crop duster in charge of controlling my unwieldy growth. When it came to me, it seemed his focus was always on pruning—never on growing.

At times my father was a simmering volcano of insensitivity. A man whose razor-sharp words and vitriolic accusations often left me feeling scorched and diminished. He was the fire that licked at my heels and taught me to be vigilant. An ever-present force to be reckoned with, it was his flame that helped forge the tenacity in my spirit that gave me the will to reach higher and prove him wrong.

I grew up setting my life achievement bar high, partly because for me, my father set it painfully and constrictingly low. "Get down off your high horse, Vicki Denise. Who do you think you are?" he often shouted. He also called me "a stupid kid"… a lot – I'm not really sure why. I don't remember being stupid, but I always seemed to give him a reason to say it.

I really did want to learn how to cook and sew, "acceptable" aspirations for a girl. Because of that, I was always involved in home economics classes at school. But I had greater aspirations and passions—I also wanted to play an instrument, be a great dancer, actress and singer, and learn other languages and cultures, and I had a growing desire to know spiritual matters, especially as a teenager. Dad didn't understand any of this. He frequently said I "thought too highly of myself," and chided me to "walk a chalk line." When I would express my aspirations, both parents would say, "Well, la ti da!"

I often wondered what that meant.

When he snidely called me "Queen Esther" it wasn't with respect for what she did in biblical times. Esther represented her people to the King of Persia. She had a respected and persuasive voice that saved her Jewish people from death.

Years later, my doctoral thesis included Queen Esther as a positive role model. I wrote, *Immersed in Myrrh,* a Hebraic guide for preparing young girls for adulthood.

I don't know why I was such a disappointment to my father – why he wanted so little from me, and when I strove to give him more, why he strove equally as hard to hold me back. Seems that all my friends complained of the opposite. My desire to prove my father wrong percolated in my spirit until the day he died.

But it was my mother's utter resignation to life and her self-imposed exile to the sofa in our living room that, in retrospect, had a far more profound effect on me. My mother lived in a hazy kind of existence under the smoldering ashes of a life seemingly without passion or purpose. I wanted to live life zealously. She didn't… or maybe for some reason - she couldn't.

I was about twelve when we stopped going to church every Sunday, because Mom often felt too bad. It seemed she always had a heating pad on her stomach and a wet cloth on her forehead. The house was kept dark, and she slept most of the time. She became a frail and fearful woman who worried about everything.

Her scent of sadness filled the air. When she died of cancer some years later, I wondered if perhaps that period of intense melancholy was when the disease first reared its ugly head.

Despite what I may have felt was an emotional disconnect, my father was a hard-working man who took care of his family. He never failed to come to the plate and provide for us. The roof over our heads was secure, our tummies were always full, and the summer vacations we took were filled with Kodak memories, if not warm and fuzzy feelings.

My parents were proud of all they had. They worked hard to achieve a comfortable middle-class status. They were vocal about being "normal," about not having too much or too little, and they were happy being "average."

Yet I knew in my spirit that life wasn't about being average.

My father worked hard and was satisfied in his success. When I was six, he built his 3,000 square foot *brick* dream home (a big deal back then) on an acre of land. He met his expectations—reached his personal goals, which he had set higher than those of his own parents.

So, why couldn't I? I never understood why it was okay for him to want more than what he had grown up with, but it was wrong for me. Was I really so terrible to set my goals higher—to want more?

My dad's boss bought a new Cadillac every few years and Dad often bought his older ones. He was truly proud of those second-hand cars. When I voiced my dream to one day own a new Corvette, you'd have thought I was committing a cardinal sin.

The double-standard really confused me.

I've never questioned the range of my voice, only the authority over which I feel permitted to exert it. Sometimes a part of me still thinks of myself as just a little girl who should be seen, and not heard, and happy to be "average."

## Adopted by God's Spirit

I was adopted as an infant. After Mom had several miscarriages, a private adoption was arranged by a friend of the family and his co-worker. The year was 1959 and adoption was a very taboo situation. My sister Rhonda was adopted a few years later. Being adopted wasn't really a big deal for me growing up; I didn't feel different because of it. In fact, being adopted actually helped me when I came to understand I had a covenant with Israel's God *through* adoption. And that actually made me feel special.

The way we relate to God is often skewed by our relationship with our earthly father. Learning the character of my Heavenly Father was a challenge to me as my earthly father portrayed quite a different standard. I always felt I had to "perform" but *not too much* so as not to intimidate my dad. God, on the other hand, expected my best. And I so wanted to please them both.

I learned an interesting tension and balance growing up, which later in life I saw in scripture as a good quality. Many think there are contradictions in the Bible. I found that not so. The Bible is a book of balance.[9] God is a God of grace and yet a God of wrath to the evil ones who oppose Him. There is light and darkness. Good and evil. Zealousness for God can become radicalism. And then there is faith and works. Balance is important. He may not have realized it at the time, but my earthly father's unconventional ways actually taught me valuable life lessons.

The first thing we must learn as a child of God is that God loves us. He is our *Abba* (Hebrew, literally for *Daddy*). *Abba* cares for His children. He provides for His children. He teaches and counsels His children. Yet He also disciplines those who carry His name. Just as a child takes the last name of his earthly father, our Heavenly Father places His name upon us.

When God felt I was ready to make this head-heart connection, He revealed this *Abba*-Father truth to me in a profound way.

I was in eighth grade and going through mandatory Lutheran catechism classes every Wednesday night at Concordia Lutheran Church to prepare for my first communion. In the Lutheran church, going through confirmation was a major achievement. I was thirteen and had no idea these classes would have such an impact on me, or the foundation that was being laid for the greatest journey of my life.

It was the year Elton John sang *Good-bye Yellow Brick Road*, and I was about to find my future would lie somewhere beyond that wide and beaconing golden path.

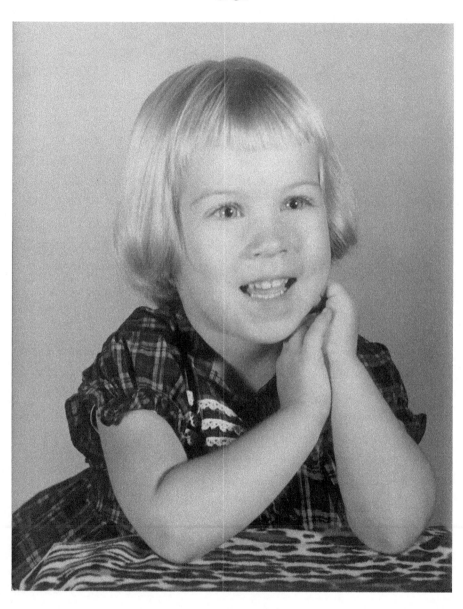

**Two-year-old Victoria Denise Hopkins.**

*Chapter 3*

# GOD-IN-THE-BOX

**Chanoch**: To focus more intently, dedicate

*"Go in through the narrow gate; for the gate that leads to destruction is wide and the road broad, and many travel it; but it is a narrow gate and a hard road that leads to life, and only a few find it...*
Matthew 7:13-14 CJB

*C*hanoch means to dedicate. The deeper meaning goes on to denote we must narrow our focus. When we choose to go down the narrow road, we are dedicating ourselves to the standards of God. Having a true faith focus is all about making intentional choices, understanding the consequences of those choices and accepting responsibility for them.

My editor and friend, Allison Bottke, says at one point during her life, she was so spiritually open-minded her brain slipped out.

I know what she means. There was a time during my life as a teen when I looked for answers anywhere I could get them—not giving much thought to the doctrine behind the choices I made.

As a teen, I played on the Ouija board, read books on witchcraft and mythology. I loved to read horror stories, but I always knew in the back of my mind it wasn't a good idea to put those words and word pictures into my mind and heart. Sometimes they gave me bad dreams—*really* bad dreams. There was a time in junior high when I was tormented at night by a negative spirit who wanted me to curse God, but I refused. I remember placing a pillow over my head trying to drown out the negative thoughts. In retrospect, I believe this was the result of playing with the Ouija board, an assumed harmless game of pretend.

I eventually renounced playing on the devil's playground once I learned it opened doors to the enemy in my life and offended God. However, the path to enlightenment on the subject of dedicating myself to the standards of God was a long one. It took many years to get to a place where I had the facts and focus I needed to make healthy spiritual choices.

## A Growing Sensitivity

Growing up I was unusually sensitive to spiritual things. I had an enhanced awareness of the spiritual realm of life—a prophetic sense of God in all things. Like a moth to a flame, I was drawn to anything spiritual, particularly things with Catholic or Jewish themes—subjects that, for some reason, intrigued me. This is when I read the *Diary of Anne Frank,* discovered Corrie Ten Boom, and began to learn about the Holocaust. I don't remember knowing any Jewish people as a girl, but I wished I did. I had so many questions.

For as long as I can remember, I gravitated toward the theatrical and creative arts—and I always sensed there was a part of me that "felt" things on a different level than most of my other friends. Not that I was better—in fact, there were times when I thought it was a little freakish—how I saw a spiritual component in pretty much everything.

I loved movies like *The Ten Commandments.* I was drawn to religious history—stories like the ones depicting the life of Joan of Arc and those about the Salem witch trials. And I was completely fascinated by Debbie Reynolds in *The Singing Nun* and by Sally Field in *The Flying Nun.* Both Debbie and Sally were young, pretty, funny, a tad ditzy, and they loved God. And then there was the nun who made me sing at the top of my lungs and twirl around my living room as the hills came alive with *The Sound of Music.*

My mother put the love of movie musicals in my heart. I fondly remember watching *Singing in the Rain, White Christmas* and the *Wizard of Oz* with her on television every year before VHS and DVD technology made them available to view any time. I learned a lot about my mom—and life—from the movies we watched.

The older I got, the more I realized a great many Christians have based what they believe and know about faith on what they learned from movies or on television. Unfortunately, not all of those theatrical depictions accurately tell the story.

I believe we are all born wanting—needing—to connect to God. Having our identity in Christ gives us a purpose, direction and function in life. A number of paraphrased quotations exist regarding a God-shaped hole—or vacuum—in the heart of every human which cannot be filled by any created thing, but only by the Spirit of our Creator.

As a young girl, I longed for something to fill that empty place. I knew answers were out there. I knew there was an angel watching over me. I just didn't have all of the puzzle pieces connected yet.

I can see now how my God was preparing me. He is preparing all of us for a higher purpose—a calling. He desires for all of us to have true happiness that comes when we walk in covenant agreement with Him. Covenant agreements with God are facts-of-life that the people of the Bible understood, but modern man has forgotten and has yet to grasp again. I often wondered how and where we lost this concept.

## Becoming a Woman

While my heart was seeking something more, my body was changing—and it definitely had a mind of its own. In fourth grade, I wore a little girl size 6X and by fifth grade, I wore a child size fourteen. I grew eleven inches in my tenth year and officially "became a woman" at eleven-and-a-half years old. By twelve, I had a curvy body, and I was growing up quickly—there was a lot going on inside of me.

My first girl-boy party was my thirteenth birthday celebrated in our two-car garage, where I decorated the entire space with pink crepe paper streamers and balloons. My friends and I had a blast. I was ecstatic when my parents gave me a quadraphonic stereo that played my albums and forty-five RPM records. It was a common sight to see me singing and dancing around my bedroom pretending to hold a microphone.

## Remarkable Revelation

I attended catechism classes every Wednesday evening at our church during the entire eighth grade. The classes started in September at the beginning of the school year and ended with my confirmation on the last Sunday of May, just before I graduated from junior high. During the first seven months of class, I learned about Martin Luther, the man responsible not only for founding the Lutheran church, but launching the entire Protestant Reformation in the 1500s.

Luther had the revelation that one could not earn his or her salvation by good works, the sale of indulgences or self-flagellation but rather is received only as a free gift of God's grace through faith in Jesus Christ as redeemer from our sin. His theology challenged the authority of the Pope by teaching the Bible is the only source of divinely revealed knowledge from God.

In 1517, Martin Luther nailed a list of ninety-five statements (thesis) to the door of All Saints' Church in Wittenbergon, Germany, and sparked the entire Reformation of the church as it was known. While I believe God used him to lead people out of the corruption of the Catholic Church, I later found out how anti-Semitic he became when he couldn't convert the Jews to Christianity. I was perplexed- how could anyone be a Christian and "hate" any people group? That made no sense to me.

## Not a Trivial Pursuit

I was taking in—breathing in—the catechism teaching every Wednesday night. After about seven months of classes, something amazing happened.

I had been seeking deeper spiritual meaning for years. I prayed to God, talked to my guardian angel (or at least to the painting on my wall) and went to church on Sunday.

Although we had a big Bible on the coffee table in my house, I seldom read or studied it. Frankly, it was like reading another language; I couldn't understand it. However, one evening as my pastor spoke the words of the Apostle Paul—words that proclaimed we were saved by grace through faith, not of works lest any man should boast[10]—I suddenly understood it!

The Word of the Lord is powerful, and He will make it known to us when He knows we're ready. Apparently, I was ready—and God's Word did a miracle in my heart. That was the Word that transformed me.

I felt like Helen Keller, who miraculously comprehends the meaning of the word "water" as it was spelled out in the manual alphabet by her teacher Anne Sullivan. Pastor Eifert was like my Anne Sullivan that day as he spoke the perfect Word at the perfect time that cut through the wall around my heart.

I was blown away by the spiritual revelation God loved me and His relationship with me (and vice versa) is the most important relationship in my life. Suddenly, the Spirit of God became real to me in a deeply personal way, and I knew in my heart that life would never be the same.

I began to weep from the overwhelming feeling of love and appreciation for what Christ did for me. I saw Him like a Secret Service agent who would take a bullet for me.

Pastor Eifert noticed me crying while our class of about twenty kids were playing paper football games and doing homework.

He asked his wife Judy to take me out of the class to talk to me.

"Is everything okay at home, honey?" she asked quietly. I nodded yes.

"Is someone in class bothering you…is anyone…hurting you…?"

"No ma'am." I said.

"How about at school? Did something happen there?"

"It's not that," I choked out as tears welled up and continued to gently fall.

*It wasn't anything that happened at home or at school—something just happened here in my catechism class!*

"I'm just so thankful for what Pastor Eifert said." I wiped the tears from my cheeks with a tissue she handed me.

"What he said? What do you mean, sweetie?"

All of this honey, sweetie and prodding—I was starting to feel mildly irritated that she talked to me like I was a little girl in grade school. Today, I can appreciate she was concerned and just trying to be helpful. But back then I couldn't believe she didn't get it. Wasn't that the point of catechism class? To affect some sort of spiritual change—a graduation of faith as it were? Could it be possible I was the only teenager to ever feel God's love in such a powerful and transformational way?

I was always a dramatic person, and maybe it was hard for her to believe the reality of what I was really feeling. I tried to explain, but the level and depth of my spiritual revelation were as foreign to my pastor and his wife as it was to me—and something about that didn't feel right. They were good people, kind and encouraging, but it seemed like they should be prepared for this kind of emotional response to a spiritual epiphany.

## On Fire for the Lord

I went home that night and dug through my white ballerina jewelry box and found what I was looking for—a colorful psychedelic button with the words "Jesus Freak" on it. I'm not sure where I got it, maybe at Spencer's gifts where my friends and I went to buy strawberry incense and check out black light posters.

I wore it to school the next day with a blue knit body suit, hip hugger bell-bottom jeans, a wide black belt and platform clogs. In 1973, this was very high fashion.

As I walked into school, I was certain everyone would be able to tell something major had happened to me. Certain I must be glowing with a transcendent level of new direction and understanding.

I wanted to share what I was feeling with everyone. I gladly told my friends about my new spiritual identity. God was giving me a new zeal as I shared my testimony, an action that made some folks—including my parents—very uncomfortable.

## Born-Again Boldness

The kids in school called my friend Ricky "Hoot Owl," not necessarily because he was wise but because Hoot was his last name. We were in Science class the day, and he listened to my story, leaned back in his chair and made a proclamation.

"Sounds like you got saved!"

I stared at him blankly.

"What do you mean?" I whispered. "Saved from what?"

"From going to Hell," Ricky proceeded to explain as Mr. Kujawa slammed his pointing rod on our table and caused us both to jump.

"Have your religious conversation after class!" he boomed.

"Yes, sir," we both said, as the other kids snickered.

We agreed to meet after school.

After school, I got straight to the point. "What do you mean by "got saved?" We took a walk at a cemetery across the street, sat under a tree, and he told me about the condition of man. This was my first experience of being "discipled" by someone.

"Everybody is lost and needs to find God. I think you just found him," he said.

"Okay, but what should I do now?" I asked.

His advice was wise for an eighth grader:

1. Go to church every Sunday
2. Give fifty cents of my weekly $2.00 allowance to the church each week
3. Pray every day

## No More God-in-a-Box

Over time, I came to understand my early thoughts about faith were distorted. I grew up believing there were several components in life you were born with—some unchangeable and undeniable truths—kind of like DNA. My parents were staunch Democrats, Lutherans, and loyal Cadillac owners. Therefore, I was born a Lutheran Democrat with brand loyalty to General Motors. It never dawned on me these were not genetic predispositions—but choices—choices I could one-day make for myself.

True faith is not dependent on our parent's religion or political values.

I loved my parents, but for people who had been going to church for so many years, I was finding it amazing how little they actually knew about their faith.

It was the first time I realized going to church does not make you a Christian. I was beginning to realize a person can possess a great deal of knowledge and still navigate life with a serious deficit of wisdom.

The Word of God ministered to me in a new and vibrant way that summer, and for confirmation my mother bought me a white leather Bible with my name engraved in gold on the cover. That year the Bible took the place of *Teen Beat* magazine on my nightstand. I would lie on my royal blue velvet bedspread at night and read stories alluding to my identity as a daughter of the King, yet I still had serious challenges understanding the Bible. No matter how I tried—and I did try—the language and idioms confused me.

However, as the Spirit of God began to pursue me, I began to experience firsthand the conflict of walking in God's truth versus following worldly paths. The choices weren't always easy—or clear—to me.

I asked God how I could use knowledge to make wise choices. It took Him years before He revealed the answer to me. Or maybe, could it be… it took me many years before I was ready to hear it?

## Get Up and Dance

Dance was something I really loved. As a young child, I had always been in ballet, tap, jazz, acrobatics, and gymnastics. I modeled for a while, played a little sports in junior high, but mostly I spent my time in dance and the performing arts. I was the leading lady in many of our dramatic productions at school.

That summer—the summer of my spiritual epiphany—the summer before I started high school, I tried out for the high school dance team. The Gold Dusters was a military-style drill team with a decidedly jazzy flair, and making the team was a really big deal. When I got the news I made the team, I was ecstatic! Mom was as excited as she could be considering her melancholy, but I shouldn't have been surprised when my dad's response was completely unenthusiastic.

"So, what's all this gonna cost me?" he asked with obvious distaste.

Although I attended church regularly, my true fellowship that epiphany-summer was with my drill team dance group. I felt powerful and popular. Dancing and performing made me feel alive—and I was good at it. When I started high school that September as a fresh-faced ninth grader, I felt ready to take on the world. I was like Maria leaving the restrictions of the Abbey—heading for adventure and dancing through the streets of Austria—I, too, had confidence in me—and in God.

In *The Sound of Music*, Maria's life changed when she met the formidable Captain Von Trapp in the foyer of the mansion that would become her home. Mine changed the first week of high school when I met Paul Jay Sarvadi in Spanish class.

*Chapter 4*

# I'M NOT YOUR FATHER

## 𝔎eṭubah: Covenant Agreement

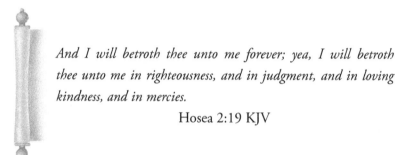

*And I will betroth thee unto me forever; yea, I will betroth thee unto me in righteousness, and in judgment, and in loving kindness, and in mercies.*

Hosea 2:19 KJV

Starting high school can be a scary time—fraught with anxiety—for some teens.

The start of my freshman year at Jersey Village High School was anything but scary. It was filled with excitement and promise.

I'd been practicing all summer with the Gold Dusters, and I'd made friends with a lot of the upper classmen who were already popular in high school. I loved dancing on the team, and I looked forward to performing before every football game and at various special events throughout the year. We were dancing to some of the hottest music of the time by the Doobie Brothers, Rod Stewart, and Chicago. The times were awesome.

They called me "cute and sweet," what I thought of as euphemisms for short and average. Nonetheless, I hung out with all the popular kids, I had a popular athlete boyfriend, and I had God—although the first blush of my new spiritual romance was beginning to wear off.

I didn't know it at the time, but when a person comes to trust in Christ, it's really important that a more seasoned believer is close by to disciple them. I had no one to teach me. I tried to do what I thought was faithful to God, those three things Ricky told me. But the pull of the world is a great force, and that doesn't suddenly change when someone is saved, especially when that someone is a teenager. I lacked affirmation, love, and encouragement. I needed people around me who were truly motivated by the Spirit, who would offer me comfort, counsel and direction in love. I didn't have that.

The stage was set for me to find what I lacked.

## Meeting Paul

There was a guy I heard every morning on the PA reading the announcements. He had a strong voice, clear and articulate, without a hint of Texas-twang. I soon found out he was in my Spanish class and sat behind me. In short order, he began to "accidentally" drop his pencil near my desk, so he could get up and retrieve it—a typical guy trick—just an excuse to get close to a girl.

However, Paul Sarvadi wasn't a "typical" guy. He was different—way different.

First, he was an upper classman. Very popular with all the students and teachers, smart, friendly and outgoing, with mesmerizing green eyes. He was student council president and voted most likely to succeed. He was in the Spanish club, science club, and a member of Mu Alpha Theta (MAΘ- the United States mathematics honor society for high schools, and two-year colleges). He was on the golf team and was a second string quarterback on our football team. He also had his own lawn care business where he worked after school and on weekends. And let's not forget his green 1970 Pontiac LeMans, a car he called "Fred."

Clearly, this was a man who had big plans.

He said he knew I was "the one" when he saw me that first day of Spanish class. Paul knew what he wanted in life, and he quickly decided what he wanted was me.

I'll admit, I was taken aback by his confidence and presumptive nature.

I had never met anyone like him, and I was intrigued by his sense of purpose and passion for life.

## About Paul

All four of Paul's grandparents came from Romania just after the turn of the 20th century. They were hard working people who came to America for opportunity and settled in the Erie, Pennsylvania and Chicago areas. Paul's paternal grandparents owned a vineyard and a grocery store in Erie. Paul's father, George, was the first Sarvadi to be born on American soil, and his family worked hard instilling into their son a high sense of self-worth, which was passed on to Paul and his siblings.

George and Trudy were married in their early twenties and had nine children with Paul being the seventh child and fifth son. They came to Texas from Ohio when Paul was in the eighth grade.

Truthfully, Paul's parents intimidated me—they had strong opinions. My body language in photos from our early years together shows a meek and fearful little girl, with shoulders slumped and eyes cast down. My posture changed over the years in photos as I got to know this wonderful family and grew more confident and appreciative.

Our families were as different as night and day. Trudy made pasta from scratch and took all day to make her homemade spaghetti, while my mom opened a can of Chef Boy-Ardee that came in a complete boxed meal. Yes, my mom cooked and sewed, but it wasn't quite the same.

My dad was a blue-collar worker that came home dirty every day. Paul's dad was an engineer with an advanced college degree. My parents were Democrats, Paul's were Republican. We were Lutheran, the Sarvadi's were Catholic. The list went on ...

None of that mattered to Paul.

## Unplanned, Unexpected and Undeniable

I had never felt so special—so accepted and appreciated. Paul's love and encouragement filled me with a sense of power and purpose I had never experienced. Our courtship happened so fast our parents didn't have time to approve or disapprove. We were on a trajectory that was impossible to stop.

We met in early September and by our first phone call a few days later Paul asked me about naming our first child. Our first official date was at the local Dairy Queen in early October. By Christmas, he proposed marriage, and by the New Year we behaved as though we already were.

Our time was that of the 70s, and we were experiencing the leftover effects of the "make love not war" generation—a mantra I'm afraid many of us decided to take literally—without really thinking of the consequences spiritually or physically for that matter.

I didn't know for sure if I was pregnant until I was about four months along. I had some occasional spotting, which made me question the probability. But then my mom suspected and approached me with the question.

"Could you be pregnant?"

I didn't show until midway in my fifth month, but even then the baby growing inside was only a tiny bump on my 102-pound teenage body. I still danced with the drill team, and in May, the Gold Dusters performed in a national competition at the Hoffienze Pavilion in Houston, with little me high kicking right along with them.

We took First Place.

Something was definitely in the air, because that summer seven girls in my high school class got pregnant. In fact, the next year our school provided a Day Care program on site.

## Breaking the News

My parents were old-fashioned, they felt the baby needed a last name (one that wasn't mine), and therefore, Paul and I needed to be married. Paul's parents weren't so convinced. They felt marriage would shatter Paul's chance for a good education at a good school.

Paul convinced our parents of our love for each other and our commitment to marriage and parenthood, and with their (signed) agreement we planned to get married. Truthfully, my dad really liked Paul, *a whole lot more than he liked me*, I remembered thinking.

Yet their signatures alone weren't enough. Because of my age, we had to go before a judge to get a waiver for me to get married. The judge was kind but reminded me a little bit of my father as he looked at me and gruffly explained what I would be facing. I felt like a little girl being reprimanded for being disobedient.

"Why do you think you can beat the statistics?" he asked me.

"Because I'm not a quitter," I quickly answered, head held high.

He stared at me over the edge of his reading glasses, made a peculiar grunting noise and shook his head affirmatively as he signed the form.

"Good luck," he said as he handed me the paper and motioned for us to leave.

I held on tight to my affidavit and outpaced my parents to the exit. I felt I needed to leave before the judge changed his mind.

One more hurdle down in a seemingly insurmountable list of obstacles we faced.

Paul was still doing some lawn care, but mostly working for his dad's company painting offices. He had a construction job lined up after that. He had no problem finding work.

The problem we now had was finding someone to marry us.

"Did you call the Father?" Paul's mom asked when we met to share our newest decision as a couple with her.

"Yes I did," Paul said. "He won't marry us in the Catholic church ... because of the ... circumstances."

I cringed at how I thought the conversation would proceed.

"What? He refused to marry you?" Paul's mother was clearly angry and muttered something in Romanian I didn't understand.

The Sarvadi's had been members of their local parish since they moved to Jersey Village three years before. When his priest refused to marry us because of our situation, I could see Paul begin to question his Catholic alignment. We had discussed our options before meeting with Paul's mother.

I was holding my breath and biting my lower lip, but Paul's voice was steady as he reached over to hold my hand and told his mother our decision.

"Mom, we're getting married at Vicki's church. We already talked to Pastor Eifert. He said there wouldn't be a problem as long as we attended premarital counseling with him."

His mother looked at us for a few moments and seemed unusually calm. You could have knocked me over with a feather when she finally responded. "Okay, good. That's good."

I took a deep breath and squeezed Paul's hand. The fact his mom acquiesced to a Protestant wedding was a sign to me—to us—that in joining our spiritual lives we were heading down the right path—albeit in a roundabout way.

We attended pre-marital counseling with Pastor Eifert and in June, Paul officially left the Catholic Church and converted to Lutheranism.

We were married at Concordia Lutheran Church on June 28, 1974, I was all of fifteen—definitely just a little girl—and Paul was a very grown-up seventeen.

## A Day to Remember

I found my wedding dress in the first store I shopped in. It was a long flowing white sheer linen dress with a silk lining. Long ribbons of pink and baby blue hung down from just below the bust line, which was perfect because the classic empire waist somewhat camouflaged my small baby bump. It wasn't a secret I was expecting, but we didn't feel the need to flaunt the fact either.

About eighty people attended the wedding, which included some of our friends from school, a few neighbors, a couple of our parent's friends and some family members. We received a lot of wonderful wedding gifts and quite a bit of cash. That was great because we had hospital and doctor bills coming up. The reception was held at my parent's home, which was typical in that era. Back in the 70s, most wedding receptions were held in someone's home or in the fellowship hall of a church. The bridal party typically served punch and cake and the only available food was tuna or pimento cheese sandwich triangles, potato chips and butter mints. In my parent's home, we had all of that plus some wonderful Romanian baked pastries, rolls, and cookies. You could say we took the standard fare up a notch.

## Marriage is a Covenant Agreement

Marriage is a covenant with shared assets and liabilities, and I quickly learned the importance of meshing "you and me" into "we." I was so young, but ready for the challenge. What I told the judge was true—I have never been a quitter—so I took on the challenge with purpose.

Pastor Eifert gave us several passages in Scripture that pertained to marriage, and I read them in my little white leather-covered Bible and prayed about them. Mark 10:7-8 reads: For this reason, a man should leave his father and mother and be united with his wife, and the two are to become one flesh. Thus they are no longer two, but one (CJB).

It didn't take long to realize being of "one flesh" is far easier said than done. Especially when the assets and liabilities you bring to the table are so diverse, as was the case with Paul and me.

Marriage is a covenant agreement, and a covenant is best explained from its original Hebraic concept of two entities becoming one in the same. In Hebrew, the marriage covenant is called the *ketubah*, a document that stated the specific terms of the covenant (but not to be confused with our modern culture "prenuptial agreement," which is another thing entirely).

In ancient biblical as well as in modern Jewish culture, when a man wished to marry a certain woman, he approached her father (or the rabbi) to negotiate a price. In Bible times most families lived in an agrarian society—the son worked for the father. Those who lived in the city often had businesses, and the son helped, learning and carrying on the family business (or craft). However, things were different for girls. After learning the family business and developing skills and education instilled by her parents, the daughters would leave the family and join her husband's family trade. With the giving of her into a marriage came certain skill sets and possessions. Hopefully, what she had learned growing up would benefit her husband and his family. The negotiation was based on what the bride brought to the union, and all things were recorded in the *ketubah*.

When we got married, the only thing I brought to the union was my commitment, tenacity, fertility, and frequent hostility. Small in stature but big in attitude, I was just a little girl with a lot of pent-up anger toward her father that was quickly misdirected at her new husband.

At the time, I didn't understand what a *ketubah* covenant was, but I did respect God. We were married in a church and made vows to Him. That was enough to keep me committed to the marriage—no matter how tough things might get.

## Two Become One Mindset

Our plan when we got married was to save up enough money to rent and furnish our own apartment, but until then we would stay with my parents.

Paul seemed to have a better grasp on the "two shall become one" concept—but I had to work harder at sharing my life.

Things were good at first. Yet as the first blush of wedded bliss passed, we began to have some communication problems.

No matter what Paul said I took it as criticism, and I would react to him in a hostile way. I was very sensitive and defensive.

"I'm not stupid, I do have a right to feel what I feel, think what I think, and do what I do," I often shouted.

Paul didn't know why I reacted to his comments, differing opinions or our disagreements the way I did. He didn't understand, and frankly, neither did I at first. I couldn't explain why I was frequently offended by something Paul said.

All I knew was my dad had criticized me all my life, and now I felt the liberty to say, "I will not stand for this!"

I reacted to Paul in a way I dared not react to my dad.

I wasn't going to be put down, squelched, limited, and demeaned any longer—even if that wasn't Paul's intention. In retrospect, I know Paul had not intentionally meant to hurt me, but I was hurt nonetheless.

One day after a particularly nasty argument, Paul said five simple words that resonated in my spirit.

"Vicki, I'm not your father."

Anything constructive Paul said, or any difference of opinion he had—because of how my dad treated me—I reacted toward him, as though he had attacked me. My interpretation of feedback of any kind was usually negative, and my response was most often defensive. I took out years of frustration I felt toward my father on my young husband.

Developing constructive communication styles was sometimes challenging. Many couples don't make it through this learning curve, but God had a plan for us.

It took me a while to learn Paul wasn't trying to hold me back—I didn't have to prove him wrong in anything. But just like the relationship with my Heavenly Father can be skewed by how I related to my earthly father, I learned my relationship with my husband can also be skewed by my relationship with my father as well.

It took a while for me to disassociate my father's attitudes from those of my husband. Paul wasn't my father. He was my husband. And he hit the ground running with his desire to be the best husband, father, and provider he could be.

## And Baby Makes Three

A lot of people judged me for having a baby so young—and they judged us for getting married. A lot of "Christians" shook their heads as if to say– "babies having a baby," or "look at those two kids playing house." We had to ignore a lot of people, especially the naysayers. I think people were making bets on how long we would stay married.

Everything went so quickly—from meeting Paul to getting married to having a baby.

In fact, the doctor said I was having a big baby. At full term, I was barely one hundred twenty pounds, and he was (rightly) worried about the size of my pelvic structure. When I went into labor, I couldn't progress past five centimeters of dilation.

I was prepped for a Cesarean section and fifteen minutes later, on September 18, 1974, our eight pound, three ounce baby girl came into the world.

Our entire family was there, and you would have thought someone had just given birth to royalty for all the pomp and circumstance being displayed. Personally, I was so overwhelmed with everything I didn't know what to think.

Paul was elated and over-the-moon in love with his little daughter.

We discussed names—a lot. For a boy, I liked Brandon or Brendon. Paul just liked Paul. For a girl, I liked Shannon or Chessa, and Paul liked the name

Michelle. My mom kept saying Chasma instead of Chessa, so we nixed that one. When our baby girl was born, we decided on Shannon Michelle, but from the day she took her first breath, we agreed to call her Michelle.

The first months of our marriage had been somewhat curious and out of the ordinary, as we learned to blend our routines and live with the opinions of my parents. Mom helped out a lot in the early months of Michelle's life. I'm not sure how I would have made it without her.

For my first school semester as a married mom, I studied on a homebound program. I made quick progress and aced every subject. My new goals were to finish school early and get a job as soon as possible. The driving age is sixteen in Texas, but after submitting all the necessary paperwork I qualified at fifteen for what is known as a "hardship license" so I could drive to work after the baby was born. Having this freedom was critical.

We were a capable couple—determined to do as much as possible on our own. We didn't ask for financial help and we paid for everything ourselves including Michelle's baby furniture, diapers, food, formula and baby accessories.

## Building Our Own Nest

Paul graduated fourth in his class from High School in 1975. We now had enough money saved to move into our first apartment. I was "Sweet Sixteen" and Michelle was eight months old. Because Paul served as a junior board member at our local bank in conjunction with a special school program, we qualified to rent the apartment on our own credit, a really big thing back then (and still is today).

Paul was awarded a full scholarship to Rice University, which was subsequently revoked when they discovered he was married. It was a devastating blow to us, but one that inevitably made us stronger. Except for a grant and a small loan, we paid for his college classes for a year at Rice. He then transferred to the University of Houston, which was much more affordable.

Because his dad was an engineer, Paul decided to pursue a degree in engineering. However, in time he would come to discover this wasn't really his dream profession. He was actually a gifted communicator, and his skill set was in sales and leadership.

I worked a series of part-time jobs while going to school and taking care of Michelle, and she was nineteen months old when I finally graduated from high school.

We continued to save our money and eventually bought a brand new Toyota Corolla as a second car so we could both get around.

Life was challenging—but good.

## Chapter 5
# BECOMING A MOTHER

**Imma**: Mommy

*Her children arise; they make her happy; her husband too, as he praises her .*

Proverbs 31:28 CJB

*G*od has been a partner with women in the "creation business" for a long time. Childbirth is holy. Being a mother is holy. It's an amazing blessing that also carries an unimaginable weight of responsibility—as does parenting in general.

Paul and I were so young and basically ignorant of this fact, but we were both committed to making this work. Together we would prove the naysayers wrong.

One day Michelle woke crying from her nap in her crib. I was walking down the hallway to pick her up when I heard something that caused me to stop in my tracks.

"Momma, Momma, Momma..."

She said her first word. Not once, but three times.

As I was bearing the weight of that moment, I suddenly realized this tiny person totally depended on me—for virtually everything.

*I am a mommy.*

As I walked up to her crib, she stopped crying and looked up with her big blue eyes. Her chubby little arms reached out, and it was at that moment I decided to step up to the challenge and be the best mommy I could be.

*You can depend on me, little one.*

I was on a homebound education program with my own private tutor provided by the school district for the first semester. I could concentrate on schoolwork and progress on a much faster pace than the classroom. When I went back to the classroom for the second semester, I had achieved enough credits to be ranked as a junior, and in completing as many credits as possible in both sessions of summer school of 1975, I had the luxury to be in an early graduation program during my senior year.

I had a few different jobs during my last two years of high school, which included wearing the dreaded brown polyester uniform with the orange bandana as a cashier at What-A-Burger, as a central credit representative at the Montgomery Ward Department Store, and as a bakery attendant at Target. Believe it or not, working in a bakery can cure you of any desire for donuts. I hated the smell of them for years.

Paul and I worked diligently and saved most of our income, so we could afford our own apartment. Because I had classes in the morning, I would work late hours, often getting home after Michelle was already asleep. The only time I saw her during the weekdays was before school and during lunch before work. On the weekends, we took Michelle to the park or the zoo. Back then the zoo was free, which fit our budget perfectly.

We were faithful to attend the Lutheran church. Paul completed an adult Catechism class and was confirmed. Since I had a better understanding now of his Catholic roots, there were times I could see Paul mentally processing the newfound freedom of the Lutheran doctrine. Now, there was no longer a need for Paul to "confess to a priest;" he could instead go directly to God. I could sense Paul openly receive and appreciate this new type of spiritual relationship.

Now with our own place, our schedule and budget became even more challenging, but we were committed … and determined. Our church family was supportive of us and made us feel welcomed.

~

Michelle was a good and happy baby and a smart toddler. She was always a joy and brought great cohesiveness to the entire family.

One Sunday morning when she was about eighteen months old, Paul accidentally closed a door on her tiny ring finger. We both freaked out as we responded to her terrified cries, finding the tip of her finger at the first joint just below her nail barely attached—hanging on by a thread. I frantically called an ambulance and the paramedic calmly wrapped up her finger. After reassuring us she wasn't going to bleed to death, he told us we needed to take her immediately to Texas Children's Hospital in Houston.

"I think the chances are good a plastic surgeon can re-attach her finger, but time is critical." He said.

"Plastic surgeon? Re-attach?"

I thought I was going to faint.

When we arrived at the hospital, I'm sure we looked like a couple of ragamuffins. I had just gotten out of the shower when this happened, so my long hair was still damp and uncombed. I had no makeup on, and I had thrown on one of Paul's T-shirts and a dirty pair of jeans I pulled out of the hamper. Paul didn't look much better. In the chaos and haste, we forgot diapers and had to ask the hospital staff if they had any extra. Almost immediately, they proceeded to x-ray every part of Michelle's little body. They asked about every cut or little bruise they found. I was so taken aback by their interrogation. Eventually, they took her to surgery and successfully mended our baby, but it was quite a process.

We didn't realize it at first, but eventually figured out they suspected us of child abuse. I would assume our age and how straggly we looked was a possible flag for investigation. Finally, around midnight they were convinced we weren't beating our child, and they let us take her home.

Her tiny finger healed beautifully and one evening as Paul and I were talking, I made a point to stop and thank the Lord that everything worked out so well. At this stage in our marriage, we didn't make a habit of audibly praying together, and our faith was mainly expressed in the formality of the Lutheran church. My audible declaration of thanks seemed to humor Paul when at the end of my prayer, he said, "This is where I'm supposed to say 'Amen,' right?"

## Leadership in Action

Not long after Michelle's accident, Paul and I were introduced to a business opportunity that would change our lives. Paul was attending college during the day and selling appliances for Sears at night. With his incredible salesmanship skills, he was making an adequate income but was open to anything that could bring in another dollar. Paul insisted we take a stab at this "wonderful opportunity," but I was a bit reluctant.

We "officially" started our Amway business in December of 1976, and success came pretty quickly. Paul loved the entrepreneurial dynamic; he was in his element. In fact, he got so caught up in climbing the Amway ladder and making money, he never returned to school.

He was like a college athlete being offered a contract with the big-league. Do you spend two more years in training (i.e. stay in school) or grab the gold ring being offered?

He opted for the gold ring and never looked back.

Other than the times when we disagreed because I misconstrued Paul's words or actions and confused him with my father, we never really had a major conflict between us—until this point in our marriage. As he was catapulted into the Amway stratosphere, something in Paul changed. The more entrenched he got into the sales and leadership training of Amway, the more arrogant he seemed to become. It was like he was being brainwashed and thrown into hyper-sales mode. When he began to tell me how I must submit to all of his decisions without question, the fights ensued.

There was one particular female leader in the organization who had a very conservative viewpoint of a woman's role and encouraged her fellow female distributors to be waiting at the door when their husbands came home with their slippers, to have dinner on the table, the house perfectly clean and the children dressed neatly and quietly awaiting their father's arrival. This female leader was obviously a big hit with the men in the organization.

"I don't think it's asking too much to expect this," Paul said to me one day after returning from one of his weekly open meetings.

"Are you serious?" I asked.

Uh, yeah, he was. Very.

I grew up in a conservative household, but the "you must submit unconditionally" attitude was foreign to me, and I quickly grew frustrated with how Paul treated me. I felt there was a difference between being spiritually obedient to your husband and subservient to his unrealistic demands. Paul was turning into someone else before my very eyes.

We began to have Amway meetings almost every night, and I constantly had to ask my mother to babysit for us. Soon, we were too busy for church, and I was spending more and more time unpacking shipments and sorting products. I remember thinking, "This isn't what I signed up for." And it scared me that for the first time I had doubts about whether our marriage would survive. Conversely, Paul was feeling confident everything was perfect and on track.

The Sarvadi family seems to deal with a familial trait of extreme confidence. It served his ancestors well when they came to this country as immigrants, and confidence is always something good to have. The problem with *extreme* confidence is it often comes out as arrogance, judgmentalism and bossiness. Paul displayed those attributes in full measure, and absolutely crossed the line as far as I was concerned.

～

After Michelle was born, I tried numerous methods of birth control that all had negative effects on my body, and Paul and I mutually decided (and in many ways were both convicted,) not to use contraception. We were prepared for the possibility of a second baby, but we were not specifically planning for one.

I was working in the billing department of a big oil and gas company in Houston, about the same time we started in Amway. I enjoyed working there for another six months until shortly after my eighteenth birthday when I found I was pregnant. In fact, that was the last "official" job I ever had outside of the home until I opened my own performing arts center many years later.

When we discovered I was pregnant, it wasn't a complete surprise.

Other people were surprisingly accepting of our news, even excited. It seemed our growing Amway business and financial success had somehow validated our "against all odds" relationship.

Our second baby's due date was February 10, 1978.

On the outside, things looked great, but our increasing marital problems over the subservient role Paul now wanted me to take had reached a point where I was talking about divorce. I didn't think I could live with this kind of pressure. However, with a toddler and a baby on the way, it was the worse time to think about a break up. After many passionate and emotional exchanges on both sides, we decided to keep trying to work out our differences. So, we did what any young couple with more money than sense would do when faced with marital challenges, we spent money—a lot of it.

I was in my first trimester when we bought our first home, a brand new twelve hundred square foot home in northwest Houston. We also bought a new Chrysler Cordoba. My father tried to keep his opinions to himself, but every now and then he would point his big finger at me and say, "You better be saving some money little lady."

In the meantime, we were planning a big third birthday party for Michelle. She requested to have a party at Peppermint Park Amusement Center. Her little blond bob bounced as she ran from one ride to another. She smiled from ear to ear as her friends clamored to be the one to sit next to her. She was so cute. Just as my mom always dressed me in pretty little girl's clothes, she continued the same tradition with her first granddaughter. Between her seamstress talents and thrifty shopping skills, Mom always helped to make Michelle look like a princess.

**New Year Promises**
We started the New Year in 1978 with high hopes and big dreams, even though I was still plagued with morning sickness and extreme fatigue that often lasted well into the afternoon and evening.

As I prepared the nursery for our "new" baby, I began to question some of the choices we were making with the "first" one.

The Bible says in Proverbs 22:6, Train up a child in the way he should go, and when he is old he will not depart from it (KJV).

*What does that mean exactly, Lord? Train up a child?*

Were we doing things right with our daughter?

We dressed Michelle up in pretty clothes, took her to church on Sunday and taught her about God. She went to Sunday school and to Vacation Bible School, where I volunteered as a helper. She was learning all of the Bible stories I had learned as a little girl. We were teaching her how to pray and give thanks at meals. But at the end of the day, were we really teaching her how to have a dynamic and loving relationship with the living Lord?

As a couple, we were faithfully committed to going to church, but I couldn't say we were growing spiritually.

In fact, I began to feel increasingly uncomfortable at our church.

It appeared to me almost everyone was anti-Catholic, anti-Baptist and anti-everything that wasn't Lutheran. Over time, I had learned (from very vocal and dogmatic parishioners) that only Lutherans were "correct." I didn't necessarily believe this, but I kept my opinions to myself. Family and faith were important to Paul and me and we were following the "Lutheran agenda" together, including Lutheran night at the Astrodome and Oktoberfest celebrations.

I was very pregnant and sitting in a rocking chair admiring our baby's nursery when I had an epiphany. I suddenly realized we were just going through the motions of the "formality" of faith, functioning in a kind of spiritual amnesia, just as my parents had done for so many years.

The fiery passion I once had for God had become barely-glowing embers—the Jesus Freak girl was gone.

I missed her.

## A Date with Destiny

When I was approaching my last month of pregnancy, Paul's grandmother came to spend time with us. She spent all day in the kitchen making Romanian dishes such as cabbage rolls, chicken paprikash, and homemade chicken soup. Her international cuisine created the most sumptuous aromas as she baked wonderful goodies such as kifla, pasca, donuts, placinta, and phyllo dough pastries. She was a fabulous cook, but I often found myself unable to eat her delicacies, even more so as my pregnancy progressed.

A week before my due date I had an x-ray to gauge the size of our baby in order to schedule a date for my Caesarean section. At that time, ultrasound technology was expensive and not in widespread use.

Paul was with me when we got the results.

"We're not going to schedule a date for the Caesarean," the doctor said. "Your baby is very small, less than four pounds. We think it's best to wait until you go into labor naturally to give your baby as much time as possible to grow. Let me see you back here in one week."

Shortly after that radiology appointment I started to feel poorly. I thought perhaps I had picked up a flu bug at the hospital.

"Are you sure you don't want to go back to the doctor?" Paul asked one evening after I'd had a bout of nausea.

"Yes, I'm sure. It's probably just a touch of the flu. I'll be fine," I assured him. "My next appointment is Monday. I'm sure I can hold out for a few more days."

I had a rough week.

I counted down the days, and when I wasn't in the bathroom getting sick or asleep on the sofa or bed, I found myself feverishly contemplating the sanctity of life, the knowledge God has a plan for every child–every person.

I wondered what our baby would be like. I prayed Michelle wouldn't feel neglected with a new baby in the house, and I hoped Paul would stop trying to turn me into someone I wasn't and accept me for who I was.

But who was I?

I thought back to my eighth-grade catechism class—to all the spiritual revelation God poured into my heart. He had a plan for me back then. What happened to that fiery passion? I felt I understood so much then—what happened to all of that enlightenment? Only five years had passed, yet it seemed like a lifetime ago.

I had so many questions for God. What did He want me to do with my life? How could I live the kind of life He wanted me to live? Was the problem Paul, me, us, or our marriage? I knew something wasn't right—what was missing and how could I find it?

We were about to add another child to our family, it should have been a joyful time, but as my health rapidly declined we were living in a kind of hazy fog. A fog that accompanied us to my scheduled doctor's appointment that turned into an emergency that sent me to the ICU and brought me literally face-to-face with my guardian angel.

**Our first home, 1977**

# Chapter 6
# TALK TO THE HAND

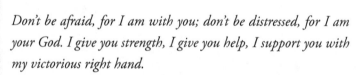

**Yad**: Hand

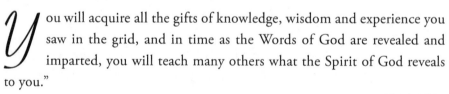

*Don't be afraid, for I am with you; don't be distressed, for I am your God. I give you strength, I give you help, I support you with my victorious right hand.*

Isaiah 41:10 CJB

*Y*ou will acquire all the gifts of knowledge, wisdom and experience you saw in the grid, and in time as the Words of God are revealed and imparted, you will teach many others what the Spirit of God reveals to you."

These last words from *Peretz*, my guardian angel, would echo in my spirit for my lifetime. However, they (and the entire experience) would remain elusive for the days immediately following my near-death experience.

At the moment my spirit returned to my body, I took a long deep breath that caused great commotion around my ICU bed.

"We've got her back!" I heard someone exclaim, followed by a lot of noise and activity.

For a moment, I felt severe pain as God became a miraculous tapestry maker and rewove my sick and wounded body to my enlightened spirit. As my mind, will, and emotions settled back into my physical body, the pain subsided, and I drifted into sleep.

Paul told me later he was pacing and praying in the waiting room when a nurse approached him.

"I heard the Code Blue," he said to her, "was that my wife?"

"Yes. But they were able to resuscitate her quickly, and she's breathing on her own. That's a good sign. Her vitals look good," she said as she led him to my room. "The doctor will be in shortly to talk to you, all we can do now is wait … and pray." She gently patted him on the arm before leaving him alone with me.

Paul said he was unprepared for how I would look amidst the overwhelming mass of high-tech equipment surrounding my swollen yet frail body.

After they removed the breathing equipment, I came out of the coma sometime later to see Paul's face. He was sitting next to me when I opened my eyes and began to mumble.

"Paul, I need to acquire more knowledge and help people understand," I said in grueling staccato.

Despite all the times I felt I was present throughout the ordeal, this was actually the first time I had been conscious in three days. As I laboriously spoke my first words, Paul stared at me, as though I had grown a third eye on my forehead. I had no idea how grateful he was to hear my voice—how hard he had been praying.

"Hello, honey," he said quietly as he stroked my arm. I was unaccustomed to seeing tears in my husband's eyes, and as he tried to talk to me about our son, I held up my hand to stop him and then drifted back to sleep.

When I woke up a little while later, he tried again to tell me something about our baby, but again I held my hand up and refused to listen. My mind and spirit were consumed with the spiritual truth I had learned from *Peretz* and I wanted nothing of earthly reality. Not yet.

Each time Paul tried to bring the subject up, I raised my hand as if motioning him to keep his words to himself. I touched his lips and said, "Shhhh…"

I now know my condition was so fragile, and my response so vehement, no one dared confront me with the truth. It was "talk to the hand," or don't talk at all.

As I gained strength, I intermittently mentioned seeing my guardian angel, but few took me seriously.

Because I had adverse reactions to every medicine they gave me, the doctors had to take me off all medications and treatments. They were amazed that instead of getting worse, I recovered quickly from the brink of death. Three days after gaining consciousness, they transferred me from intensive care into a sterile isolation room to undergo extensive tests.

The doctors were mystified at how well my body was healing. My mental status, however, was questionable.

Over the next two weeks, the doctors poked, prodded, evaluated, tested, observed and analyzed—and all they could determine was I had some type of extreme liver dysfunction, and it was healing rapidly. I was the topic of discussion as many doctors met together during those two weeks. At one point a doctor asked if I believed in God because there was just no other explanation.

He had no idea how much I believed in God and in His plan—how much His divine intervention played a part in my miraculous recovery.

Not long after I began to get some of my strength back, Paul noticed that I was staring intently, marveling at my ability to control movement in my hand.

"What are you looking at, hon?" he asked.

"Isn't it amazing?" I opened and closed my hands and swirled my arms around in the air. "Look, I can decide to move my body parts, and they move at my command!"

Paul looked more than a little concerned with my observation.

There were days when breathing seemed unnatural, and I often felt as though I had a wad of cotton in my throat.

I told a nurse, "You know, this body isn't really me, it just carries me around."

Whenever Paul visited, he appeared increasingly frightened by random things I said, such as the time I told him my tongue felt thick and awkward, and I didn't like the cumbersome effort of talking.

"Communicating telepathically is so much better." I declared. "*Peretz* and I did it so naturally."

As I mentioned different aspects about my guardian angel experience to Paul, I was completely unaware he was growing more distraught about my mental state, fearing he'd lost me. In fact, it really disturbed him when I told him how a place on my back continued to "open up" and that's where I felt "I exited my body."

This sensation would happen from time to time for years afterward – even to this day.

Because of this entire unique experience, I was suddenly conscious of the energy entity—the spiritual entity that was *truly* me—a feeling I have never completely lost.

So many things were different after I saw *Peretz*.

Now, I was extremely aware of my flesh, my sins, and of a very gracious and compassionate God. I wasn't afraid of death—I'd already experienced it. I babbled incessantly about my life grid experience. But the single most disconcerting issue during the entire time was that I refused to acknowledge the death of my baby. Instead, I patted my still slightly swollen belly, content with the idea of still being pregnant.

It's strange when I think about it now, but at the time I desired an enhanced level of transparency and truth about everything going on around me—except when it came to discussing my son. I didn't allow anyone to talk about the baby—I think my heart simply wasn't ready.

Instead, I lay in my hospital bed and imagined feeling life in my womb.

For almost two weeks, I lived in a delusional bubble of denial before I could face the devastating loss of our child.

To lose a child is an incomprehensible pain. Something words cannot describe. We both lost a child—but it was Paul who buried our baby—our son. Paul cradled our son's tiny lifeless body in his hands, stood graveside as the impossibly small casket was lowered into the ground. My young husband wrestled first with a wife whose life hung by a thread, and then with her dysfunctional denial.

I refused to accept the reality of death.

But these were the days that changed the heart and soul of my husband. A time God used to set Paul's heart on a journey of discovery, dependence, and leadership that would serve him in infinite and indescribable ways.

Decades later, I still feel sadness that Paul had to experience this stage of grief on his own.

He told me later he never felt so far apart from me—or so close to God. He knew God was going to somehow turn this horrible tragedy into a powerful triumph. It seemed the further away from reality I traveled during those weeks after my death, the closer Paul got to his Heavenly Father. Perhaps that was God's plan all along.

In retrospect, it's impossible to deny God was using this time to shape the entire spiritual integrity of my husband. A man who would eventually be responsible for the livelihood of thousands of employees and countless consumers. However, that time was a long way off, as Paul prayed for a miracle at my bedside.

*God, Michelle needs her mother. Please bring her back to us, help her face reality. Please fill Victoria with the spirit of Your love and joy once again. I need my wife, and we need a miracle.*

Ten days later, the miracle came—like mother's milk to a starving child.


## Saturation Point

It was a Sunday morning … and I remember it like it was yesterday. I awoke to my hospital gown and sheets completely saturated with a wet substance, and I couldn't tell where the liquid was coming from.

Alarmed and confused, I called for the nurse.

"There's something wrong," I said as I motioned to my gown. "I think my I.V. bag is leaking."

The nurse slowly lowered the side rail on my bed and placed her hand on my arm.

"Victoria, this is breast milk," she said quietly. "Your body is returning to normal. It's a natural progression."

I stared at her, taking in the information and looking back and forth from her to the front of my gown. My breasts ached as did my empty arms as I wrapped them tightly across my chest and began to rock back and forth.

"But I haven't had my baby yet. *It's too soon,*" I cried.

The precious nurse sat on the edge of the bed, placed her hands on my shoulders, and with great compassion said the words of truth my heart was finally ready to hear. "Sweetie, your baby was born ten days ago. He didn't make it."

Reality collided with delusion and crashed my protective shield to pieces. I couldn't lie to myself anymore. The evidence was unmistakable. A vice gripped my heart, and I felt it ripping out of my chest as an unearthly wail I didn't recognize as my own shattered the silence. The tears came. Grief had finally found me.

The nurse held me until my wails turned to a steady stream of tears that didn't subside even as she gently helped me shower, changed my gown and linens and wrapped me in tight bindings to ease the pain in my breasts and stop the flow of milk. After she helped me back to bed, the nurse gave me a cup of grape juice before she left. The juice reminded me of communion, but when I tried to pray I felt numb. Paralyzed.

Alone.

A few minutes later a friend knocked on my door and entered. Gwen saw my tears and distress.

"What's the matter, honey? What's wrong?" She dropped her things and rushed to my side.

"My breast milk came in ... but I know my baby will never ..." I couldn't finish the sentence as tears once again filled my eyes. Gwen held me and said a prayer that ministered to my heart. By no accident God had sent a Christian friend into my room as I was finally being reconciled to the tragedy I had been ignoring, and demanding everyone else to ignore.

The doctors had lifted the isolation quarantine a few days before, and I asked Gwen to take me outside to get some sunshine. As she wheeled me down the hall, we passed the hospital chapel.

"Wait. Will you take me inside?" I whispered.

"Absolutely," she said and pushed my wheelchair right up to the front of the altar. She took a seat a few rows back and gave me private time at the foot of the cross. I sat there in silence for what seemed a long time. I waited to hear from God but I felt nothing. I wanted to say something to Him but the chapel felt empty-void of God. Where was He?

"Okay, I'm ready to go," I finally said. "Can you please take me back to my room? I don't feel much like going outside now."

When she got me back in my hospital bed, I was ready to ask her some questions.

"Was there a funeral?"

"Yes," she said. "There was a lovely grave side service."

"Who was there?"

She named some of the friends and family members. Then, she took a deep breath and proceeded gingerly. "Vicki, Paul asked me to pick out what your baby would be buried in. I chose a little blue night gown."

As she described it to me, I tried hard to remember which one it might be, but I couldn't place it. It bothered me I didn't know which blue nightgown she was talking about—as I'd touched and stared at all of the tiny clothes for months.

After a long pause, I asked another question.

"Was he wrapped in a blanket?"

"Yes, I picked out the blanket, too."

Michelle and I would often sit on the floor in the nursery and admire all the tiny little clothes and blankets. I knew them all by heart. "Which one did you choose?" I asked.

"The white crocheted blanket with silver threads."

"Oh, yes, I remember that one, it was very pretty."

This quiet exchange of information was a healing balm on my broken heart. It was good to know my baby was wrapped in a beautiful blanket. But when she started to tell me about the tiny white casket, my protective hand went up.

I didn't want to talk about it anymore.

"Gwen, I think I need to talk to Paul about this part."

She completely understood and, after a while, she hugged me good-bye. I just laid there in silence and darkness until Paul arrived. He knew what to expect as Gwen called to tell him I was ready to talk at last.

## A Great and Tiny Sacrifice

That evening when Paul got to the hospital, his relief was visible and our emotions were raw as we finally talked about our son.

I asked him some of the same questions I asked Gwen. He told me about the blue nightgown and the pretty blanket. He told me about the tiny casket, and the small cross of yellow roses that had lain on top of it. He talked about the service and the comforting words of our pastor.

"There must have been fifty people there, honey."

He recounted the friends and family who had come, even though the burial had taken place on a bitter cold and rainy February morning.

He then gave me a stack of sympathy cards he had saved.

"You won't believe how many plants and flowers people have given us. Our place looks like a greenhouse." He laughed to lighten the mood. "We have pots and vases everywhere."

Not very amused, I asked "What about in the baby's room? Did you put some there?" I tried to picture flowers in the room I spent so much time preparing, and wondered how I was ever going to be able to enter it again.

"No, that room is pretty much empty." He cast his eyes to my bed linens. "Some of our friends came and took down the crib. They packed up the clothes and most of the nursery items."

"*What?* Why would they do that? Why would you let them do that, Paul?" I cried.

"I—I—I guess I wasn't thinking … when they offered I thought it sounded like a good idea. I'm sorry, honey, I'm sorry…." I didn't have to question the genuineness in Paul's words.

I came to realize my friends thought it would be too sad for Paul and me to put everything away. However, in retrospect, I think we needed to do some of those things ourselves to get through the various stages of grief. I felt grief in every part of my being. There is no cure for grief. It's not something you can pack up in boxes and haul away. You just have to walk through it.

Grief was the helium that filled my empty heart and helped it continue to beat.

The *Yahrzeit* is the Jewish tradition that marks the first year of mourning. I entered that year with indescribable pain. I missed not only the funeral of my son, but also the ability to say good-bye to him while removing his personal belongings from the nursery.

## A Picture and a Promise

On the evening Paul and I had our first discussion about the baby, he took my hands in his and quietly told me he had some Polaroid pictures.

"Do you want to see him? You don't have to…"

I took a deep breath "Yes, I do. It's okay…"

We stared at the pictures and marveled at how precious our tiny son looked. His face seemed angelic. Seeing he resembled Paul's dad, we decided to name him George after his grandfather. We had originally thought Christopher Paul would be his name, but instead we honored our fathers and decided on Rodney George. We still refer to him as Little George.

That night after Paul left, I was exhausted and tired of crying. As I tried to calm my spirit, I began to hear words inside my head as though someone was talking to me. Unable to ignore the words, I grabbed some of the envelopes from the stack of get well soon and sympathy cards people had sent me, and I wrote the words swimming around in my head.

"In about a year, and less than two, I will give you another child. Perfect and healthy. Do not fear for you will not be sick, and you will have no complications. This child will be mighty in the eyes of the Lord and do great things for My Kingdom. Many will come to the knowledge of God and be healed and delivered. For this child will hear My voice, have a heart after Me and do great exploits for My Glory. Many will be blessed."

I looked with stunned amazement at the words I'd written. I never had such a phenomenon happen to me, never mind the fact I communicated face-to-face with my guardian angel. I wasn't familiar with prophecy or how it worked, and I wondered if this was how life would be from now on? Would I always hear these silent voices? Have visions? See angels? Had some secret doorway been opened? I didn't know, but I treasured this note from God. I read and re-read the words

I was compelled to write, then tucked it away and trusted God would bring it about in His appointed time.

I had no idea this would be the first of many prophetic messages the Spirit of God would reveal to my heart and mind—and manifest in reality. Indeed, a doorway was opened—ushering me into a spiritually supernatural life.

## The Gem of Baptism

When our pastor learned I was now able to acknowledge our son's passing, he came to visit me just before I was released from the hospital. Paul was there, and the pastor prayed with us and read some scriptures. Then, he told me before little George passed away, a delivery room nurse noticed on my identification bracelet that I was Lutheran.

"She took the liberty to baptize your baby according to Lutheran tradition," he said. From his demeanor, this was apparently a significant thing.

"Was that the nurse sitting at the end of my bed crying?" I asked.

"Yes, it was," the pastor said, then looked at Paul, astonishment on his face. He and Paul were both surprised by my question—since they could attest to my being comatose at the time. But I remembered it all clearly.

"Why was it so important to baptize an infant?" I asked.

"Because it is a tenet of the Lutheran faith," he said, and explained the position of the church regarding infant baptism.

"Are you saying if the nurse hadn't baptized our baby, he wouldn't be in Heaven now?"

He nodded affirmatively.

I simply could not believe this to be true. I respectfully told the pastor he was wrong. He said he had his "personal beliefs," but this is what the Lutheran faith supported.

This prompted Paul and me to question the doctrinal beliefs of our church for the first time. To us, this Lutheran "tenet of faith" didn't feel right. It also didn't seem right a pastor would "personally believe" something different from what his "professional faith" supported—as his vaguely ambiguous comment seemed to indicate was the case.

While something in my spirit didn't seem right, I had no idea how conflicted people were on this entire subject of infant baptism. In fact, on the issue of baptism in general. I never knew this was one of the key issues that caused the splintering of Protestant denominations in church history. It certainly splintered me and I needed answers.

This is where our journey for spiritual truth really began for us as a couple.

We never returned to the Lutheran church, and vowed to become more aware of the doctrinal differences in denominations—something neither of us had ever really considered.

Our son would never see the sun, never know his big sister, and never experience the fierce and protective love of two young parents who were ready to welcome him into their growing family- at least not on planet earth. Our baby was in Heaven, and at only twenty-one and nearly nineteen, Paul and I were just babies ourselves. For all of our seemingly responsible bravado, it was our first experience with grief in all of its pain and glory. Yet out of this devastation came a desire to know God more deeply, the beginning of a glorious journey.

God promises us His strength, His support, and His victorious right hand. His right hand is idiomatic for absolute power. There is no god greater. He is a God of miracles, and He is a God of healing.

God used this tragedy to breathe life into our faith, conviction, and marriage. He used it to move in miraculous and prophetic ways in both of our lives. Like the children of Israel who had wandered in the desert, God gave us another chance.

Paul's spiritual epiphany during this time was as cataclysmic to him as my death and angelic visitation were to me. No longer the little girl from Texas and the smart boy from Ohio, we were now set upon a course to be warriors for God, on a mission to find truth and wisdom.

No matter how many times I held my hand up to Paul in desperate denial, God was holding His hand out to us.

We would never be the same again.

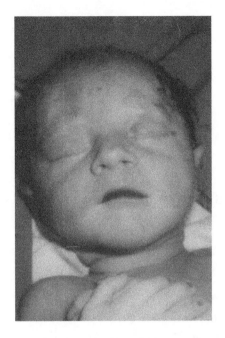

**Rodney George Sarvadi, February 13, 1978**

## Chapter 7
# LIFTING THE FOG

𝕸ikveh: Immersion in waters of new birth, Baptism

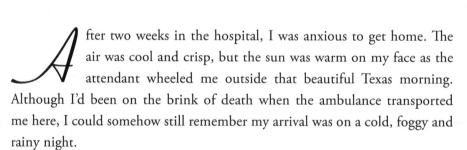

*Through immersion into his death we were buried with him; so that just as, through the glory of the Father, the Messiah was raised from the dead, likewise we too might live a new life.*
Romans 6:4 CJB

After two weeks in the hospital, I was anxious to get home. The air was cool and crisp, but the sun was warm on my face as the attendant wheeled me outside that beautiful Texas morning. Although I'd been on the brink of death when the ambulance transported me here, I could somehow still remember my arrival was on a cold, foggy and rainy night.

So much had happened since then—it seemed a lifetime ago.

As I waited for Paul to bring the car around to the entrance, I felt a cavalcade of conflicting emotions. I lost my baby boy and there was a deep sadness in my soul. However, there was no denying I also found something miraculous—a new sense of direction—a heightened spiritual awareness. Polar opposite feelings of both grief and gratitude tugged at my spirit.

God not only healed me from a deadly liver ailment, but He also sent an angel to help me find purpose and clarity of mind. And He began to reveal prophetic words to me—a supernatural communication that would intensify over the years. For some reason, God had turned His attention toward me.

As soon as I arrived home, I went straight into little George's room to find it empty, except for Winnie-the-Pooh curtains and one piece of furniture. The folding changing table with empty bins underneath sat like a lone sentry in the room. I don't know why my friends left this, but I'm glad they did.

Michelle came bustling in, but her bright smile faded when she saw my face.

"Mommy, why are you crying?" She tugged on me. "Are you sad?"

"Yes, sweetie. Mommy is sad."

I sat on the floor and held her in my lap. The last time we sat together in the same place we were marveling about how tiny the baby clothes were, and we had a long talk about what it was going to be like to have a new baby in the house.

Now, I tried to explain to my three-year-old her little brother was in Heaven. She was very quiet. Concerned and trying to understand why the baby wasn't going to be living with us, she crawled from my lap and squatted to look inside the changing table bins.

"Where are the baby clothes?" She tilted her head as her bottom lip started to quiver.

I mumbled quietly—something like he needed all his things in Heaven—as I got up to look in the closet. There were still a few things remaining on a shelf, and I grabbed two receiving blankets and held one out to Michelle as I clung to mine and sank back to the floor.

We just sat there with our baby blankets and stared at the Winnie-the-Pooh curtains still hanging on the window. We discussed the colors of the balloons Winnie was holding. My arms literally ached, and I found myself clutching my chest as I had the day I first realized my baby was gone. The grief overwhelmed me. I tried to stay strong for my little toddler, but I couldn't contain my tears. She climbed back up in my lap and wrapped her little arms around me and said, "They're red mommy, the balloons are red."

Not long after this conversation Michelle "created" two imaginary friends, Cambie Bambie and Cambie's friend, Nay Nay. These "friends" quickly became residents at our home. We had to accommodate both friends, which included opening doors for them, fixing plates of food at lunchtime for them and remembering to say good-night to them all. Children often create imaginary friends, especially after traumatic events I was told; this was normal and maybe even healthy.

Sometimes it unnerved me. But these little friends seemed to be Michelle's therapy, and they made her happy. Many months later, they faded into oblivion and were gone.

As days turned to weeks, I held on to the hopeful prophecy I'd felt compelled to write down while in the hospital. And a particular scripture verse I highlighted in my Bible brought me great comfort: We remember before our God and Father your work produced by faith, your labor prompted by love, and your endurance inspired by hope in our Lord Jesus Christ. For we know, brothers and sisters loved by God, that he has *chosen* you, because our gospel came to you not simply with words but also with power, with the Holy Spirit and deep conviction (1 Thessalonians 1:3-5 NIV).

I was always a hopeful person, always looking for the best and trying to stay positive. Although it's hard to find anything positive in the death of a child, the prophetic words I received in the hospital gave me hope, and this scripture confirmed what I was going through was part of something much bigger.

*Had He chosen me?*

Yes, I lost a baby, but there was no denying what I also gained. I had been given a supernatural opportunity to pass through my life and see it displayed before me like a blueprint—a timeline grid filled with amazing gifts that would one day be mine! I'd seen an angel who talked to me—who revealed powerful truth with great conviction. And I later heard what was like a voice deliver prophetic words about my next child. I had crossed over into a spiritual world that would change my life.

I was trying to process all of this information as I read from a yellow pad Paul had given to me at the hospital.

I had written copious notes during my recovery, recounting every detail of what I remembered from the time Paul accompanied me to my routine doctor's appointment to the point when I died. I recorded every word I could remember that the messenger *Peretz* said. As I kept rereading my notes, I began to understand the earthly restlessness I felt was caused by the heavenly revelation I experienced.

Then I realized I had a choice to make—remain confused and question the reason of the experience, or have faith and accept it. And because God doesn't lie, my choice was clear.

"Okay, God," I said aloud, "let's do this!"

It would be many years before I really had understanding and clarity about the depth of revelation I had received from *Peretz*, but choosing faith and acceptance at that time gave me an insatiable desire to search for answers in the Bible. A true hunger for Bible study was born in my spirit—a hunger that would eventually become my life's work.

At the time, I still couldn't process God's Word very well, it was filled with idioms, analogies, and foreign words, but what I did understand made me hopeful.

And as more time passed, I realized God was indeed watching over me. He was answering many of my prayers, and He was definitely healing my body. Perhaps even more important, He was healing my marriage.

It was miraculous—Paul no longer seemed intent on making me into a Stepford wife. Something changed in him when I got sick, a change that brought us so much closer together.

## A New Denominational Direction

At the invitation of a friend, we began attending Fellowship Baptist Church, later to be renamed Metropolitan Baptist. I was impressed and a bit taken aback by the casual approach to faith in this new flavor of Christianity we discovered.

My view of worship was to be silent and reverent in a high liturgical formal service in which every congregant knew when to stand, kneel, sit, sing, and recite the creeds. As Lutherans, we even knew when to leave the service as the organist launched into *A Mighty Fortress is Our God* and ushers appeared and nodded for each row to exit in a formal recessional as the song played on.

This new Baptist experience was different—*completely* different.

Here, people would sometimes shout "amen" or "praise the Lord!" Audience interaction was a bit of a culture shock, but I quickly adapted.

This church also incorporated theatrical drama in their worship services with full stage productions and re-enactments of the Passion and Nativity Stories and special solos sung by talented congregants. To someone who loved theatre as a schoolgirl, this opened up a brand-new dimension to me. This new kind of living faith was vibrant—no longer just a formal rote routine. I was ready for the progression.

We elected to be water baptized *in Christ* right away, as it was an outward expression of our inward decision to follow Him. This was different from the sprinkling done in the Catholic and Lutheran churches which symbolized being baptized into the *church*.

The issue of baptism was the main reason we left our Lutheran church, and this public profession of faith and what the Bible said about it felt right to us. We were joyfully caught up in the Baptist experience of salvation and the new birth through the womb of baptismal waters.

I later found the doctrine of Baptism comes from our Jewish matrix of a similar custom called *mikveh*. The idea of *mikveh* is also likened to being born again like a baby coming out of the waters of the womb.

Although the entire body is immersed, it's not just the physical act of baptism alone that is important, it's also about the conscious decision one makes spiritually and emotionally to be a new creation in Christ. When we make a conscientious decision to repent of our sin and to trust Him, water baptism becomes the announcement to the physical and spiritual world of our heart decision. It is the formal ceremony or picture of our dying to self and rising anew in Christ. Because He was Jewish, *Yeshua* was fully immersed in baptism as is the Jewish custom. It was at this event God, the Father proclaimed Christ to be His Son, and the Holy Spirit lighted upon Him in the form of a dove. In fact, the moment of Jesus' baptism fulfilled a great prophecy as it was then that the Great King of all the universe, the Crown of all creation announced audibly by what Jewish custom calls the voice of a dove that the One being delivered out of the waters of the *mikveh* to be the King's Son, the Prince of Peace.[11]

~

We settled into our new life as Baptist believers as we continued to process the grief of losing our son by immersing ourselves in our Amway business. Our group became so energized and impassioned. They rallied behind us—due in part to Paul's increasingly adept leadership ability to encourage and empower others and maybe just because of compassion. Regardless, it was exciting to see the numbers of people sign up and the orders increasing.

As weeks turned into months, I begged my doctor to allow me to get pregnant again. I desperately wanted to see the fulfillment of the prophecy I had been given—the one initially written on the back of the pastel yellow envelope I kept in my Bible. However, the doctor insisted I wait until my bilirubin blood count was back down to near normal.

Four months later, I got the green light, not that I think the doctor expected me to conceive right away.

But I did.

## A Child of Prophecy is Born

Our beautiful daughter Cynthia Pauline (Cindy) was born less than thirteen months after we lost our son. Our child of prophecy weighed a little over six pounds, was perfectly healthy, and we were thrilled!

Paul got involved teaching "college-and-career" Sunday-school classes with his good friend Richard Rawson. Then, he started to serve at our church as one of the leaders of Evangelism Explosion, a program that nurtures believers to share their faith in Jesus. He was a natural-born teacher and encourager. I became involved with the nursery department, helping to teach toddlers about Jesus.

It was 1979 and Paul eventually stopped wearing three-piece suits to church, as was the Lutheran custom. Instead, he now wore button-down shirts with an open collar or a leisure suit. I traded dresses for fashionable blouses with big shoulder pads and high-waisted, front-pleated pants. The heels were clunky, and the hair was big.

My Lutheran upbringing taught that our relationship with God was a private matter and shouldn't be mixed into the secular aspects of our lives throughout the week. But we learned a different view about sharing our faith from our new church community and fellow Amway distributors. We learned that hearing spiritual testimonies in the context of our everyday lives is often how the Lord comes into the hearts of many non-believers, transforms their lives, and compels them to faith. We realized "telling our testimonies" glorified Him.

Our up-line distributors were also outspoken about their faith in the public arena. Fortunately, the Amway culture embraced this. So it was in large Amway conferences Paul and I began to share our testimony of faith on a grand scale.

Many were brought to tears as we shared about Paul's life-changing ambulance ride, my poignant conversation with a heavenly host and the miracle healing that even the medical community admitted could have only been God's doing. We were now following in the ways of Christ by spreading the good news of salvation to all who would listen.

It was then our Amway business exploded—in a good way.

Within a year of losing our son, we had four personal direct distributors with several more directs down line from those. We were now profit sharing, voting members and had reached the level of Emerald—a big thing in the company. The exponential growth of our distributorship was mind-boggling.

With the addition of little Cindy and our growing network of down line distributors, our twelve hundred square-foot home became cramped. We had about one hundred people in our group and couldn't have many distributors over without bursting at the seams.

"Let's build a house." Paul said one day, and I whole-heartily agreed.

We put our little house on the market and to our surprise, it sold right away. The new owners needed to take occupancy immediately, so we had to make a quick decision. We ended up signing a one-year lease on a four thousand square-foot home with five bedrooms until we could figure out what we were going to do. The house was more than we needed at the time, but being the lady of such a grand manor made me feel quite grown up.

Although I felt grown up, I quickly learned I didn't look it.

I answered the door one day to a service vendor I had called.

"Hi. Is your mother home?" he asked.

"My mother?"

"She called about a problem with …"

"That was me." I laughed. "I called, I'm the mother."

"No way." he shook his head. "You're just a little girl!"

It wasn't the first time I would be mistaken for a child, nor would it be the last, and I couldn't wait to share this with Paul when he got home.

## Sharing Vision and Faith

In almost no time, we were busy on the speaking circuit. Paul was a charismatic and captivating speaker. We were sort of a sensational phenomenon. Since we were in our twenties, we were known as the "diaper directs," an image I was not fond of. We were asked to speak all over the country, and went to several incentive trips and conferences each year to places like the Caribbean and Hawaii. This was a far cry from the vacations I grew up taking to the Texas coast. I never knew ocean water could be such beautiful shades of aqua or turquoise.

Paul began to buy me diamond rings, furs, and new clothes from fancy boutiques. His love language is giving, and he was in his element.

As a girl, I spent countless hours on road trips in the back of a Cadillac. My dad loved his cars, but I never shared his sentiment. A Cadillac was a car for older people, not for a young mom like me. Yet suddenly, Paul and I each had our own. I drove a brand new, blue Cadillac Fleetwood Brougham. At times I felt silly driving Michelle and Cindy around in what felt more like a big boat.

However, this type of luxury automobile motivated the group, so that's what I had to drive. Soon, I began to feel like everything we did—everything we bought—was to "motivate the group." We were the official "dog and pony show."

One December morning I realized my monthly cycle was late, so I bought a home pregnancy test. This was long before instant pregnancy tests were available, and I remember waiting anxiously for the fifteen-minute results. Michelle had just turned five in September and was at a pre-K class, and nine month-old Cindy was on my right hip smiling at me as I paced in the bathroom, holding the plastic strip in my hand.

"Do you want to be a big sister?" I cooed with mounting excitement.

As I stared at the positive sign on the pregnancy test, my eyes got big, and I shouted with joy.

"Oh my goodness, oh my goodness!"

Cindy squealed with delight, almost like she was saying, "Oh yeah, this is gonna be fun."

I remember thinking, "I'm going to have two babies and a preschooler, and everyone still thinks I'm just a little girl myself."

Our lease would soon be up on our house. We had originally thought we were ready to buy or build a new home, and we already gave notice to our landlord. However, being pregnant changed our plans once again, since having no health insurance meant paying cash for a cesarean section.

"The house will have to wait a little longer," Paul said.

We set out to find a home to lease and, in almost no time, we found a nice house on a golf course and signed a one-year lease.

Diana Andree was born ten days before Michelle's sixth birthday. Cindy was eighteen months, I was twenty-one, Paul was a worldly twenty-three, and our lives were moving forward with a velocity that defied logic and normality.

As part of my post-baby exercise, Paul and I decided to take dance lessons from a school a few blocks from our house. We dropped Michelle off at pre-kindergarten, Cindy at preschool, and took Diana, our newborn, in her carrier with us to class.

Our teachers were old enough to be our parents and were an unusual match. She was tall with the longest legs I had ever seen. A former ballerina, she was elegant and graceful, and with several sashays she could be from one side of the dance floor to the other. She had black hair, always in a bun, and typically sported a sweet smile. He, however, was a short cowboy with stubby legs, mostly bald (with a little gray hair on the sides). For eight weeks this interesting couple worked with us several times a week. We learned to waltz, foxtrot, and tango, as well as "The Swing" and "The Jitterbug." I recalled the pleasant memories I had of watching my parents dance around our living room. Paul and I gravitated more to the swing of the 40's and 50's and my mom and dad seem to be happy about our desire to learn "their kind of dancing."

~

Our Amway business continued to thrive. We loved our life together, and we loved being parents. Our kids brought such joy into our lives, and oh so many funny moments.

I remember one spring day when Cindy and Diana were toddlers, Paul was enjoying the nice weather with the girls on the back patio. Cindy sat on his lap and Diana was perched on his outstretched legs while looking back at the two of them and sucking on a pacifier.

"What do you like about your sister?" Paul asked Cindy as she leaned back on his chest.

"She's pretty," Cindy answered.

"Yes, she is," Paul said. "What else?"

Cindy, barely three, thought for a moment and said, "Well, she's funny."

Paul smiled at her response. "Yes, I agree. What else?"

Cindy shrugged her shoulders and put her little palms in the air said, "I just love her!"

Paul was relishing the beautiful moment when Diana pulled the pacifier out of her mouth and said, "Wha yelse?"

Perhaps it was our laughter that fueled our youngest. From that moment on, Diana forged her niche as our comedian, actress, and all around drama-queen—always wanting the laughter, limelight and attention.

Cindy, on the other hand, was quiet, compliant and so gentle. Being true to the prophecy of the promise, she often prayed for people she knew were sick. When she was four, I told her that her little friend, David, had broken his arm. She immediately fell to her knees and with tears asked God to heal his arm. I always marveled at her faith as a small child—it was a natural part of who she was. Seeing homeless people on the roads, she would beg and plead with us to help them. She talked about Jesus to her classmates in kindergarten. She was a perfect student and role model even through her teenage years. I have to admit we rarely had to discipline her. Just a slight raise of an eyebrow caused her to repent.

Growing up, Diana and Cindy were always extremely close, perhaps because they were so close in age—barely a year and a half between them. Michelle adored her little sisters, but was very independent. I always looked for ways to make my oldest know how special she was—how much I cared. When she was in grade school, I became a scout leader for her Brownie troop (the precursor to Girl Scouts.) Brownies gave us a wonderful opportunity to spend time together, and I had a great time leading these sweet little girls in craft activities, songs, field trips, and yes, in Girl Scout cookie sales! By then, the two little imaginary friends who had come to live with us after baby George died had been long gone.

~

Paul was now working Amway full time. Having him home during the day was nice, but at night he was in everyone's living room but ours, recruiting more and more distributors. The more successful our business became, the more administrative work I had to do in processing orders, unpacking boxes, and preparing product for our down line to pick up and distribute. Although I did feel a special connection with the crowd when I could share my testimony from the platform, the glow of being an Amway celebrity was wearing off for me.

We had a successful business and more material goods than I ever dreamed of, but something was missing in our life.

Our church attendance had become sporadic, and I felt like our involvement in Amway was competing for our time with God ... again. I had grown lax in keeping God and His Word as the center matrix of my life; we both had. There seemed to be a struggle in our ability to keep a balanced perspective. When I identified my spiritual emptiness, I became hungry for the deeper things of God's Word that can only be found by studying it faithfully.

One day, a couple we knew in Amway invited us to their church to hear a special speaker, Norman Vincent Peale—renowned author of *How to Win Friends and Influence People*. We had recommended his book to all our distributors, so we really wanted to hear him.

Although his talk was powerful, something about the church didn't feel right to me. It was intriguing, and the people we met that evening were without a doubt philosophically and intellectually deep, but I just didn't feel the power of God in this place. God gives us peace of mind when His Spirit is present, and both Paul and I lacked peace of mind during our visit.

Though we didn't visit the church again, we decided to give this couple an opportunity to teach us some visualization techniques. The next weekend they invited us to attend what they called a "Mastermind Meeting" at their home. As dogs barked in a frenzy outside the house, we sat around in a circle and "meditated" together and then shared the "visions" we were having. We even began having our own "Mastermind" meetings in our own home.

For a few months, we dabbled in the teachings of the New-Age movement that swept the country. New-Age is an umbrella term used to describe many diverse groups that share an enthusiasm for the creation of a new era (i.e. "New Age") exemplified by harmony and enlightenment.

The New-Age movement grew in popularity during the 70s and 80s through the teachings of David Spangler and other metaphysical religious groups, but it has existed in various forms since the second century, beginning with Gnosticism. New-Age ideas have many different origins from a variety of places, but most of them can be traced to Eastern religious traditions such as Hinduism, Buddhism, and other ancient religious traditions. New-Age groups are often distinguished by their occult practices of psychic readings, tarot cards, yoga, meditation strategies, and astrology.

There is no standard doctrine within the New-Age movement, as many of their teachings focus on individual autonomy, relativism, and spiritualism—and it's because of that foundational ambiguity, we felt unsettled—unsure of who was really being exalted and worshiped.

There was something in both of us that was nagging and uncomfortable with this "metaphysical expression" of religion based primarily on pursuing personal enlightenment. Paul and I knew we needed to reconnect with God, and within a few months decided this path definitely wasn't it.

And so, we defaulted back to what we knew—to our comfort zone—and headed back to our Baptist church where we took refuge.

Our nation was changing. Under Ronald Reagan's presidency, we welcomed Sandra Day O'Connor as the first woman Supreme Court Justice. It seemed everyone was singing and dancing to one of the many hit songs from *Thriller*, Michael Jackson's record-breaking album. And a collective belief that fairy tales can come true swept across the world as Lady Diana Spencer married Prince Charles, becoming the much-beloved Princess of Wales.

After leasing two homes, we finally bought a new home in Terra Nova West in the Northwest Houston area. It was a busy year for us. It was also an exciting one, as we traveled to Europe for the first time. That was the year my boat-size Cadillac was replaced by a new Lincoln Mark IV, and I was ecstatic.

## A New Adventure

Paul and his friend Richard had friends who were brick masons, and it seemed they were all working overtime to keep up with the building demands in Houston. Neither Paul nor Richard knew anything about the building business, but the dynamic duo were certain they were on to something big when they started a brick masonry construction company.

About the same time, we moved all the Amway products and our distributor operations out of our home and into rented offices.

My husband is an optimist of the highest order—a true positive thinker. We invested a lot of money into the masonry company, which had just officially launched. When Paul came home from work one day looking defeated and sad I prodded him to tell me what was wrong.

"I went to visit little George's grave today," he blurted out with tears in his eyes.

I was shocked at this revelation. I had only visited the grave a few times, because my guardian angel assured me our baby sat on the lap of the Father. And even though five years had passed, Paul's sadness instantly brought back memories of the hardest time of my life.

It was difficult to watch Paul cry, but I knew in my spirit everything was going to be okay. I thought back to what *Peretz* had revealed to me, how there were so many more blessings left to experience on my timeline grid of life. We had been married for almost a decade, and our youngest child (Diana) was now three.

"Do you want to have another baby?" I quietly asked.

Truthfully, we both missed the joy a baby brings into the world. Call us crazy but at that moment, we decided to try and have another child. We didn't have to try long. I often teased Paul I got pregnant that time because we shook hands and agreed on it.

Fortunately, fertility was (obviously) not an issue.

## Good-bye Michelle - Hello Shannon

I was six months pregnant when a tragic event happened.

Our sponsor in Amway had a little girl who was Michelle's best friend. Lisa and Michelle had been inseparable since they were two, and both girls were about to turn ten. They were talking on the phone one day and when Michelle hung up, she was very troubled.

"Mom, you have to pray for Lisa," she said.

"What's the matter, honey?" I asked.

"She's going to Knoxville for her birthday to visit her grandparents..." Michelle began to cry. "Mom, it felt like she was saying goodbye to me for the last time." Tears streamed down her cheeks.

"Oh sweetie, it's going to be fine. You'll see her in no time." I tried to comfort her, but it was apparent Michelle was greatly affected by the phone call. I prayed with her and told her we had to trust God to watch over Lisa.

A day later, Paul and I were awakened in the middle of the night with a phone call. Lisa had been killed earlier that evening in Knoxville by a drunk driver.

*Lord, how are we going to tell Michelle?*

After breakfast, we broke the news to the two older girls.

Cindy started to cry, but Michelle looked at us blankly, almost as though she knew it was coming. She responded with a fierce stoicism that frightened me.

"Can I go to my room now?"

At that moment we lost our Michelle, as though a part of her died *with* Lisa. In short order, she dropped her middle name, Michelle, and took on her first name, Shannon, all the while informing us she never wanted to be "Michelle" again.

"Shannon" didn't want to talk about Lisa, or anything remotely personal or serious. When baby George died, her imaginary friends kept her company. This time, she took on a new identity. Life (at least on the surface) was all about laughter and levity. She retreated from conflict and decided to be "happy," have fun, and stay as busy as possible. After Lisa died, conversations never got too deep before Shannon put up the protective walls to keep emotions away. I knew this tactic all so well. I had thrown up my hand to keep negative words away. Shannon resigned herself to a life of fun. Cyndy Lauper's hit song, *Girls Just Want to Have Fun* became the anthem in our home.

We encouraged Shannon to get involved in the preteen group at our Baptist church, and around this time Cindy and Diana decided to make a public profession of faith. Shannon elected to join them. Although she was still struggling with her grief, I could sense her honest desire to feel God in the same way as Cindy and Diana.

So it happened that all three of our girls were water baptized at the same time. Three little girls declaring Jesus is Messiah were immersed in the *mikvah* waters of baptism. As parents, we were so blessed, yet a familiar sense of unrest began to trouble us.

We were beginning to feel something in our spirits about the dogmatic restrictions of our Southern Baptist church. Something just didn't feel right. After Paul's Catholic upbringing, our past Lutheran experience and now a waning Baptist affiliation, we began to wonder if we would ever be able to find a spiritual home for our searching souls.

"Are we looking for something that doesn't exist?" I asked Paul one day.

Compelled to seek the deeper things of God, we thought we would venture out again to find a new level of spirituality. Our friends, Dave and Patty invited us to their charismatic Assembly of God Church. The place was packed, and the worship was lively to say the least. People even danced in the aisles. This was something new to transplanted Lutherans-turned Baptists. We had never seen dancing in church.

At one point during the service, a lady sitting next to Paul shot up and began to yell out a message in a garbled language neither of us recognized. Paul's eyes got big, and he squeezed my hand really hard as if to say, "What the heck is going on?"

Although I wanted to comfort him, I have to admit I was a bit unsettled, too. I wasn't ready for *this* type of public expression either. Actually, it all felt a bit manic—a bit crazy to me.

"It's okay," I whispered to him. "I don't think her head is turning a 360…"

Paul smiled, but I could tell he was extremely uncomfortable with all the demonstrative activity going on around us. Although I couldn't say I blamed him, I found the entire experience somewhat fascinating as well. Nonetheless, we went back to our now 1500-member Baptist church the next Sunday.

"I like it here, Vicki. Nobody really knows if were even here," Paul said midway in the generally predictable service. "And I don't have to worry about … unexpected things."

~

Unfortunately, there were a lot of unexpected things Paul *did* have to worry about, primarily our failing brick masonry business. Just a year out of the gate and the chips (or rather bricks) began to fall. Clients began to have a harder time paying their bills and Paul and Richard were juggling significant debt they had guaranteed with their own names.

Our Amway business was still prospering, although Paul hadn't spent much time introducing the opportunity to any new potential distributors.

Sometimes it's the unexpected things in life God uses to speak to us—to shake us up and dust off the cobwebs of complacency or erroneous thinking. That's what was happening to us, as I entered the last trimester of my fifth pregnancy.

It was during this time I began to get a glimpse of faith not only as a personal choice, but as a cultural influence. Organized religion shaped our culture in so many ways, as did the issue of Protestant denominationalism. Suddenly, I began to see that a denomination is not my identity. My identity is in Christ—not in what denominational dogma I followed. And for the first time, I found myself asking very serious questions: "If the various Christian denominations focus on different aspects of how to interpret the Word of God, were they perceiving different facets of the same God of Truth, oblivious to the other's revelations? If they were *all* seekers of Truth, would God throw them curve balls?"[12]

I don't think so. I think they all had some validity.

But where exactly is the central hub of truth?

More questions followed. Was I walking in the call God placed on my life? Was I following the mandate *Peretz* had revealed to me when I died in the ICU?

What would quench the thirst I always seemed to have to know God in a deeper way? Why am I still asking, "What am I missing?"

"I think there's so much more to being a Christian than simply calling yourself one and belonging to a church." I said to Paul one day. I was amazed it had taken me so long to realize this.

As a Lutheran, I understood grace and salvation[13]. As a Baptist, I understood baptism and evangelism[14]. And now I was beginning to understand there is more to the journey of faith than just getting saved and baptized. I wanted to move on through the cross—but I felt the majority of the people in our current church were stuck there. Wasn't the Messiah *off* the cross, raised from the grave and mandating us to receive and walk in His Spirit? What was this promise of the Father Yeshua mentioned before He ascended?[15]

I knew there were more gifts on the timeline grid of my life that God wanted me to have, I just didn't know how to get them.

I started listening to cassette tapes and Christian television speakers such as Pat Roberson and Derek Prince. All this teaching about the power of God through the Holy Spirit intrigued me. I heard about people getting healed and delivered from addictions and even witchcraft. I had questions—a *lot* of questions.

"What are these Gifts and Fruit of the Spirit listed in 1 Corinthians 12?" [16]

"What exactly is intercession or travail?"

And, "Why does someone fast?" [17]

I had a growing list of questions, yet no one at our Baptist church could give me viable answers, no matter who I asked.

I had been so certain of God's will after *Peretz* came to me, but it was years since my guardian angel sent me back from death, and I knew I wasn't totally fulfilling the call God placed on my life. I understood the Father and Son, but I couldn't quite grasp the Holy Spirit. Although I longed to know God in a fresh new way, I wasn't sure about the charismatic expression of Spirit-filled people, I didn't want to be perceived as a crazy person babbling in tongues and completely out of control. No, that wasn't for me.

One Monday morning I prayed a heartfelt prayer: *God, I really do want more of You. I want to go further with You, but not in a crazy way, okay? Please reveal to me what Your will truly is! Who are You, Holy Spirit?*

Maybe a half hour went by when my neighbor from across the street rang my doorbell.

"I'm sorry to bother you," she said timidly, "but I haven't been able to get you out of my mind all morning and I feel compelled to invite you to a Christian ladies group I belong to. Would you be interested?"

Taken aback by the coincidence, I was at first speechless, but then I told Geri about my morning.

"I just prayed that I wanted to go a little further with God. I asked Him to make Himself known to me in a new way," I said.

She smiled and slipped a brochure in my hand as I agreed to go with her later that week. I closed the door and read the brochure about the group called Women's Aglow[18]. I stopped in my tracks when I read they believed in speaking in tongues.

*Okay, Lord, which part of "I didn't want anything too crazy" did You not understand?*

I felt a little uneasy at this type of expression. After all, the supernatural is scary to the mere mortal. My heart was beating a little faster, and I wasn't sure if this unusual fluttering came from the fear of the unknown, or the sheer possibility it held.

Who could have guessed my life—our life—was about to dramatically change. Again.

*Chapter 8*

# TRANSFORMED HEARTS

## 𝔔uach 𝔥a𝔎odesh: Holy Spirit, wind, breath

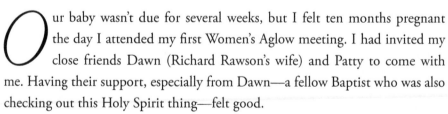

*He asked them, "Did you receive the Ruach HaKodesh when you came to trust?" "No," they said to him, "we have never even heard that there is such a thing as the Ruach HaKodesh."*
Acts 19:2 CJB

O ur baby wasn't due for several weeks, but I felt ten months pregnant the day I attended my first Women's Aglow meeting. I had invited my close friends Dawn (Richard Rawson's wife) and Patty to come with me. Having their support, especially from Dawn—a fellow Baptist who was also checking out this Holy Spirit thing—felt good.

We sat in the back of a packed church sanctuary. The ladies were friendly and seemed genuinely happy we were there. The music was beautiful. Not the big organ like the Lutheran church I grew up in or the piano like the Baptist church we were currently attending. In actuality, it was a small band, and instead of familiar hymns, they were singing Bible verses with snappy contemporary melodies.

At one point, we moved into something I had never heard before, but later learned was called "residual praise." Everyone seemed to be lifting up a personal song, a private melody, an individual praise unto God simultaneously. It sounded heavenly, as if a choir of angels were joining in a glorious rhapsody along with us mortals on earth. This was my first experience with true unadulterated praise and worship unto God—an amazing organic experience that captured my heart and ushered all of us into the presence of the Almighty Creator. This time of singing unto the Lord was not just an agenda formality as I was accustomed.

After this transformative worship experience, a lady named Billie Brim began her message.

"Today the Lord is going to lead some of you in a new direction," she said as she looked around the room. "Today, it's time for some of you to move forward!"

And then she said an unbelievable thing that took my breath away.

"Today, I'm going to talk about 'Going *a little bit' further with God.*"

I could have fallen off my seat when I heard the title of her message. *Really God? Could you be that specific?* Clearly, He sent this woman to answer my exact prayer from three days before.

I listened with great anticipation to one of the most profoundly impactful messages I've ever heard, and I took in her words with an open heart. After her powerful message, she asked us three critical questions:

"How many of you ladies have confessed your sins and asked Jesus to come into your heart, cleansing you from all unrighteousness?"

Without pause, I raised my hand high. Yes, I'd accepted Him as my Savior as a young Lutheran girl in Catechism class. I looked around; it appeared every lady raised her hand.

*Whew—I passed the first test.*

"How many of you have been obedient to His Word and followed the example of Christ by being baptized in water showing forth your new faith as a witness to others?"

My hand shot up again. *Yes! I had been obedient just seven years before when Paul and I joined the Baptist church.* We both made a public confession of faith and were fully immersed in a baptismal in front of hundreds of people proclaiming our sins were washed away and we were new creatures in Christ.

*So far, so good. I was two for two,* I thought.

"Of those who have been born again and have been obedient to be baptized in water, how many of you have *not* been baptized in the Holy Spirit and wish to change that now?"

While her third and final question took me by surprise, I once again raised my hand.

I shot to my feet and found myself somewhat shocked as Dawn and myself (along with another lady) practically ran down the aisle to the front of the church.

That day, I asked for the Messiah Jesus to refine me with an unquenchable fire. To burn up all vestiges of the flesh, to strip away anything that was hindering His perfect way in me. To equip me for every good work He has called me to do, to take away the impurities of my heart and pull out the dross. To burn away the wood, hay, and stubble within my soul, and receive me as a burnt offering[19] before His holiness, and to baptize me in the fire of His Holy Spirit![20]

As I said these words with the speaker, tears rolled down my cheeks.

Suddenly, my entire body felt like a lightning bolt jolted through me. My knees grew weak, my body felt overwhelmed, and I heard another language pour out of my mouth as I physically sank. Someone nearby reached out and helped me and my unborn child to the floor. I wore a knee-length white linen maternity dress with pink and blue ribbons, it reminded me a lot of my wedding dress—rather apropos considering what was happening.

I don't know how long I remained on the floor. Someone placed a blue modesty cloth over my legs. A few of the ladies wore long skirts, and I felt what I thought must be their hems brushing me as they walked around me.

*Or maybe they were brushing me with feathers?*

Not that I spent time trying to figure out what was brushing against me. Instead, I was enveloped in a beautiful experience with God. I felt wonderful peace, perfect love, and unspeakable joy. After some eight to ten minutes, I tried to get up. I needed help as I was weak, shaking all over (not to mention nine months pregnant).

Someone helped me to a chair where I sat next to a lady who introduced herself. "I'm Judy," she said.

As someone read announcements, I leaned over and quietly asked Judy, "What was the meaning of brushing me with feathers?"

She looked at me strangely. "What do you mean? No one was near you," she said.

"No one?" I whispered. "Are you sure?"

"Absolutely sure—you were lying there alone."

She was wrong. I knew I had not been alone, but what exactly had I felt? *Could it have been angels? Or was it the very breathe of God?*

"Holy Spirit" in Hebrew is Ruach Ha Kodesh, which can be translated to the wind or breath of God. Just as Adam received the breath of God after he was created, it is also received after one becomes a new creation in Christ—when the Ruach (or breath of God) comes in to give new life, a new life of power. The Holy Spirit does not just breathe one breath into your physical lungs, but rather new life into your entire being. Because you are crucified with Christ, nevertheless you live, and the Holy Spirit now lives in you and gives you His constant breath. He—the Holy Spirit—actually is the breath you breathe.

Without His Spirit, we cannot clearly hear God's voice.

The anointing of the Holy Spirit gives us a supernatural power that causes a renewing of the mind—and the mind is where conflict is fought.

I had been experiencing inner conflict for years, but my season of confusion was about to end. At last, I could finally begin to walk in the purpose Peretz had shared with me when I died.

### The Missing Piece/Peace

While Apollos was at Corinth, Paul arrived at Ephesus and asked 12 disciples if they had received the Holy Spirit since they believed in the Messiah.

And they said unto him, We have not so much as heard whether there be any Holy Ghost.

And he said unto them, Unto what then were ye baptized? And they said, Unto John's baptism. Then said Paul, John verily baptized with the baptism of repentance, saying unto the people, that they should believe on him which should come after him, that is, on Christ Jesus. When they heard this, they were baptized in the name of the Lord Jesus.

And when Paul had laid his hands upon them, the Holy Ghost came on them; and they spake with tongues, and prophesied (Acts 19:2-6 KJV).

Like these disciples, I had received what was similar to the message of John's baptism, which was to repent and believe upon God's giving of the Messiah. During my public profession of faith with Paul at our baptism, I had repented of my sins and made a confession that I *believed* Jesus gave His life for me as God's atoning Lamb. But at that time, I wasn't told that God requires more – because even demons believe.[21]

Before Billie prayed with me she told me God desired to give gifts to all His children.

"It is the gift of the Holy Spirit that changes and transforms us," she said. "You were right to confess your sins and proclaim Jesus as your Savior and be water baptized, but now you must allow Him to take away the bondages that keep you from giving Him your all."

Then, she asked if there were things in my life I still needed to give to God, if there were still areas where I didn't trust Him. "If so," she said, "you must surrender them, allow His Spirit to reside in you. You must include the Holy Spirit in your covenant relationship with God. And then, He will equip you for every good work, whether it would be healing, counsel, wisdom, even deliverance as the Spirit takes up residence in you."

Being in a covenant with God is definitely like a marriage, the two parties exchange assets and liabilities. When we enter into a covenant with Him, we come with a lot of baggage, imperfections, unrighteousness, bad habits, vices and problems. However, God comes to us in authority, perfection, holiness and power. His Son, Jesus, took my guilt of not keeping His Holy ways and paid the price of death for me according to Torah. He took the liability of my sin and the Laws that were written against me upon Himself to be buried with Him in the grave. In this covenant exchange, He gives me His power by His Spirit to overcome every weakness. I now have His mind and His authority because like in marriage we share in assets and liabilities. I also have His name. The Word says His name is actually written on my forehead evident in the spiritual dimension.[22]

In order to walk fully in God's glorious promises, it is necessary for me to give my life back to Him, not living for myself any more, but rather allowing His Holy Spirit to live *through* me—to empower me as I obey His commandments and instructions. It is this partnership of me (a mortal being) and Him (the all-powerful Spirit, God) that is life-changing.

However, this covenant relationship (a marriage *ketubah*, if you will,) could only transform me to the degree I was willing to "give up" my own ways and desires. Receiving His Spirit requires me not only to die to my sinful ways and selfish will, but to also ask for the refinement that will transform me into a new creation. A refinement that will allow the Living Word or Torah to come alive in my heart—to mesh like a tapestry with my physical body as the very ways of God course through me.

With the breath of the Holy Spirit within us, He then equips us with His power called the Gifts and Fruit of the Spirit.[23] It is then we are truly able to do "all things through Christ."[24] Heal, discern spirits, prophecy and receive godly supernatural wisdom by His Spirit.

I was ready. Life as I had known it was over—a new season had arrived.

I would soon learn that the Baptist church where Paul and I were baptized and considered ourselves to be members did not believe in the charismatic ministry and gifts of the Holy Spirit as something one receives today. They believe dispensation occurs at different times in history and we are not in *that* time.[25]

Wow, I had to disagree. Something was definitely dispensed and I was more on fire for God now than I had ever been in my entire life.

My heart was open that day. I was ready to experience the Lord in all of His fullness. Ready just like the believers in the Upper Room when the Holy Spirit came upon them with supernatural power. [26]

I departed the Women's Aglow event that day a far different person than when I arrived. I couldn't imagine why I had ever been afraid of this wonderful promise of the Father. God is so good—He loves me so much. He didn't want to leave me a saved, weak human. He didn't want to bring me to the foot of the cross and leave me there. He wanted to fill me with His life force and power beyond human understanding. The same force that raised Christ from the dead.

On that day, I willingly accepted the precious gift of His covenant Spirit in me.

### Sharing the Gem of the Spirit

My spiritual high was the direct opposite of Paul's professional low when I returned home that afternoon.

I knew he was worried sick about our brick business. The bottom had officially fallen out of the oil industry in Houston, and subsequently the building industry followed. Many of our clients were unable to pay their draws and several were about to file bankruptcy, which meant we would never be able to collect what they owed us.

"Paul, you have to listen to this." I waved the cassette tape I got from the meeting as I walked in the door and marched over to the stereo where I inserted the tape. I knew it would help him in the midst of this financial threat. This was, without doubt, a precious gem on my life grid.*

"It's me, from the meeting today," I said, as I hit play. "I didn't know they were recording it, but I'm glad they did. You won't believe it—I can't believe how the Holy Spirit…"

"Not this Holy Spirit thing again…" Paul interrupted. "I don't have the time or energy for this, Vicki. Give it a rest, will you?" He took a deep breath and growled.

"Paul, you can hear me praying at the end—listen! That's me and the manifestation of a holy language by the Holy Spirit. It isn't an act. I felt it—it was *real*—the Holy Spirit is real! Please, you have to listen…"

My husband listened at first with incredulity, but he listened.

Then I shared my revelation about the Holy Spirit with him.

"Paul, don't you see? God sent the Holy Spirit to remind me of the promises He showed me on the grid when I died in the ICU. *This* is what *Peretz* meant when he said I would acquire special gifts of knowledge God intended me to use for His plans and purposes. I can't do anything in my own power. I need

---

\*      Visit VictoriaSarvadi.com for Precious Gems articles and teachings.

supernatural help. No wonder we've been so restless. We've been walking in our own understanding and our own power."

My spirit cried out as I poured my heart out to my husband.

"Paul, this is where God wants me to be—where He wants *us* to be. I know it...I believe it...I feel it...please—just listen to the tape again—and pray with me."

As Paul listened to the tape over and over again, I could see his heart softening.

My experience earlier that day had been life changing—I knew I would never again be the same. I desperately wanted Paul to feel the same freedom, power and joy of the Spirit that pulsed through my body.

This was a far different baptism than what Paul and I had experienced together years before. Back then we were on the same course at the same time, and as transformational as it had been, it was a decidedly different experience. This time we were on different trajectories, and I prayed fervently our paths would quickly merge. I couldn't bear to think we had come so far together, only to be spiritually split apart. Surely that could not be God's plan.

This could have been a challenging fork in the road for us—had Paul hardened his heart.

Thankfully, that wasn't the case—as God continued to knit our hearts on one path—one course. The fact is, God had already chosen Paul—I was just the conduit He used to ignite the flame in his primed and ready heart.

# Chapter 9
# A TEACHABLE SPIRIT

### 𝕷ilmod: To learn

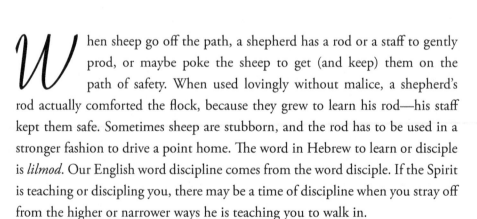

and you have forgotten the encouragement that addresses you
as sons and daughters:
*My child, don't make light of the Lord's discipline or give up when
you are corrected by him, because the Lord disciplines whomever
he loves, and he punishes every son or daughter whom he accepts.*
Hebrews 12:5-6 CEB

hen sheep go off the path, a shepherd has a rod or a staff to gently
prod, or maybe poke the sheep to get (and keep) them on the
path of safety. When used lovingly without malice, a shepherd's
rod actually comforted the flock, because they grew to learn his rod—his staff
kept them safe. Sometimes sheep are stubborn, and the rod has to be used in a
stronger fashion to drive a point home. The word in Hebrew to learn or disciple
is *lilmod*. Our English word discipline comes from the word disciple. If the Spirit
is teaching or discipling you, there may be a time of discipline when you stray off
from the higher or narrower ways he is teaching you to walk in.

God's grace is like a rod that teaches us to stay on the narrow road—the right
path. Grace isn't freedom to sin but rather grace is a supernatural power that

convicts you to come out of the ditch and get back on track. That is what our conscience does. It either affirms or convicts us of our behavior.[27]

Thinking back to those many times when we felt there was more to our calling and we were just not where we should be spiritually, we realized this was what God was doing to us—getting us back on the right path.

Business was bad, times were hard, and we were buried in debt. Things looked really bleak, but we began to see how the Good Shepherd was working amidst the chaos and crisis. He was orchestrating everything with the love and guidance of a firm—but a gentle Shepherd—doing what He does best — getting us back on track.

The Spirit of God was so alive in my heart I couldn't see the demise of our business as anything but His good and perfect will. I knew He was in control, and somehow it was all going to work out. However, failure (in anything) was never an option for Paul, and this was completely unfamiliar territory for him. He didn't have the same peace of the Spirit that made me feel like I was walking on air—despite my heavily pregnant body.

I longed for Paul to have this same lightness of spirit—the burdens he carried were so great.

Spiritual growth and personal struggle can (and most often do) co-exist simultaneously. As Paul continued to listen to my tape, repeatedly, I could sense he had questions I wasn't prepared to answer. So, a few days later I asked my friend Patty if she could bring someone to our home to minister to Paul—and me. I knew she had several friends well-versed in ministering the biblical aspect of the Holy Spirit.

When the Apostle Paul talked about Jesus, he "persuaded the Jews" with the Scriptures they were familiar with, and told them how Yeshua had fulfilled all those prophecies as the Redeemer, God's Passover Lamb. [28] The Gentiles knew nothing of the Words of the prophets, so with them, his technique was different. He just told them what Jesus had done and they believed by faith. When Tommy came to our home, he approached the topic with Paul as though he were a Jew versed in Scripture. They opened their Bibles together and began to talk at great length. Tommy systematically took Paul through the Word and showed him this phenomenon of the Spirit was a promise to believers recorded by the prophet

Joel.[29] He showed him in the Bible how even the Apostle Peter had to remind those who were confused (just like my husband) that this spiritual fog was bound to happen. However, if we kept ourselves open to instruction—course correction—we could come safely through the darkness.

Paul listened, asked questions, and considered all Tommy shared with him. More important, he had a teachable spirit and was completely open to God's will. He laid his heart on the altar of prayer and supplication.

During the five-year period of our success in Amway, we had acknowledged God and believed in our Savior Jesus Christ, but we had not asked for the refining fire of the Holy Spirit. Truthfully, we didn't know much about the Holy Spirit—it wasn't a subject our denomination expounded upon. Back then, we were operating as believers in Jesus but mixing our message of the good news with the teachings of prosperity that glorified success not God.

Truthfully, success is a benefit not a destination and prosperity is a by-product not a goal. We had made a wrong turn when we began to cater to our fleshly desires of things and the pride of life. We had to learn when you are truly in alignment with the Lord you can find joy in lack or in plenty. Blessings are not just financial. It's a blessing to be healthy, healed, delivered, and at peace with God and others in our relationships. We learned some powerful life lessons from our Amway experience, lessons we were still learning as we struggled with the ever-increasing nightmare of our failing business.

However, God's grace gives us the power to overcome any adversity, and His loving rod of influence and direction helps us find our way back on the path of safety.

As Tommy shared more about the influence of the Holy Spirit, I think Paul and I suddenly realized together that we were *both* being disciplined as well as discipled, *and* redirected. We were in danger of getting off track, and it was course correction time. Perhaps God had allowed us to go through hard times as an act of His grace to bring us back into His ways. The demise of our business did not mean the demise of the gifts He placed in us or the purpose He had for our lives. In fact, we relied on them now more than ever.

This was a deeply profound revelation for me, as I began to relive in my spirit the time I spent with my guardian angel. His words echoed loud in my heart and soul, and I knew without question this gift of the Holy Spirit was a significant component on the course I was intended to walk. But I began to realize that there's always going to be more. I will never "arrive" and know it all. God is so much bigger than man and we could never receive all that He is in our entire lifetime. He made me realize a very profound truth. Always be open to the teaching of the Spirit. We go from line to line and glory to glory.

However, it wasn't just time for me to walk in the prophetic wisdom *Peretz* had imparted to me; it was time for Paul to walk in his destiny as well. A destiny that began years ago in the front seat of an ambulance when he gave his heart to the Lord.

Suddenly, I could see all the questions, concerns, and worry fall from Paul's face, replaced by a sweet smile of true sincerity.

"I'm convinced." Paul suddenly declared, as Tommy laid hands on him and prayed that the Messiah, Jesus would baptize Paul in His Spirit.

I thanked the Lord profusely as I looked at my husband with deep respect and relief. This wasn't a man defeated or broken by the influence of a powerful teacher. Tommy did not lead Paul to a place where he wasn't ready—and willing—to go. Paul wasn't a husband pressured by a wife to conform. I merely held fast to the revelation I had been given. I prayed with all my heart and soul for my husband to see the same light I was now walking in—and God answered my prayer.

Anyone could see, by just looking at him, that Paul *personally* realized the work Jesus did on the cross was confirmed after He ascended—so the Holy Spirit would come as a promise of the Father.[30]

Since that day, I have witnessed my husband operate in a power of wisdom and faith that has not been his own—a miraculous transformation that integrated rational logic and spiritual truth on a deeply intimate level of personal understanding and commitment. I believe this personal revelation is the primary reason Paul Sarvadi has become such a powerful and influential force to be reckoned with in the corporate world. Today, my husband is one of the most respected CEOs in the country—perhaps the world. I am constantly amazed at what God has done in Paul's life, and in the lives of the countless people he influences every day.

## Another Heart Miracle

We knew it would be impossible to return to our Baptist church environment.

Although but a few days had passed, it seemed a lifetime of revelation had poured into our hearts. I had asked Judy, the lady I sat next to after I pulled myself off the floor at the Women's Aglow meeting, about the church she attended. She told me it was Trinity Church, a non-denominational Spirit-filled church. Remembering our last experience at a charismatic church, I drew in a deep breath before I suggested to Paul perhaps we could give it another try and visit this church. The fact he wasn't the least bit reluctant to do so gave me added confirmation we were on the same course.

At that time, Trinity Church was temporarily meeting in a school cafeteria, something that strangely brought a more spiritually organic and less traditionally structured feel to the entire experience. It was all about the message—not the physical trappings of structure and formality.

And what a message it was!

The sermon was incredibly enlightening and again unlike any I'd heard before.

The pastor talked about how it was because God had mercy on His children that He sent His Spirit to empower us so we could actually walk as Jesus walked. How we could do even greater things than He had done because He was going to the Father?[31] How could we do anything greater than what Jesus did in laying down His life on our behalf for the atonement of our sins? The only way we could do greater things would have to be by His Spirit working and continuing to live His life in us and through us.

Growing up, the Lutheran liturgy filled me with a deep appreciation for religious tradition. But as an adult, I was unable to fully embrace all the restrictive tenants of the denomination once I began to understand them. Especially after our son died.

The years we spent in the Baptist church confirmed their solid focus on bringing people to the cross of salvation. But what happens once they arrive? It seemed to me like I always heard the same message at our Baptist church—like I was always being fed the nourishing appetizer but denied the meat of the main course. There was a hunger in my soul to go further into God's Word, and I found myself empowered and enlightened by the timely message we heard at Trinity Church that day. Paul felt the same. At last, we were moving on by way of the cross to minister to the sick, the hurting and the tormented in the power of His glorious Spirit.

It took us so long to get to this place. Thank God we were here at last.

At the end of the service, the pastor extended an open invitation to join him up front for prayer—no matter the need. It was almost time for our baby to be born by Caesarean section, and Paul and I eagerly went forward to receive the prayer of faith for a safe delivery.

Just a few days later on November 28th, Paula Kristen was born—we would call her Kristen. Her sisters Shannon, Cindy, and Diana were ten, five, and four respectively. Had he lived, little George would have been seven. I was twenty-five to Paul's twenty-seven, and we had been married for ten years.

"But you're just a little girl!" A member from Trinity Church exclaimed when we returned later that week with our new baby girl and our entire family of beautiful daughters.

Although I may have looked young, I certainly wasn't feeling it the day Kristen was delivered. After giving birth five times, I felt this would be my last delivery. I don't know why, but I felt my body would not be able to handle another pregnancy and live. After talking with Paul, I confirmed with my doctor that after he delivered this baby, I definitely wanted a tubal ligation.

My doctor was in complete agreement and the delivery of our fourth daughter confirmed our concerns.

After cutting through the layers of skin and muscles during the Caesarean section procedure, my doctor was about to place the scalpel on my uterus when suddenly it ruptured. He quickly got the baby out and handed her to a nearby nurse, and began to work feverishly on the profuse hemorrhaging.

"Begin blood transfusions, STAT!" he ordered. Time was critical as I was bleeding out in front of him.

I began to experience the all-too-familiar feeling of falling and floating. I felt my back opening and my tongue thickening as I slowly drifted in and out of consciousness. My spirit did not leave my body this time, although there was a part of me that longed to see my guardian angel again—to ask *Peretz* questions I hadn't thought to ask so many years ago.

Doctors worked feverishly to control the bleeding and repair the damage. To have this happen in the operating room gave me the advantage I needed to survive. Had my uterus ruptured before that day—something that could have easily occurred considering the condition it was in, the internal bleeding would have most likely killed me and our daughter.

Once again, God guided the hand of a skilled doctor and directed a team of dedicated professionals to save my life.

Later that day the pediatrician came to visit us in my room.

"I'm afraid your little girl has a ventricular septal defect, we call it VSD," he said. "In layman's terms, it means your daughter has a few small holes in her heart. You can take her home but the first thing Monday morning, I want to see her at Texas Children's Hospital for a pre-surgery visit and another ultrasound."

Surgery? On a newborn? As scary as it sounded, we weren't afraid. In fact, we had a level of peace that surprised both of us, not to mention everyone around us. You see, we were now equipped with the power and gifts of the Holy Spirit—and this made a decided difference. One of those gifts was the gift of faith. A supernatural assurance that God is in control, is not lacking, and can, in fact, heal our child.

We believed that truth with every fiber of our beings.

That Sunday, just one day after I was released from the hospital, we took all of our daughters and our four-day old infant back to Trinity Church. At the end of the service, we took little Kristen up for prayer. Judy's husband Dean was the elder who laid his hands on our newborn baby and prayed an anointed prayer of faith.

When Monday came the doctors at Texas Children's Hospital were astonished as they looked at comparison tests and ultrasounds.

One previously significant hole in Kristen's heart was completely gone, and the other was now so tiny surgery was deemed unnecessary.

"We can't explain it … it looks like a new heart," the doctors muttered.

But we could. The healing in our daughter's heart was nothing short of a supernatural miracle.

~

As we continued to ask for the fire of the Spirit to fill and enable us, God continued to purge the leaven (aka: the ways of our evil nature) from our lives. More than just Kristen's heart was healed. Paul and I both received a clean heart and the mind of Christ, something that allowed us to better grasp God's will for us.

We began to discern situations and experiences with *His* mind. Our minds became enlightened with revelation, knowledge, wisdom and prophecy as our fleshly thoughts and ways were burned up and removed—supernaturally.

Little did we know as God was saving my physical life and giving us new spiritual lives, He was also preparing us for what He was about to take away. Something we once depended on more than Him—our financial security.

It finally happened. Due to plummeting oil prices, bankruptcy was happening all over Texas and several clients who owed us money filed as well. This action protected them and prohibited us from any further action to collect their debt, inevitably leaving our masonry subcontracting company broke. The hemorrhage was beyond our control—the company bled out and died. Paul and Richard scrambled to develop other sources of income, but entrepreneurship is a high risk game and the failures compounded. So now with four children, a large mortgage and many doctor bills, we were faced with a looming financial crisis and Paul was actively looking for a way out.

## A Life Changing Phone Call

About a year into our financial decline, Paul received a phone call from a friend who knew Paul was looking for a new gig. He offered him a sales agency position in a new company that provided services for small businesses combining payroll and employee benefits. Paul didn't know much about this new business but the more he thought and prayed about the opportunity, the more certain he felt there was a great potential in helping small businesses such as his (that had recently failed for example)!

Paul put it this way: "The idea of providing payroll and benefits to small businesses by combining them into one large group sounded like an interesting idea. But right from that first phone call I envisioned a much broader service that would provide instant infrastructure to help small businesses deal with the wide range of challenges and opportunities that come with being an employer. I had no idea at the time I would eventually have the opportunity to make that vision a reality."

Paul loved his new role and he thrived getting the agency off the ground and establishing over a dozen new clients for the company he represented, Omnistaff. One of the new accounts was owned by a gentleman named Jerry McIntosh who was so excited about the new service, he sold his company and joined Paul signing up new customers.

The new accounts were sold, enrolled, and running payroll, which meant the last step in the process was for the commission to be paid so we could finally get some breathing room on our own financial situation. Then Paul received another life-changing phone call with even more immediate effects.

Jerry McIntosh was driving when he heard on the radio that Omnistaff was filing bankruptcy! Just about the time we thought we saw our ship coming in, we watched it go up in flames.

We had to severely cut back on expenses.

We looked for a house to lease as our beautiful home went up for auction. No more Cadillacs or Lincolns, we needed smaller car payments. We cut corners wherever we could.

"Paul, lets sell some of this," I said one day as I was going through my closet. "I don't need fur coats and diamond rings…"

"No." Paul said gently. "Not yet. Those were my gifts to you, Victoria. I don't want you to sell anything. You've sacrificed enough and I *am* going to get us out of this mess."

## Our Trinity Turn-Around

In addition to the strength our growing faith provided, our girls were also the reason we not only survived but thrived during that season. The combination of their joyful spirits and the love and support of our church family got us through those lean times.

Through our involvement at Trinity Church we learned to live by the power and direction of the Holy Spirit. In order to walk through life on these terms, both Paul and I had to learn to listen for His voice and to daily seek His calling for our lives. Sometimes, in order to learn to listen, God needs to get our undivided attention. Our financial challenge was exactly the wakeup call Paul needed to begin to walk in the Spirit and seek God's help to get out of our mess instead of trying to do it on his own.

Our financial situation reached the low point when the Omnistaff agency came to an abrupt end without receiving the earned commissions. The pressure Paul felt to provide for the family was so severe he was up all night worrying and pouring his heart out to God, asking for direction and mercy. Then in the quiet of early morning hours Paul received a direct answer by the Holy Spirit.

"I had been up all night praying and crying desperately seeking an answer about what to do to feed my family," he told me later. It was then he picked up his Bible and noticed that I had placed a sticky note on the front cover for him to read Psalm six. I would often do this if I felt the Lord had "a Word for him." He told me that he was sure he had never read this passage in his life, but was stunned that it expressed his exact emotions from that very night, even using words he had spoken from his own mouth!

The Psalm ends with: Depart from me, all ye workers of iniquity; for the Lord hath heard the voice of my weeping. The Lord hath heard my supplication; the Lord will receive my prayer.

Let all mine enemies be ashamed and sore vexed: let them return and be ashamed suddenly (KJV).

Paul felt faith rise up in him by receiving a specific passage of scripture that, although written ages ago, was exactly on point for his circumstances.

Perhaps the most important part of this time in our lives was Paul's involvement in a men's prayer meeting that met at 6:00 every morning. His commitment to this time was a priority and he was very transparent with these men of God, bearing his pain and humility of his financial situation. These men prayed with him and for him every day.

My husband has always been a man of high integrity and values, but I watched God do something miraculous in him during this time as He prepared him for his purpose—for his life calling.

In his humility, Paul made a new commitment to a life of faith based on a fresh revelation about the Holy Spirit. We knew from our Baptist foundation that when we came to Christ we had the promise of the fullness of the Holy Spirit deposited in us.[32] But the question is not how much of the Holy Spirit do you have but rather how much of you have you allowed to be governed by His Spirit?

Paul was ready to "be neither to the right nor the left" but in the center of God's will each day. He asked for wisdom and then tested his decisions against God's Word, choosing what he felt God wanted over his own desires.

A pivotal example of such a decision came as Paul prayed for a job to meet the need for immediate income. The answer to the prayer came in the form of a sales and marketing role working at a labor relations consulting firm. This company had been one of his former clients that felt the blow from losing a full month's payroll in the Omnistaff bankruptcy. Although Paul wasn't at all happy in his new work situation, God had placed him in a perfect place for a crash course in employment law—a major component of the plan God had for Paul's life. He soaked up knowledge, kept his eyes, ears, and heart open, and continued to pray for wisdom and discernment about his next step. Our involvement at Trinity church profoundly impacted our lives. Paul taught on Wednesday nights, and once again it was evident he had a gift. I taught children's jazzercise classes using Christian music combined with lessons for life, and was involved in the leadership of the women's ministry.

I even volunteered as a phone counselor for the Christian Broadcast Networks telethon under the direction, at that time, of Dr. Richard Booker, a man who would one day become a personal mentor and friend.

At Trinity we learned the power of prayer and obedience to the Holy Spirit and how God would orchestrate His plan for our lives if we let Him. His plan is always better than ours and He always puts together the right team to accomplish it. Two couples from our young married group were a critical part of God's plan for us. Steve and Charissa Arizpe, and Jay and Sally Mincks became covenant friends by divine appointment at Trinity Church.

Not long after that Paul became an elder in the church—an unprecedented invitation considering his ripe old age of twenty-nine!

## New Revelations

Almost seven years had passed since *Peretz* and my spirit-self hovered together over my lifeless body in the ICU, but I could hear his words like it was yesterday.

"You will acquire all the gifts of knowledge, wisdom, and experience you saw along the grid, and as the Words of God are revealed and imparted, you will teach many others what the Spirit of God reveals to you."

As I continued to immerse myself in God's Word and pray for the wisdom and knowledge *Peretz* predicted I would one day share with others, I began to understand the Bible in ways I couldn't explain.

During this season God began to lay the burden of denominational legalism on my heart. A burden that caused me to study Scripture in a different way—a deeper way. I began to understand the traditions of man often molded the minds of believers into doctrines that differed from church to church and especially from denomination to denomination. I began to see the body of Christ was divided by denominational dysfunction, and not united as Jesus had prayed in John 17:22: The glory which you have given to me, I have given to them; so that they may be one, just as we are one - (CJB).

I knew I had been called for a higher purpose—*Peretz* had told me so. I still didn't know quite what that was—not yet. But I was learning, and God was using me.

I was asked to speak several times at ladies Bible studies. I gave a teaching on the deeper meaning of tithing that was a divine revelation of His Word. [33] In fact, I elaborated on how the verses of the Bible can teach us truth on many levels—not just one. [34] When I finished with my talk, one of the older women in the group came up to me.

"You have incredible insight into God's Word. It's an obvious gift," she said.

"Thank you," I said.

"I'm actually quite surprised," she added. "I learned something new, and I feel God has given me a fresh revelation in His Word from what you shared."

"Why are you surprised?" I asked.

"It's just that you're so young ... you need to get older honey, then maybe you will really have people's ears ... right now you're just a little girl." She patted my arm gently and walked away, completely clueless how condescending and contradicting she sounded. What did my age matter if God gave her a Word of wisdom through my message?

As God began to show me deeper levels of scripture and revelation, I often found myself facing comments like this and even more severe objections that mystified me. Apparently, how young I looked somehow contradicted the fact I could have anything intelligent to say.

Although God filled me with prophetic revelations, I grew more discerning in sharing them with anyone other than Paul and a few close friends.

However, I also felt the wind of change in the air as I forged ahead.

Perhaps I *was* just a little girl, but I was a little girl with a *mighty* Father. I was a little girl who deeply loved the Lord and completely embraced the power of the Spirit within my soul.

And I was a little girl ready to let God use me to make a big difference.

# Chapter 10
# CROSSROADS

**Tshuvah**: Repentance, to return

Here is what Adonai says:
*"Stand at the crossroads and look; ask about the ancient paths,*
*'Which one is the good way?' Take it, and you will find rest for*
*your souls. But they said, 'We will not take it'...*
Jeremiah 6:16 CJB

As 1985 came to a close, we found ourselves walking in a steady cadence of faith and obedience. We were making ends meet with a much smaller but steady income. However, Paul couldn't let go of the entrepreneurial spirit that is so much a part of his makeup.

Paul and Jerry McIntosh met together between Christmas and New Year's still trying to help former clients find a new solution to their employment woes due to the Omnistaff bankruptcy.

These former clients suggested Paul and Jerry start their own company providing payroll and benefits. They knew these men cared about them and their companies even though they hadn't been paid. Paul and Jerry, on the other hand, were impressed at how much the clients thought of the

115

service provided. The problem? There was no longer any company providing such a service.

Well, there were actually two more problems; one named Victoria and the other named Bobbie (Jerry's wife) both of us were still recovering from the last entrepreneurial roller coaster ride and not inclined to hop on another. Our husbands were well-aware of our "*preference*" for steady income.

"Jerry, you know we've agreed *not* to start a new company right?" Paul asked one day.

"Right. Absolutely not. Our wives have made that perfectly clear ..."

A long pause followed.

"So, since we are definitely *not* starting another company there can't be any harm in just asking the question. *If* we *were* going to start a company, what would it be like?"

With that, Paul and Jerry had another entrepreneurial seizure but this time with quite a twist. Instead of going straight to the numbers and the nuts and bolts of sales and service and pricing and profits, the discussion went to "people and faith."

Paul and Jerry wanted to live their lives through the week walking out the same faith they practiced on the weekend. But could work and faith co-exist?

Paul wanted to hire people for their input, not their output. He wanted to treat them with the respect for their inherent worth as children of God.

Both men envisioned a company where faith and family were properly prioritized ahead of work. They wanted to see what would happen in a company if it was built on biblical principles and values. "Instead of compensating people for coming to work early and staying as late as possible," Paul mused, "how about if we compensate people for finding better ways to get results faster so we can all spend more time with our families?"

Paul and Jerry described a corporate culture that became the foundation and fuel for a company that would be the cornerstone for an entire new industry ... *and* help thousands of small businesses across the country.

"The reason we started the company was to help improve the success equation for small business," Paul would one day report. "We just felt like it was way too difficult to be successful in business and we wanted to improve both the odds of success and the degree of success, and that was what caused us to put together a comprehensive service based on a new legal construct we called co-employment."

Co-employment allowed client companies to join a relationship with a company sharing and bearing the legal and regulatory issues of employment, offering better benefits to employees to level the playing field with large companies, and even relieving the administrative hassles of payroll and government compliance. This company would stand shoulder-to-shoulder with business owners and help them succeed.

When Paul shared the idea with me, I winced. I knew he could be a success. He had proven that over and over again. But was the timing right? I wasn't sure if Paul was ready, especially not after fighting and climbing his way back to financial equilibrium. We both knew the past year had been hard on him, and he readily admitted it.

"I love the idea of helping small businesses succeed, but I'm reluctant to put my family through another start up," Paul told me. "And truthfully, I'm exhausted on so many levels it isn't funny."

"Then what do you really want to do?" I asked him. He looked thoughtful before responding.

"Vicki, I'm not sure if I'm ready psychologically, emotionally, physically, or financially to start a new business …" he paused, "but I have to say that for the first time in my life I am completely ready spiritually. But only if it's God's will."

In the natural, Paul really had no business jumping into such an endeavor. However, he wasn't operating in the natural—as God was supernaturally preparing him on every front.

That fact alone was the key element that changed the entire scenario.

Sometimes we have to be at the end of ourselves to completely trust God.

And my dear husband of almost twelve years was at the end of himself. He was ready to hear from God, walk in faith and trust, and start a new business. Paul was always a good provider, even when we were financially strapped he seemed to manage to get us through the rough waters. But this time he would use the entrepreneurial gifts God had bestowed on him in an entirely different way. This wouldn't be like Amway or the masonry business. This time, God was at the helm navigating, and wherever we traveled, it would be God who received all the glory.

## A New Era

Administaff was founded on March 6, 1986, and on April 1st, Paul and his partner Jerry McIntosh officially signed their first new client.

With God and their shared spiritual principles and values at the helm, the business became very successful very quickly. God was clearly in control.

These brave and determined men of faith started their new company in a humble six-hundred-square-foot office in Kingwood, Texas, with one phone they shared at a partner's desk. Paul soon put together a fabulous management team of experts in their field, and the company began to grow and prosper.

That summer, we closed on a new house in Ponderosa Forest. It was the third home we had owned as a couple, but in many ways it felt strangely like the first, insofar as being a gift from God we fully acknowledged in every way.

We had come so far and our three oldest girls, who were eleven, seven, and six, loved the home and the backyard pool. They quickly settled into the neighborhood. Our fourth, little two-year-old Kristen, was having a harder time. Although her heart had miraculously healed, she had a lot of upper respiratory health problems. I prayed for answers.

Paul upgraded his car from a Ford Tempo to a Buick Park Avenue. I didn't particularly like my six-year-old station wagon with the ceiling head liner starting to fall in, but I didn't complain. I could see we were moving forward and making progress.

As I thought back it became apparent to me that we had approached financial success the first time with an attitude of ungratefulness and spiritual immaturity. We allowed flattery and the love for money and "things" to be the chief indicators of achievement. Over time we came to learn that being the ones who give (and not only the ones receiving) as the true indicators of success.

One of the hardest lessons to learn in life is to be self*less* instead of self*ish*. Our testing taught us to depend on God. It's in humility that God lifts his children up. Just like the prodigal son, after he spent all his inheritance and found himself desiring the food he was feeding to the pigs he was hired to care for, he realized it's all about relationship. He finally desired to return to his father.

In Matthew 19:24, Jesus said, And again I say unto you, it is easier for a camel to go through the eye of a needle than for a rich man to enter the Kingdom of God (KJV). I now knew what He meant. When everything is going well, and you are excelling in life, you have a tendency to forget about God. The Bible says, "Seek ye first the Kingdom of Heaven and his righteousness; and all these *things* will be added unto you" (Matthew 6:33 KJV- emphasis added by the author). The Hebrew word *t'shuvah* means to repent and turn back to God, inferring you were once with Him, but left.

For a time I guess we were gone from Him, pursuing our own will—but now we were back.

Yes, we were replacing and upgrading some of the material things we needed, but this time it wasn't to impress or motivate anyone. This time things were decidedly different as we gave God all the glory, honor, and praise for every breath—every blessing.

From our Holy Spirit baptisms and the profound moment when we experienced our baby Kristen's heart being supernaturally healed, our faith in miracles grew strong. We continued to grow in the Lord and learn about our authority in Christ. We continued to share the good news of Christ at every opportunity, pray for the sick, help the poor and do the work God equipped us for as a blessing unto the Lord.

When Paul finally replaced both of our cars with new Lincoln Town Cars, I marveled at the fact God was clearly restoring what the locust had eaten.[35]

## Not a Stepford Wife

I always loved being a corporate wife and a stay-at-home mom, but I never felt constricted by those roles. Quite the opposite.

Not working "officially" outside the home was something that enabled me to focus on my family, education, and volunteer projects. But make no mistake, I wasn't sitting home watching soap-operas and eating bon-bons (most stay-at-home moms aren't). In addition to caring for the countless needs of our growing family, I also volunteered my time as the administrator of Trinity Christian Academy. In this capacity, my responsibilities included countless administrative and admissions duties, such as registration and accounting.

My heart was truly in ministry, although at that time the thought of acquiring any formal theological education hadn't firmly entered my mind. In fact, when

I began to take classes at North Harris County College (whenever I could fit a few in,) my first goal was to get an Associates Degree in Nutrition, as the topic had always been interesting to me. Paul was supportive, and I loved my time as a "student."

Our entire family thrived at Trinity Church, and we were all growing strong in the Lord.

Shannon was involved with a dynamic youth group and was learning to cope with the sadness she still carried after all these years from losing her best friend. She had some new close friends and seemed to be healing. Cindy and Diana were balanced and healthy, strong in the faith, excellent students and played soccer competitively.

Kristen's first two years of life had been miserable as she suffered with severe allergies that caused constant bronchitis. She even fought pneumonia—twice. But now, Kristen was growing into a healthy and sociable little girl. She was my little buddy, and we often ran errands together when we discussed every kind of subject under the sun. She loved to think of herself as "big" so she asked me to teach her "college words." Her favorites were "espionage" and "cornucopia," although rarely was there opportunity to use either of them; she just enjoyed saying them. I can't recall how she learned the former, but she learned the latter as a result of asking about an arrangement on our table.

"Why does that basket shoot out fruit?" she asked one day, her little expression as serious as it could get, while I tried hard not to laugh.

~

I was reminded again of my guardian angel's words when he challenged me to acquire more knowledge in the Lord, so, I dared to ask the Lord once again to take me further.

This time, instead of sending a neighbor to my front door, He placed a homing device in my spirit that caused me to consistently open my Bible to thematically related passages. In short order, a pattern began to develop in my daily quiet time and Bible study. I was clearly being drawn to scripture that talked about seasonal celebrations and feasts—about the traditions the Jewish people—and Jesus Himself—found so special. Truthfully, in all my "church years," I seldom gave thought to the Jewish Jesus and how my own faith was actually rooted in *His* ancient Jewish faith.

I had been reading the Bible for years, but I had no idea there were so many seasonal feasts celebrated by the Lord. Thirsty for understanding the mysteries in His Word, I asked a ministry leader about the feasts of the Lord as written in Leviticus.

"Why don't we celebrate these feasts?" I sincerely asked.

"Leave all those Jewish celebrations alone, Victoria," my mentor said. "Old Testament holidays don't concern us. They belonged to the Jews. As Christians we have our own holidays."

Frankly, I was stunned.

The Bible is God's Word, and it had become my life and my breath—how could *anything* in it not concern me?

The apostle Paul said all scripture is good.[36] I knew Paul was referring to the First Testament because, when he penned those words, the Second Testament didn't exist yet. On closer inspection of Leviticus 23, I noticed it is the Lord that says, "These are *my* feasts". Clearly, these weren't "exclusively" Jewish feasts (although it is the Jews who have been faithful to observe them). These were the *Lord's* feasts, and I knew in my spirit I had to learn more about them. Perhaps even more so now that I had been admonished by a respected church leader to "leave Jewish things alone."

Seriously? Jesus was Jewish—was I supposed to leave *Him* alone, too?

As I studied the feasts of the Lord, I found myself thinking more often about the Jewish roots of my own Christian faith—something I had never specifically and intentionally focused on. Of course, I knew Jesus was Jewish, but suddenly I realized knowing and truly understanding are two entirely different things.

I explored how different it must have been two thousand years ago. I couldn't even relate to what the world of Jesus must have been like. He, in no way, stopped being Jewish. I found scriptures of Him celebrating Passover (Matthew 26:17), Sukkot (John 7:2,14) and Hanukkah (John 10:22). As I thought more about Him in this context, I began to wonder something that quickly grew into a cavalcade of questions:

How is it I had been active in several Christian churches since I was a young girl and knew so little about the roots of my Christian faith?

Had I been absent all those days?

Did I not pay attention?

Or—could it be—the connective tissue between the two was intentionally severed?

And if so—why?

My prayers became focused on God revealing His Word to me—the unadulterated, unbiased truth. The more I studied, the more I saw many of our modern Christian interpretations concerning the Word were simply not lining up with what the Word actually said. If God is the same yesterday, today and forever,[37] what happened? Jesus was so eager to celebrate the Passover with the Apostles, to share with them what was about to be fulfilled by the prophets in the next few days ... and hours.[38] That particular cup of wine *after* the supper and the unleavened bread held a significant meaning. [39] What was dawning in the minds of the disciples at a meal they had rehearsed for centuries?

Why had the modern church let Passover go? And when did it happen?[40]

As Christians, we champion ourselves for "progressing forward," but the more I studied God's Word, the more acutely aware I became of the gnawing feeling we were going the wrong way. What was it about "when at a crossroad choose the ancient path?"[41]

The thought crossed my mind that possibly the church needed to return to the things the Jewish Jesus loved.

## Travail

While in prayer one cold winter day in January 1987, I felt a pain go through me like a knife. I doubled over in grief. Yet it wasn't a physical pain, but more a feeling of intense heartache and deep sadness. A curious connection in the spirit to something happening to someone else. I knew about travail during prayer but never experienced it until now. I felt so burdened and heavy hearted. I closed my eyes and prayed.

"God, what does this mean? What are you telling me?"

What I felt next was disturbing. It was like a knowingness or a thought appeared in my mind, something I hadn't conjured or created.

After about thirty minutes of prayer the pain in my gut released. The burden lifted, and I felt better. Not sad anymore. Over the next several years, this travail would often come over me. It was a strong underlying need to simply pray for a single tortured soul.

One time I saw (in my spirit) a little boy being neglected and crying in the dark. It felt as if this child was like a hostage who was being kept away from his home. Suddenly, a revelation stunned me. Over the years, Paul and I had discussed the possibility of perhaps one day adopting a child—a little boy. I knew the child I was feeling in my spirit was our little boy—and the home he was being kept from was ours. He was trying to get here in his spirit.

"Paul, I think I'm praying for a child we will someday adopt."

This prophetic revelation caused Paul and me to unite in prayer often for this little boy's life. We asked God to keep him safe. We had no idea the personal and spiritual growth that would occur in us as a result of these prayers. We also had no idea this little boy had actually been born in August of this same year, and it would be another four years before this tormented child would find his way into our home and into our hearts.

## God Moves in Mysterious Ways

In the summer of 1988, a series of massive rainstorms hit the Houston area. After days of rain our beautiful home flooded with three feet of water. We were fortunate to have flood insurance and proceeded to conduct a major renovation. This was just the motivation we needed to buy a different home and relocate closer to our new company in Kingwood where Paul was spending more time. A shorter commute would be better for him—and the time seemed right. Knowing the change would have significant ripple effects, we prayed fervently about the decision and felt this was the path God wanted us to take.

We bought our fourth home in the Bear Branch Village in Kingwood.

Although we planned to remain members of Trinity Church and attend on Sundays, the long commute made it harder to be active in other areas of ministry as we had been. We dearly loved our church family, but we felt God calling us to let go of the reins. Therefore, we resigned from all of our volunteer duties, including my work as the school administrator and Paul's responsibilities as an elder.

We—all of us—missed our active involvement in church, but the younger girls adapted well to the move, enjoying their new schools, soccer, gymnastics and new friends.

Shannon, however, had more difficulty adjusting. She missed her friends, and the transition from a small Christian academy to a public high school with over thirty-five hundred students was hard on her. She struggled with the stigmas of affluence and competition among the Kingwood teens. I saw her changing, and it wasn't good. She really needed to be plugged into an active youth group near our home—all of our kids did.

Over the years, we had been led to one church after another on our journey of faith as a result of following a trusted believer. We had never been what you would call "church shoppers." We both felt the conviction in our spirit it was time to look for a new spiritual home, but this time there was no one around to give us a referral. No one, that is, except God.

"Paul, let's visit that cute little Victorian-era church we always comment on when we pass by it." I said one day. "I have a really good feeling about that one."

"Sure, let's go." he said.

Chapel in the Forest was an Assembly of God church nestled in the woods of Kingwood not far from our new house.

Our girls were fourteen, ten, eight, and four on the Sunday before Easter when we all dressed up and ventured out to the lovely little chapel, unaware of the visual impact our large family would make as we visited that day. The church was packed. There was no large band like at Trinity. No special effects and no laser lights. Just an awesome message and Spirit-filled praise and worship music supplied by an anointed duo who also happened to be the pastor and his wife. He played the piano like a virtuoso, and I'm telling you, wow—could she sing.

# Chapter 11
## CHAPEL IN THE FOREST

### S'hma: Listen

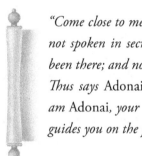

*"Come close to me, and listen to this: since the beginning I have
not spoken in secret, since the time things began to be, I have
been there; and now Adonai Elohim has sent me and his Spirit."
Thus says* Adonai, *your Redeemer, the Holy One of Isra'el: "I
am* Adonai, *your God, who teaches you for your own good, who
guides you on the path you should take…*

Isaiah 48:16-17 CJB

O ne of the most difficult things to do in life is listen to the wisdom of
others, our own intuition, and especially to the still small voice of God.
In my experience, the ability to listen to God's prompting becomes
infinitely easier with the anointing of the Holy Spirit. Having the Spirit of the
living God inside your heart makes the choice to disobey Him much harder. He
keeps you safely on the narrow path.

There were a lot of churches in the area of Kingwood, but Paul and I both
felt we were being supernaturally called to Chapel in the Forest, especially after
our first visit.

This new focus would be the start of an epic era in our life, and God directed
us to the exact place where He wanted us to be as the seasons of change unfolded.

We felt an immediate connection with the pastor and his family. It was apparent to us from the day we met this was a wise, humble, and anointed man of God. Pastor Bron and Darlene Barkley were just a little older than Paul and me. They had a son, John Paul, age ten—the same age as our Cindy. We smiled when Pastor Bron later told us his son, John Paul, had tugged on his sleeve when we entered the church for the first time and said, "Dad, look at all the pretty girls!"

On our first visit that beautiful Spring morning, I immediately noticed a different dynamic operating at the Chapel. Trinity Church was now a large and growing congregation of about six hundred members with leaders and congregants primarily in their thirties and forties. However, the Chapel was less than half that size and from what we could see was led by leaders in their fifties and sixties who appeared to attract people in that same age range.

We decided we wouldn't let the older demographic distract us as we trusted God would enable us to make a difference in this special place. And perhaps, we reasoned, this is why we were called there.

The decision was an easy one; we "officially" became members the next week on Resurrection Sunday—a rather fitting day to start our new life in Kingwood—ushering us into almost a decade of ministry with the Chapel in the Forest community—and into a lifetime relationship with Bron and Darlene Barkley, and their wonderful family.

~

Shortly after we joined Chapel in the Forest, Pastor Bron conducted a Passover Feast Celebration at the church. He was drawn to explore how the church was an extension of the ancient Jewish faith. This would mark our first time attending a celebration steeped in Jewish tradition and history. I was elated and Paul and I found the entire experience enlightening.

We became active in the church very quickly.

Because Pastor Bron and Darlene were close to us in age (well, at least Darlene was), we spent more time with them than any of the other church members. We had lively discussions about the early church and shared our respective opinions on why there was such a disparity of recognition in Protestant circles to the Jewish heritage of Jesus.

After getting to know me and becoming familiar with the volunteer work I had done at Trinity, Pastor Bron asked me to oversee the church's missionary administration and communications. It didn't take a rocket scientist to see the pastor desperately needed help with administrative tasks, but like many churches, there just wasn't enough money in the budget to pay for a qualified assistant.

In retrospect, I shouldn't have been shocked by the resistance some of the older church leaders had when I agreed to join the ministry efforts and help as a qualified volunteer. I should have been used to it by now. I couldn't seem to get beyond being viewed as "just a little girl."

"Why is it no matter what I do," I said one afternoon to Pastor Bron, "I always seem to be under scrutiny from all of the older leaders?"

"It isn't *all* of them, Victoria," he said. "And if it makes you feel any better, it's not just you. You don't have the market cornered for making some people uncomfortable. Pushing outdated boundaries and challenging stagnation is supposed to be uncomfortable. Sometimes God puts us in places to intentionally shake things up. Just keep doing what God is calling you to do and remember you answer to the Holy Spirit, and not to someone else's ego or misinformation."

I was so grateful for his advice. For the first time in my adult life, I had a spiritual mentor who poured wisdom and encouragement into my heart and mind. Pastor Bron's mother was an evangelist, and he had great respect and admiration for women in ministry—he considered it an honor to nurture my spiritual growth and exploration.

I considered it a blessed gift from God.

～

Paul's company grew exponentially, with annual revenues exceeding all expectations. In December of that year, he officially became the CEO and Chairman of the Board of Administaff—our company that years later would be known worldwide as Insperity Inc..

Although his professional responsibilities increased, Paul never lost sight of keeping God and his family first.

Paul taught a junior high Sunday school class, where he lovingly called his kids, "Tweeners." I taught Missionettes, a Christian discipleship program for girls, joined the intercessors for prayer once a week and worked with Darlene in the women's ministry. When she discovered I had a decent singing voice, it wasn't long before I joined her and Pastor Bron on the platform as part of the new praise team.

Paul and I assisted the youth pastors for special youth events until, a few years later, we became the senior youth directors. In almost no time, we had up to sixty teens meeting weekly in our home. This was a wonderful group of young people. I wanted to think it was because we were great teachers ... but then I noticed a larger number of teen-age boys who regularly attended. It didn't take long to figure out it was our girls (and not necessarily our stellar teaching skills) attracting them.

So many great things happened during this time—but there was also a shadow of concern as Shannon began to hang out with some strange-looking kids who attended Kingwood High School. All of her new girlfriends wore black. Black *everything*—clothes, hair, nails, lipstick, and eye shadow. Some of them had tattoos. We found her distant, non-communicative, chain-smoking boyfriend with a Mohawk ... disturbing. Though Mohawk Guy didn't hang around long, other boyfriends followed who brought more concerns. Most of her friends seemed depressed and rebellious. We were clearly perceived as the enemy, although I'm not sure we did anything specifically wrong to warrant that perception. I remembered the generation gap had existed in my home when I was her age, but in retrospect, it didn't seem as wide.

We continued to seek the Lord for direction concerning her well-being.

## An Adoption Journey

In 1990, Paul was asked to serve on the board of Depelchin Children's Services,[42] one of the largest providers of mental health, foster care, and adoption services in Texas. Paul often told me about cases that broke my heart. I heard the sad stories of poverty or drugs that broke families apart. As an adoptee and now a mom myself, I saw sides of adoption I had never explored.

I seldom talked (or even thought) about the fact that both Rhonda and I were adopted. Truthfully, I never really desired to know specifics about my birth family. I never had desperate questions that needed answers … until Paul started serving on that board.

On my landmark thirtieth birthday, I finally gave in to the new found curiosity. I decided I wanted to meet my birthmother. My Godfather (whom I called uncle) was instrumental in setting up my adoption, and when I called him, his response surprised me.

"I've been expecting this call for years," Uncle Robert said.

He gave me a contact name, and I was off.

Finding the ex-sister-in-law of my birth mother—the woman who had approached my uncle some thirty plus years ago concerning her brother's wife and an unexpected pregnancy—was actually quite easy.

She was elated to hear from me when I called, which was a relief for me.

"I've been praying for you since you were born," she cried.

"What …?" I stammered.

"I mean it, child. I've been praying for you for years."

We talked for some time, and she told me she was a member of John Osteen's Lakewood Church (before he passed away and his son, Joel, took over the leadership). She also told me something I hadn't considered—something that took my breath away.

"You have two half-brothers and a half-sister."

I was speechless at this revelation.

"If it's okay with you," she said, "I will contact them first and let them tell their mother you have asked about her." I agreed and when we hung up the phone I prayed for God's will to be done.

Imagine my surprise when my older half-brother and half-sister called immediately and said they wanted to meet me right away. When they came to my front door a few days later, it was surreal. I didn't really know what to expect.

My daughters resemble me in many ways, but growing up, I hadn't looked like my parents, grandparents, cousins, or my sister. Now, as I looked at my brother, there was no denying the resemblance.

"Mom is kind of overwhelmed with the situation," he told me. "She's kind of embarrassed to face you."

"Please tell her there is no pressure," I said. "Tell her it's okay, even if she decides not to meet me—I will understand."

My brother, sister, and I visited for a while, but sadly, I didn't feel a strong connection. They were like strangers, yet biologically connected. Then, six months later, I got *the* phone call.

My birth mother was ready to meet me.

The moment she rang the doorbell, I felt like a guest on the Oprah show. I really didn't know what I was going to say, and I suspected she was just as nervous. As I opened the door, I gave the entire situation to God and asked Him to guide my words and actions, and to reign over the conversation.

Standing before me was a short lady (surprise! I'm 5'2") with blue eyes and high cheek bones just like mine. I silently opened my arms to her and after an awkward but nonetheless long emotional hug, I welcomed her into my home for iced tea and a visit.

"I want to tell you what happened," she said quietly, avoiding eye contact.

She told me the circumstances of my unexpected conception.

"Your birth father never knew about you—I never told him I was pregnant. I was really just a young girl, and I didn't know what else to do."

*Just a little girl* … pregnant and afraid. How well I understood her situation. While I was blessed to have Paul's love and support when I discovered my pregnancy, she had been alone. I understood her awkward position and, at that moment, God gave me so much compassion for her. After a long heartfelt conversation, I ended up praying for her salvation and ministering forgiveness and peace to her. It was an emotional time.

I soon met my younger half-brother and saw them all just one more time. It may seem strange to some people, but none of us felt the need to develop our relationships any further. We were not like a TV reality show family who transitioned into becoming close friends. Sometimes life is about filling-in-the-blanks, and once that's accomplished you can move on.

Years later when I discovered my birth mother passed away, I'd like to think she did so without guilt and regret, but with joy and contentment for giving me an opportunity to live a different life.

## Our Family Grows

With a better understanding of my own birth mother's situation, Paul and I both felt the burden to be an answer to someone else's prayer. Our girls were seventeen, twelve, eleven, and seven when we went through the application and screening process to become adoptive parents.

By the summer of 1992, we added a sweet newborn daughter and a four year old son to our brood. Brittany Elise was only a few days old, and assimilated into our household with ease. It was awesome having a newborn again and her new sisters took their big sister roles seriously. In fact, Brittany always had somebody holding her and fighting to feed her and even change her diaper. Things were a bit more challenging for our son—Paul Westin.

When the adoption agency first contacted us, I got my journal out and did the math. Westin was definitely in utero the first day I interceded in prayer for his survival. There was no doubt in my mind, he was the boy I had been convicted to pray for—the boy I dreamed about. However, knowing this didn't make the situation easier to live with. When he joined our family we struggled to learn how to be parents to a child with emotional trauma we didn't understand.

We had Wes less than a week when we took our annual family vacation. This year we were going to Bermuda, and we felt certain Wes would have the time of his life. One of the excursions we enjoyed was taking a submarine tour. We had to take a passenger ferry to the submarine. The ferry was crowded and Paul and I had to separate, each of us taking three kids. I found myself sitting next to a lady traveling alone. She admired the sweet little baby I held and began to engage in a conversation with two of my young daughters. In the meantime, Paul chased Wes up and down the aisles of the ferry trying to keep him from stepping on people's feet, asking him to keep his voice down, and apologizing to everyone who seemed annoyed by the ruckus.

I tried to ignore the spectacle. The lady next to me commented on how well behaved my little girls were. She also added I must be a good parent. She paused and then pointed to Wes and said, "I don't know about the parents of that little boy though!" I thought about saying nothing, but I knew she would eventually figure it out. So I told her we just added him to our family. Then and there, it dawned on me a lot of people would judge us through the behavior of our son.

Before long we realized Westin had some very serious issues. He was extremely hyperactive and, as a result of a traumatic early childhood, he had an unusual amount of insecurities and fears. He was often oppositional and defiant, and extreme behavioral dysfunctions plagued him—and us. But we were always hopeful we could help him out of the dark place that held him captive.

The first time we took Wes to church was a disaster. It didn't occur to us he had never been in a church or been told about God. Even though we tried to prepare him for the experience, he was obviously confused. We sat in the back and after a few minutes of taking in the surroundings, Wes jumped from Paul's lap during the opening prayer and screamed.

"God's not here! Where is he? I don't see him!"

Then, he quickly dropped to the floor and crawled under the pews toward the front of the church, surprising people as he scooted among their feet. People whispered, then shouted to each other. I watched in horror as Paul tried to intercept him. Then each row of congregants realized the situation and began to help. Finally, someone caught Wes and handed him to Paul, who wrapped his arms firmly around the struggling little body of his new son and carried him out of the church. The gravity of what we were up against began to weigh heavy on me.

*God, please give us the ears to hear you. We can't help him without hearing your voice!*

Wes's biggest problem was disobedience. He wouldn't listen to anything we said. He seemed constantly tormented and agitated. He didn't trust, respect or feel safe around anyone. But through all of his defiance, I could still hear the heart of God who showed me how we, His children, are often unruly, disobedient, stiff necked, selfish, and untrusting. My heart ached for God, as I finally understood what He must feel like as He disciplines us.

I had five well-behaved daughters and one defiant son, and while I knew God loved all of them the same, I was finding it more difficult to cope. It was hard to be compassionate to a little boy who acted like he didn't want to be loved—who pushed us away at every opportunity. Years would pass before Wes could trust us as his earthly parents and acknowledge God as his Heavenly Father.

Today, Wes is a doting father to our latest granddaughter, Ariya Jordon Sarvadi. A divorcee and a full time dad, he takes his responsibility seriously, and I always smile when he calls me or one of his sisters for parenting advice.

~

After years of smoking, my mother had mouth surgery to remove cancer on her tongue and jaw. Even though my father had home health care nurses assisting each morning, he needed additional care in the afternoon and evening.

"I could help!" Shannon declared. "I *want* to help…"

Paul and I talked it over and, after prayer, we felt this might be just what Shannon—and my parents—needed. In her junior year, we withdrew her from Kingwood High School and enrolled her in a private school just a few miles from my parent's house. She moved into my childhood home (and bedroom) to care for my mother. With great respect and appreciation, I watched my daughter help her mammaw navigate the last year of her life with determination and dignity.

Sadly, I lost my mom to cancer in August of 1993—the same year Shannon graduated a year early from high school.

## A Foundation of Philanthropy

That next year, we bought a larger home in Fosters Mill Estates. As we settled into yet another new season in our life, we felt the call to teach our children more about the principles of tithing and philanthropy. God provided economic blessings beyond our wildest dreams, and so we created the Sarvadi Family Foundation to give Him thanks. Through this charitable giving foundation, we taught our children it is the Lord who gives man the ability to obtain wealth.[43] Our responsibility is to give our blessings back to others. Involving our children in decisions of giving blessed our hearts—and theirs. We researched as a family and found a number of causes we could give to. Compassion for the homeless, care for orphans, and the desire to see a cure for cancer were some of their concerns.

Giving freely with joy was—*is*—the key. Everyone embraced the goal of our family foundation with an open heart—and open arms.

The Bible says, But this I say, He which soweth sparingly shall reap also sparingly; and he which soweth bountifully shall reap also bountifully. Every man according as he purposeth in his heart, so let him give; not grudgingly, or of necessity: for God loveth a cheerful giver (2 Corinthians 9:6-7 KJV).

We had all the worldly symbols of success: a spacious and beautiful new home, four fabulous cars in the driveway, even designer clothing. We took wonderful family vacations at beautiful world resorts. But the biggest lesson we learned was to give God first place—with an emphasis on "*give.*" Proverbs 3:9 says, Honor *Adonai* with your wealth and with the firstfruits of all your income (CJB).

We feel as a result of our obedience during this time (and thereafter,) God continued to increase not only our financial health but our spiritual and emotional health as well.

In June of that year, we celebrated our twentieth anniversary. When Paul blessed me with a new convertible foreign car, I had to pinch myself to be certain I wasn't dreaming.

As I looked at my life and thanked God for all the blessings He had bestowed, I contemplated where God was leading me next.

### They Don't Stay Little

Caring for my mother gave Shannon a sense of worth and purpose. She graduated a year early from high school as valedictorian of her class (a distinction Kristen and Brittany would one day share as well), and she was studying for her BA from Baylor University, which would precede a master's degree from LSU. She had come so far from the sad little girl she once was when she lost her baby brother and years later, her best friend.

As I prayed to know God's next plan for my life, He showed me in an unexpected way.

"Mark and I are getting married," Shannon said one day.

I stared at her for a moment, took a deep breath and rolled my eyes. I wasn't fond of Mark. They had dated sporadically when she was in high school, and when she entered Baylor, he intentionally enrolled at a neighboring college to be near her. Their relationship obviously grew—much to my dismay. Mark always seemed intimidated by us, avoided eye contact and never engaged much in conversation, how would he ever fit into our gregarious family?

Paul was far more relaxed about the news. He loved his daughter and just wanted her to be happy.

I decided after a few weeks of sulking, I probably needed to love the guy my daughter loved. *God, show me how to love this young man.*

Shannon was taking a full load of classes at Baylor in both the spring and summer semesters in order to graduate early. With the wedding set for August 1995, it became quickly obvious she was not going to be able to work on wedding plans at the same time—no matter how much she wanted to.

"Mom, will you help Mark plan the wedding?" she asked.

I looked at her as memories of growing up alongside her cascaded one over another. She was a wonderful, gifted child who had now grown into a talented, driven, and beautiful young woman.

"Yes honey, I'll help you—and Mark."

In His infinite wisdom (and with keen sensitivity and a witty sense of humor,) God designed a rather unique way to knit our hearts together, as Mark and I forged a rather unusual alliance as the official Wedding Planners.

Since we knew our church would not be big enough to seat all of our friends and Paul's huge family, the first thing we needed was to find a venue. We decided to try Mark's mother's church, which was the beautiful Episcopalian church in Kingwood. I had a great deal of experience by now in planning social events for ladies ministries, church dinners, and corporate parties, and I was feeling confident on how to make everything Shannon wanted possible—to make her special day look lovely and flow with perfect ease.

Mark and I made an appointment with the wedding coordinator at the church.

This woman, who was from the UK, kept referring to the church as "The Church of England." We told her of some of Shannon's ideas to decorate the ends of the pews. She stiffened her back and responded in the most proper and emphatic Queen's English I had ever heard. "Absolutely not!"

I opened my eyes wide and kind of stuttered, "E…Excuse me…?"

"We will do nothing to detract from the altar," she said, in the same queen-like tone.

"Uh … okay …" I stammered, momentarily unsettled by her unexpected curtness. "Shannon would like to have a unity candle, where can we place..."

"Absolutely not!" Her words came a few decibels louder than the first time. "This is the Church of England … not a Hollywood extravaganza!" She actually rolled her "r" as she said "extravaganza."

Mark and I were flabbergasted as she continued, "Please remember, we have only agreed to offer the church to you as a courtesy to the grrrroom's mother..."

She referred to Mark as though he wasn't even there, and I watched as he shifted uncomfortably in his chair and looked completely embarrassed by the entire exchange.

Clearly, she didn't know Shannon and Mark had been getting pre-marriage counseling from the pastor there or that he had approved the inclusion of the unity candle in their ceremony.

"Well, ma'am," I said, "the bride has already gotten permission from the pastor to light the unity candle."

"Well, ma'am," she echoed sarcastically, "I'm the wedding coordinator, not him."

Let me say while I'm a Christian, I'm not a saint, and by this point I had my fill of being treated like a red-headed step-child. This rude woman had gotten on my last nerve. I sat up straight, leaned forward, and responded with an exterior calm that belied my interior anger. "Well then, perhaps you could clear something up for me. Does he work for you or do you work for him?"

My question, combined with my body language and tone of voice seemed to settle everything.

Shannon and Mark would have their unity candle and hurricane candles attached to the end of every other pew in the sanctuary. However, this meeting left a bad taste in my mouth. I wanted to give this woman a copy of Charles M. Sheldon's book, *What Would Jesus Do,*[44] because how she treated us was completely the opposite.

In her position, she had the ability to bless people—to exhibit the love of the Lord who would have wanted us to feel accepted, welcomed and encouraged as we discussed the plans for this sacred ceremony. I'm sure He was grieved by the attitude of arrogance and boastfulness this woman displayed.

He probably wasn't happy with how I responded either, as I felt compelled to put her in her place. I was already asking Him to forgive me as Mark and I left the uncomfortable meeting that day in silence.

When we got back home, I could see Mark was wrestling with something heavy.

"I thought she was supposed to be a Christian. Do Christians really act like that?" He looked at me with a combination of righteous adult anger and genuine childlike confusion, and my heart broke for him.

"Just because someone works at a church or even goes to church doesn't make them a Christian," I said, as I motioned for him to sit down next to me.

"Then, what does? What makes someone a Christian?" His question pierced my heart as the genuine desire for truth was apparent. I knew in my spirit God was opening a special door at that moment—He was giving me the opportunity and the blessing to bring my future son-in-law into the Kingdom of Saints. As I shared the good news of salvation, Mark began to cry.

"I want everything God has for me," he said.

That day my daughter's fiancée received his salvation and the infilling of the Holy Spirit. He was going to be my son-in-law, but on that day he became my spiritual son, and our Mark has never been the same.

The wedding turned out beautifully, and today, Shannon and Mark are the wonderful parents to six of our precious grandchildren, and I love him as my own son.

Indeed, God works in mysterious ways.

# Chapter 12

# CROSSOVER

**E'ver**: A Hebrew, one who crosses over

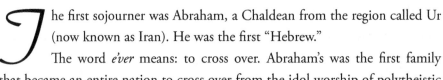

*And when he had called the people unto him with his disciples also, he said unto them, Whosoever will come after me, let him deny himself, and take up his cross, and follow me*
Mark 8:34 KJV

he first sojourner was Abraham, a Chaldean from the region called Ur (now known as Iran). He was the first "Hebrew."

The word *e'ver* means: to cross over. Abraham's was the first family that became an entire nation to cross over from the idol worship of polytheistic paganism to a monotheistic belief in one true supreme God. Generations later, Moses brought that extended family together in the form of a nation with a structure and code of law, given to him on Mount Sinai.

The history of Judaism (and why so much of this history was removed from the Christian faith) began to consume my focus.[45]

Our pastor's heart was in the same place as he struggled with his passionate desire to understand the Jewish clarifications Jesus preached and the Hebraic wisdom He revealed, while at the same time remaining true to the denominational tenets of the Assembly of God church as well. In a season of apparent testing, Pastor Bron felt convicted to enter into a forty-day prayer experience with God.

During this time I had been reading books written by respected Hebrew scholars such as Richard Booker, Marvin Wilson, and Brad Young, and information flooded my spirit at warp speed. For example, scholars have said when translating the Greek of the Second Testament to Hebrew, an amazing thing would develop as the ancient Hebrew sayings and idioms would become obvious.

It suddenly became clear to me—although the first century writers *wrote* in the Lingua Franca which was Greek —they *thought* with a Hebrew mindset.

The wisdom available in the Holy Word of God all came back to Hebrew.

Then it dawned on me. Jesus never spoke English. He didn't live in an English speaking, Anglo-Saxon region of the world. He didn't have a western mindset like me. He lived in the Middle East, in Judea—He had a *Hebrew* mindset. He was a Semite and a Jew who spoke Hebrew. I worship and adore a Hebrew-speaking Messiah, and at that precise moment, the Almighty revealed a profound truth to me as a teacher.

*How can I truly teach His people if I don't understand Hebrew, the very building blocks of the inherent written Word of God?*

I realized in order to understand the Bible and the prophetic visions God imparted, in order to really teach others what the Spirit of God was revealing to me, I had to learn the native language of *Yeshua*—I had to learn Hebrew.

~

A few days later, the phone rang and a familiar voice from the past greeted me— Mary, a member of Trinity Church. We hadn't spoken for quite some time. "God put you on my heart, and I want to extend an invitation to you," she said.

"Okay…"

"My good friend, Dr. Richard Booker, has invited several Hebraic scholars to Houston to conduct a series of lectures. I thought you might enjoy attending…"

I knew Dr. Booker's name well, as I had been reading the work of this renowned scholar for some time—ever since I met him as a phone volunteer at the CBN telethon.

Dr. Richard Booker was considered a pioneer and spiritual father in teaching on Israel, Jewish-Christian relations, and the biblical Jewish roots of Jesus. He has been a featured speaker at the Christian celebration of the Feast of the Tabernacles in Jerusalem for two decades. I had been voraciously reading his book, *The Miracle of the Scarlet Thread,* and it helped me understand the Bible in profound ways. [46] To be given the opportunity to meet him again was remarkable—the fact he would one day become a close personal mentor and write the foreword to this book was unfathomable at the time.

Containing my excitement upon hearing Mary's invitation was hard, and I imagine she had to hold the phone away from her ear as I shouted with joy. "Mary! I can't believe you're calling me … you are literally an answer to prayer. I just had the most profound revelation…"

The words tumbled from my mouth as I told her about my recent revelations and shared my compelling desire to learn Hebrew and more about the Jewish life of the first century. As Mary and I talked, something familiar flashed across my mind's eye, and for a split second, I saw a shiny box on a grid. [47] The sudden vision came and went—but the memory lingered.

As Mary talked about the upcoming lecture series, I felt that strange opening phenomenon in my back and I had a feeling deep in my spirit that I had arrived at a significant location on my timeline grid of gifts, and I couldn't wait to share this with Paul.

"Yes!" I exclaimed to Mary. "Yes, I definitely want to go, thank you so much for inviting me!" When she extended the invitation to Paul and our pastors as well, I was thrilled—and I knew they would be as well.

～

Paul, Pastor Bron, and I went to hear the famous Bible scholars Dr. Booker had brought to Houston. We soaked in the words of wisdom of Dr. Brad Young and Dr. Dwight Pryor with great expectation. The experience changed our lives as God spoke to each of us in distinct and different ways.

*Dr. Brad H. Young* is the founder and president of the Gospel Research Foundation and a founding member of the Jerusalem School of Synoptic Research. Today, he is a tenured professor of New Testament Studies in the Graduate School of Theology at Oral Roberts University. At the time I first heard him speak, his critically acclaimed book, *Jesus the Jewish Theologian,* had just released.[48] His teaching that evening blessed me in ways I cannot explain—that he would agree to write the closing to this book, is evidence of his true heart to encourage and support me.

Dwight Pryor was a distinguished Hebraic scholar as well who captivated his audience with profound perspective. He was also a popular lecturer and the founder of the Center for Judaic-Christian Studies.

The fact that all of these scholars would one day become close friends was something we never imagined.

~

That evening I learned that Hebrew has countless idioms, just like English. As modern English speakers, we understand what "killing two birds with one stone" means, or the phrase "I'm green with envy," but are we privy to first-century *Hebrew* idioms? Could it be one of the reasons we have problems understanding the Bible is because there are idioms being used that confuse us?

Do we know what it means when the Bible talks about "taking away your bow," or "a good eye?"[49]

God commanded tassels called *tzit tzit* be placed on the corners of the hem of the prayer shawl called a *talit.*[50] The corners of the *talit* are called *kanifim* which literally translates to "wings." So "wing" is an idiom for corner. That helped me to understand Malachi 4:2, "But unto you that fear My Name shall The Son of Righteousness arise with healing in His Wings." Idiomatically speaking, healing would be found in the corners or hem of the garment of the Messiah.

The more I listened, the more clarity I experienced—like turning the wedges of a Rubiks Cube and suddenly all the colors aligned.

Understanding this new meaning of hems and wings gave me new understanding to what was going through the mind of the Jewish woman with the issue of blood. She knew it was forbidden for her to touch anyone (as she was considered unclean)—but she also knew the Words of the prophet as she courageously touched the Messiah's hem. She responded in faith to receive healing according to God's Word and thereby affirming *Yeshua* as God's Messiah. She received healing by touching the "wings of the Messiah" (which were located on the hem) of the Son of Righteousness.[51]

These seminars totally changed my perspective of the Word of God.

Christianity as it is known today has gone through considerable permutations that caused it to resemble the Greco-Roman world of the fourth century, instead of the first-century matrix where it started.

So, what was faith like in the first century? What exactly did Jesus teach? How did the Jewish people receive His teachings? What were these listeners connecting His teachings to? What were their expectations? These were but a few of my questions as I began to realize I needed to have a stronger foundation of Jewish culture, tradition and language in order to apply the Words of Jesus in the proper context. And the only way to fully achieve that foundation was to go back to school and learn it.

At this point, I had a hodge-podge of college credits that equaled an Associate Degree in completely non-related fields. The Spirit began to convict me perhaps it was time to begin a more "formal" theological education.

Years had passed since *Peretz* revealed God's purpose for my life. What a roundabout route I had taken to get to this point, and it had only just begun.

During my studies, I was shocked to discover how Constantine the Great had altered the enlightened interpretation of the Judaism of Jesus to what is now known as Catholicism—and I started to see how the Protestant Reformation began to slowly steer it back.

I pondered how I walked through my own Lutheran reformation where I first found my Savior and learned of His grace. I smiled at the memory of wearing my Jesus Freak button and felt a twinge of melancholy as I recalled the doctrinal tenet of infant baptism that eventually led Paul and I away from the Lutheran church and into our season of calling in the Baptist church.

The memory of being immersed in life-giving water as I personally experienced the first command to be baptized and preach the gospel to all people was a memory that would remain forever sweet in my spirit.

Yet God was still refining and reforming us, as He moved us from that profession of faith to another of even deeper intimacy, when He introduced us to the Holy Spirit and called us to Trinity Church, a Spirit-filled community.

A place where the Lord equipped Paul and me with unexpected power and supernatural gifts as was evidenced in prayer and of the laying on of hands.

And now, it happens to be in an Assembly of God Church that we have connected to a Spirit-led pastor who desires to know his Jewish Messiah as much as we do that we climb up another step on the ladder.

From Lutheran to Baptist to Charismatic to the Jewish teachings of Jesus,—a journey of incomparable growth and spiritual revelation.

Saved by grace, identified through water baptism and filled and equipped with the Spirit. Each denomination basically emphasizing one very important aspect of a Christian's walk. It would seem He had led us to the most beautiful place of all. A place where we could embrace the pure teachings of our Jewish Lord and the clearly defined Judaic faith He so beautifully revealed.

As we began to reclaim these teachings, we flourished.

I loved my church. However, as time went by, I began to have trouble with yet another group of intolerant believers who seemed to hate the Jewish emphasis of Jesus and seemed to be anti-Semitic and anti-Israel as well. This saddened me. Would *Yeshua* have this same reaction to his own brothers and country of origin?

Additionally, there were other things happening in the body of charismatic churches that bothered me. People were flocking to big revivals all over the country. I felt disturbed to see Christians "drunk" in the Spirit, laughing with unbridled laughter, blindly following "prophets" and signs and wonders. Doesn't the Word say signs and wonders will follow *the believer* and not that believers should follow the signs and wonders? And shouldn't we be *filled* with the Spirit[52] and not *drunk* in the Spirit? Things just seemed a bit "off".

Once again, I found myself questioning my denominational alignment.

This time, however, I wasn't alone in my confusion. Pastor Bron and a small group of church members also felt the growing disparity between those who desired to learn the ways of the 1st century Jewish expression of Messiah, those who desired this strange new drunkenness that resembled the Eastern religious expression of Kundalini,[53] and those who didn't want to rock tradition in any way whatsoever—content to maintain the status-quo in the familiar Greco-Roman church model.

Despite the growing differences in our congregation, a wonderful and true supernatural wind began to blow, as a growing fellowship of believers in our church began to reclaim the lost legacy of Christianity's rich Hebraic heritage. I wondered, though, how long we could do this in an "AG" Church before things blew up.

~

As we continued to learn the theology of Jesus from Pastor Bron and the brilliant scholars whose teachings we followed, I began to understand my personal journey from reformation to restoration. God took me through my blueprint timeline grid of life and gave me handpicked gifts of knowledge. One of those gifts was a growing understanding of the first century Jesus—and of the reasons for my own spiritual journey—my own restoration. (There's a great Timeline of Church History on my website at VictoriaSarvadi.com).

Much like Abraham, I had crossed over.

With this new level of spiritual enlightenment, I saw God's plan coming into a fresh new focus. We had been bathing our ten-year-old company in prayer and trusting God for direction in every decision. We learned there were spiritual principles that operate just as sure as the laws of physics. We understood the commandment to give back and we gave a considerable amount of our income to God's Kingdom work. Our children also learned what it meant to leave a lasting legacy through the work being funded by the Sarvadi Family Foundation. We did all of these things not as reluctant obligations, but as enthusiastic blessings unto the Lord.

As we walked in obedience, God blessed and positioned us for the next stage of our life and our business. Administaff grew and prospered beyond all we could imagine; we were advised to take the company public. This was a major step with major ramifications. I have to admit I was anxious. This would mean an entirely new level in life. We would officially jump off the porch to play with the big dogs in the yard.

We asked our pastors to pray over us. Paul was certain this was the way to go, but I was fearful from the horror stories I had heard. *Was this elaborate jump going to change me? Us?* Why had Jesus said it was easier for a camel to go through the eye of a needle than a rich man to enter into the Kingdom of God?[54] We were financially comfortable now, but this would catapult us to another level entirely. If that happened, *would I forget God? Would people hate me? How would this change our kids? Would my kids be safe?*

Most people would be ecstatic about this incredible opportunity.

However, I was terrified and my imagination went crazy.

*Chapter 13*

# TRAVELING A VERY PUBLIC ROAD

## Derech: Path, Way

*...he restores my inner person. He guides me in right paths for the sake of his own name*

Psalms 23:3 CJB

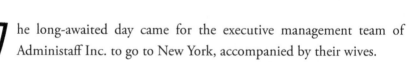

*T*he long-awaited day came for the executive management team of Administaff Inc. to go to New York, accompanied by their wives.

Known as the Four Amigos, Paul, Richard Rawson, Steve Arizpe, and Jay Mincks had prayed and labored to bring this company to where it now stood. Paul may have had the initial vision, and started with a different management team but he will be the first to say it was the collective strategy and stamina of these four men who made everything possible to reach this critical juncture in time.

Together they wrote new tax code for the IRS, navigated the often tumultuous waters of government compliance issues and developed landmark systems and procedures that changed the way the human resources industry conducts business. In fact, you could say they created the industry with all of the new legislation they were ultimately responsible for bringing to fruition.

And as men of God, it was in weekly prayer sessions where the Four Amigos would get the wisdom and discernment needed to walk in God's will and purpose—where they would get answers to many questions they had about running their business—a business that would eventually be known as Insperity, Inc..

The *Amigas* were considered just as instrumental in the success of the company due to their constant support and encouragement and unceasing prayers. Our group of dynamic women included Dawn, Charissa, Sally, and me.

As we walked among the hustle and bustle of worldly commerce on Wall Street, with the soaring skyscrapers of the Big Apple as a backdrop, we couldn't help but think we had hit the big time. Someone commented we would all become rich overnight, something that made us laugh as we all knew how long this "overnight" journey had actually taken. The pomp and circumstance of the day was a heady experience for everyone. Some of us brought our older children to be part of this momentous occasion. Cindy, our daughter of prophecy, accompanied Paul and me.

Paul rang the famous starting bell that day to signify the opening of the New York Stock Exchange. As predicted, shares of Administaff (ASF) began to trade at a feverish pace.

This monumental day exceeded all financial expectations. It's true; we were like lottery winners who, in one moment, entered an entirely different tax bracket. In many ways, a dream come true. Yet, when I look back at pictures of myself on that day, I resemble a deer caught in the headlights—as opposed to a woman looking forward to a "life of luxury."

In reality, I was in a haze and I felt unsettled in my spirit.

*Where is all of this going? What does the future hold?*

Our lives had always revolved around social events and celebrations, but when our company went public, I felt like we had moved into the proverbial glass house—we were now going to live under a huge microscope. I felt exposed and vulnerable. I've always been a person who likes her privacy, and the level of exposure we were embarking on was way out of my comfort zone.

~

At this time of great success, we were also having troubles at home.

Wes was about to turn ten. The older he got the more he acted out. He had difficulties in school with fights, horseplay, and refusing to participate in class. We tried one private school after another and even home schooling, but to no avail. Every year we struggled to find a suitable solution for Wes's education. He had an undeniable inability to socially integrate with other children.

One day we met with Wes's doctor. He said something that resonated in our spirit.

"Maybe what you folks need to do is buy some land and get him out of the suburbs—somewhere he can run around and get dirty."

We were ready to try anything, and if getting Wes out of the suburbs and into a therapeutic country lifestyle would help, we were all for it. Ushered in with considerable prayer, the plan took fruition quickly. In almost no time, we found a property in a nearby community—initially seven acres we eventually expanded to twelve.

We had never lived on acreage like this before—and certainly not in a home as grand as this. The country estate included a stocked pond, an Olympic-size swimming pool, and a seven-bedroom home where each one of our children would have their own room *and* private bath. We had been blessed to have comfortable and spacious homes—even during the lean times—but this was like Scotty had beamed us up to another world.

The property also had a 6,000 square-foot barn on it—a huge building we had no earthly idea what to do with.

Fortunately, God was way ahead of us and would soon reveal His plan.

However, a new but serious issue presented itself shortly after we moved into our country home and it all came down to a rudimentary issue of mathematics—there simply were not enough hours in my day. Period.

Wes's behavior challenges took a lot of my time and energy, but we still had four daughters at home ranging from four to sixteen and staying attuned to *their* ever-fluctuating emotions and needs was just as important. Everyone had school, homework, extracurricular events, church, and youth group activities. Hairstyles and clothing choices for five girls didn't happen in the blink of an eye. And preparing meals and keeping up with laundry for everyone was almost a full-time job in itself. The kids always had their chores, but a house this size was way beyond our collective ability to keep clean. Plus, there was also my own Bible study and ministry volunteer work, which was important to me (and my sanity). Last, but by no means least, I had a husband whose relationship I valued along with my added responsibilities as a corporate wife.

We were living in an idyllic country paradise, but we needed help.

"I have an idea," Paul said one evening after I'd had a particularly harried day. "How about if we add one more day to our housekeeper's schedule and hire a nanny to help out with the children?"

I grimaced at the thought of my children being raised by a nanny.

"Look, you don't have to do all of this on your own. Think back to when we were starting Administaff—the bigger we grew the more additional help we needed, do you remember?" I nodded as he continued. "Where would we be now if I had tried to do everything on my own?"

Pastor Bron often refers to Paul as the E.F. Hutton of Houston. "He's a quiet man of great strength, but when Paul Sarvadi opens his mouth, people listen," Bron says.

I was keenly aware of my husband's thoughtful communication style and had grown to deeply respect his wisdom and insight—so, when he leaned back in his chair and looked at me with his piercing green eyes, I knew it was time to put my fear aside and listen—really listen.

"Look, we can afford the financial expense, but we can't afford the physical and emotional expense this is costing. God hasn't blessed us so you can run yourself into the ground…"

He made a good point—a *very* good point.

The next day we talked to our housekeeper who was more than happy to work another day, and we began to make inquiries about hiring a nanny.

Funny, but when I agreed to Paul's wise suggestions, I was more worried about my father's judgmental reaction to all the changes. Since my mother's death, he seemed even more critical of my actions, and I continued to walk on eggshells around him.

Some things never change.

~

Not only was there an increase of cleaning demands with such a large home, but the extensive property had ample grounds and landscaping that required almost constant upkeep.

A lawnmower would never have the power to keep up with the acreage, so either we contracted everything with an outside vendor, or we invested in a tractor and a groundskeeper. Paul ran the numbers, and decided it made far more sense to hire a groundskeeper or two.

When Pastor Bron and Darlene's son John Paul graduated from high school, he wanted to take some time to decide on his next step, so we hired him to maintain the property. Several young men from our youth group were also looking for work, so Nathan, Adam, and Zack came to work for us as well. These young men worked really hard.

We christened our country home, "The Secret Place," after Psalm 91:1 He that dwelleth in the secret place of the most high shall abide under the shadow of the Almighty (KJV).

With a strong "home team" in place, we settled into a pace that allowed all of us to grow in amazing ways.

The younger girls started piano lessons, and soon the concert size grand piano in our living room wasn't just a decorative piece of furniture. Kristen who had excelled in competitive gymnastics for five years switched gears and followed in the steps of her two older sisters by becoming a junior high cheerleader. Stray pom-poms could often be found stuck in one of the formal floral arrangements. The house always seemed to be full of music, song, dance and cheers, and the sweeping double staircase and elegant banisters were often backdrops to song and dance rehearsals. Plus, we were still a big soccer family—as four out of five kids now played on school teams as well as in competitive and recreational leagues. There was never-ending activity under our roof as our family began to go down the many paths of life's activities.

Our priority reason for moving to this country property was to help our son—and we began to see what could be a light at the end of that dark tunnel. We hired a private teacher for Wes, who came to our home, and for a while, this was exactly what he needed.

The wide-open space did more than just answer our prayers concerning our son's needs. The timing of our move to acreage property was perfect for what God was about to do concerning the needs of His Truth-seeking children.

## Called to Follow the Rabbi

I have always treasured and respected the name of Jesus, as do all faithful believers.

However, the more enamored I became with Jesus as the Jewish theologian, the more apparent it became that there were other Christians in my church who didn't share in my excitement. When I began to refer to Jesus by His Hebrew name, I could sense the discomfort some people felt. This made no sense to me; *Yeshua* translates to "God saves" and isn't Jesus the personification of salvation? The Father's gift to mankind? *Yeshua* was also known as "Rabbi," a term that seemed to make some people equally uncomfortable.

In fact, it seemed the entire Jewishness of Jesus made some folks downright squeamish.

I couldn't understand why anyone would be hesitant to call Jesus a Jew. After all, He was.

Believers of the first century were primarily Jews—as the Apostle Paul wrote: For I am not ashamed of the gospel of Christ: for it is the power of God unto salvation to everyone that believeth; to the Jew first, and also to the Greek (Romans 1:16 KJV).

Jesus traveled across the land of Israel for three and a half years explaining the Scriptures more clearly and performing great miracles among His own people. In John 4:22, He declared, …salvation comes from the Jews (CJV).

The Second Testament scripture attests to the fact that "multitudes" of Jews followed Him. Some Hebrew scholars have interpreted this to mean literally tens of thousands of people. In fact, it has been calculated by Hebrew scholars that less than twenty years after His Ascension, over thirty thousand Messianic believers lived in Jerusalem. Can you envision a congregation of tens of thousands of Jews worshipping *Yeshua*?

According to custom, when a Rabbi went through a region, people "followed" or walked with him for a while in order to learn from him. Following a Rabbi also meant you "walked" your life according to his teachings. This walking or way of living, thinking or believing is called *halachah* from the word *holech*, which means "walk." The followers of *Yeshua* were taught the *halachah* of Yeshua. Much of His "ways" or *halachah* was passed down to the modern church. But some of it was lost. This was disconcerting to me.

What have we been missing?

## Walking a New Path

Back in the beginning of his own Jewish roots journey, Pastor Bron occasionally incorporated an analogy or parable in his sermons to reference the Hebrew heritage of our Christian faith. However, that time of "occasional analogy" had long since passed. As he became more entrenched in following the Rabbi *Yeshua*, he felt increasingly convicted by the Spirit to teach even more of the Hebraic aspect of the original church to his flock. He began many Sunday services by blowing the shofar, reading from the Torah and quoting portions from books written by Hebraic scholars. He often wore a prayer shawl, prayed Hebrew prayers and taught Hebrew words or concepts.

All of these changes made some of the older members in the church uncomfortable—and unhappy—and it soon became evident something had to change—and it wasn't going to be them.

Eventually, Pastor Bron was given an ultimatum by the church leadership. He needed to stop teaching so much Jewish history and heritage in his sermons—period. An "occasional" mention of Jesus being Jewish would be tolerated, as the church leaders were not denying the heritage of Jesus. What they were denying, however, was Pastor Bron's ability to speak freely about the Jewish foundations of the Christian faith from the pulpit of "their church."

"We're not sure what God is calling us to do," Pastor Bron and Darlene said to us in confidence one evening. "We only know that to deny the wisdom *Yeshua* is now revealing to us would be like denying His existence."

Paul and I could relate to what they were feeling. We, too, were experiencing the fresh wind of faith based on following the old dust from Rabbi *Yeshua's* feet, and it had changed our lives. We had learned so much from Pastor Bron's anointed messages and Spirit-filled teaching, and we knew this path he walked wasn't a passing fancy in his life, but a serious calling—one he did not take lightly.

"We're almost in our fifties, not an ideal time to be starting over from scratch," Darlene said, "but that is what faith is all about, isn't it? It's about trusting God to provide even when the options look bleak—especially when the options look bleak. We don't know what we're going to do, only that we're being called to do more than maintain the status quo."

Paul and I felt a tremendous burden for this devoted couple. As close friends, we knew firsthand what was happening, and it broke our hearts to watch the growing dissension among the members and the splintering of the church.

We prayed almost without ceasing to know clearly what God would have us do in this situation. We both felt God convicting us to step in and take an active role in what was happening. We talked about a possible option, discussed the associated consequences and agreed about the step we felt called to take.

When we approached Pastor Bron and Darlene with our idea, we felt a level of peace that assured us we were walking in God's will.

"We want you to know if you feel called to leave the denomination to follow the Spirit of God, we will join you—and support you." Paul said when we met privately with them. "We'd like to renovate the barn on our property as a place to grow a new fellowship, a place to share the true heritage of our faith. Until it's ready, we can meet in our home."

I was thrilled to be able to utter the next words. "We are prepared to come alongside and support you in this new ministry outreach, and we will provide the capital to get everything started and help with your expenses."

It's impossible to explain the emotions of the moment as tears cascaded down Darlene's cheeks and Bron lovingly embraced my husband and me. This time of new beginning will always be a treasured memory the four of us share as brothers and sisters in Christ—and as deeply connected friends.

We talked about the possibilities, and their agreement to our proposal was almost instantaneous. We reached consensus on the next steps to take almost immediately. Thus began the start of the Shalom Hebraic Christian Congregation.

Shortly thereafter, Pastor Bron Barkley resigned his pastoral position and we officially withdrew our membership from the Assembly of God church. It would be our last denominational affiliation. About twenty others from Chapel in the Forest joined us to sit under Pastor Bron's anointed teaching as we began to meet in our home while at the same time launching an aggressive barn renovation project.

"It has never been our intention to turn Jews into Christians or Christians into Jews," Pastor Bron said. "Our desire was simply to open people's understanding to connecting our Christian faith with the lost legacy of the Torah—the Hebrew Bible."

And that's what we did—and what we still do to this day.

Shortly after beginning our new adventure, I accepted the role of administrator at Pastor Bron's request, a position I felt privileged to hold.

I was so fearful of what might happen when our company went public. Yet going public is inevitably what made all of this possible. It enabled us to buy our country property, fund a new ministry, and begin an incredible journey started in a barn.

Could a ministry with such a humble origin as to be birthed in a barn ever succeed?

The similarity to another story of humble beginnings was not lost on us.

**The Secret Place, our country estate, est. 1998.**

## Chapter 14

# THE NEST BEGINS TO EMPTY

### Safta: Grandmother

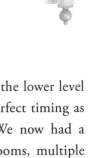

*Planted in the house of* Adonai, *they will flourish in the courtyards of our God. Even in old age they will be vigorous, still full of sap, still bearing fruit.*

Psalm 92:14-15 CJB

*W*ithin five to six months, the major renovation to the lower level of our barn was complete enough to move in, perfect timing as our home-fellowship had grown considerably. We now had a sanctuary that seated eighty-five people, three offices/classrooms, multiple bathrooms for men and women, a large storage area, a basement, and two apartments upstairs.

Our young groundskeepers, John Paul and Zack, became roommates and eventually moved in to the two-bedroom apartment above the barn/church. They also went to college nearby while they shared the workload of the grounds. Evelyn, our nanny, moved into the smaller one-bedroom apartment and her devotion to Brittany, Wes, and Kristen proved to be invaluable.

The older girls were serious students, and popular at school. They were still involved in competitive and school soccer, and in the youth group, which met in our home. With a game room, a flashy jukebox, pool table, and swimming pool, our country house became the hangout for many a teenager during Cindy and Diana's high school years.

When the time came for our little Cindy to graduate from Kingwood High School, she did so with honors—a distinction that would be shared by Diana not long afterward. With just eighteen months between them, these two were always connected at the hip.

One day, after picking Kristen up from junior high, we drove up to the house and saw John Paul pulling weeds in one of the flowerbeds. Kristen looked at him calmly from the front passenger seat and said something that took me by complete surprise.

"I'm going to marry that boy one day."

I smiled at her whimsical pre-teen prophecy, but with a six-year age difference, I highly doubted that was ever going to happen. She wasn't even a teenager yet, and John Paul had already graduated from high school and was now attending college.

I thought back to when we had first visited Chapel in the Forest on that Sunday before Easter so many years ago. Kristen was only four years old. She had practically grown up with John Paul, and I knew he thought she was a cute little girl—but that was all she was to him—just a little girl.

I didn't take her words too seriously as I pulled the car under the portico and lovingly teased her.

"He's quite a bit older than you, sweetie, do you expect him to wait for you to grow up?"

She grinned as she climbed out of the car, and her one-word reply was as solid as the sound of the car door as it closed behind her. "Yep!"

I should have known not to underestimate my "just a little girl" daughter. It turns out, she inherited her own God-given gift of prophecy. In May 2002, John Paul Barkley and Kristen were married. Today they are parents to four of our precious grandchildren, and John Paul holds a significant leadership position in our foundation. To have our good friends and pastoral leaders Bron and Darlene Barkley as fellow in-laws is an added blessing.

Yet, there's even more.

Eighteen months after Kristen's wedding, Diana married John Paul's former roommate and our other grounds keeper, Zack Alexander. Over the years, we had several young men work for us, but Zack and John Paul stayed around for more than the work. As they married our daughters and joined our family, Paul often says in addition to growing all the lush foliage on our property, we also raised our own crop of sons-in-law in the back yard!

However, when little Kristen first shared her seemingly innocuous marriage proclamation with me, her wedding and her sister's were a long way off. At that point, I was focused on Cindy's graduation. We were busy visiting colleges, ordering senior pictures, trying on graduation robes, and shopping for a prom dress. It was a busy spring, and just as we got down to the wire, Cindy made her choice to go to SMU, where (surprise) she and Diana would both receive their Bachelor's degrees.

I won't lie, I felt old when Cindy graduated—almost like I had lost my identity. And as I began to adjust to the pain of "de-parenting" my college-bound daughter and facing Father Time's selfish agenda, I received another mortality-shaking announcement.

Shannon was going to have a baby.

Now, I was really dealing with an identity crisis—a *huge* identity crisis.

It seemed like just yesterday I had a baby on my hip and was telling the exterminator I really was the "mommy," and not just a little girl who answered the door.

How had the years passed by so fast? A new generation was beginning, and I was going to be a grandmother—a grandma … a *safta*.

The first time I said that "G" word out loud I declared it would be my last.

"I'm going to be a *nana*—never a *grandma*," I said.

I liked the sound of "Nana," it rhymed with "Momma," which I was familiar with.

Shannon and Mark had been living in Baton Rouge, Louisiana where Shannon attended grad school at LSU. The baby was due in August and Shannon would graduate with her Masters Degree in July. Their intention had always been to return to Texas after graduation, and they were anxious to get back before the baby came.

Mark arrived a few months earlier to close on a brand-new home they bought in Kingwood and to get it ready before the baby arrived.

Doctors told Shannon she was going to have a girl, and we were excited about Avery joining our family. The nursery was lace, ruffles, and rosebuds, and Shannon had a beautiful Precious Moments mural painted on the pale pink walls.

So, imagine our shock when a little boy arrived.

~

I fell in love with our son-in-law all over again when Mark headed to Babies-R-Us that afternoon to exchange the pink car seat, crib, Pack-N-Play and various items of clothing for their blue counterparts before our little Christian Montgomery came home.

Our children were growing up. Our ministry was expanding. And our lives looked—and felt—like a fairy tale. The Holy Spirit gave me revelatory insight, and I received tremendously rich teaching from some of the most knowledgeable Hebrew scholars in the world. However, I still felt something was lacking. I still felt the need to seek more as the words of my guardian angel grew louder in my spirit. All I could think of was what *Peretz* had said: I was supposed to "acquire more knowledge and *teach others*."

I'll admit, as unhappy as I was about getting older, I had grown weary of being called "just a little girl." If I was destined to carry that moniker forever, I decided to do so with a doctorate degree as my companion.

"I want to go back to school," I said to Paul one night. "Real school, not just random classes and lectures. I want to get a master's degree and then my doctorate. No matter how long it takes. I want to study first century Christianity and get the credentials."

There was no need to hold my breath and wait for his reaction, as my dear husband was in complete support of my pursuit of knowledge. Paul was pursuing his own goals in business, and he saw no reason I shouldn't pursue mine.

Dr. Richard Booker offered a degreed educational study program at his Institute for Hebraic Christian Studies in Houston. [55] I registered and immediately began classes. Richard and Peggy Booker soon became close friends as they considered me their spiritual daughter.

Although life moved at warp speed, I felt I was in the center of God's will. Our children were getting older and growing more independent. I had no internal conflict about our fellowship or the pace at which it grew. I loved being a student and the ministry leadership responsibilities I had were so fulfilling. I was also involved in a great deal of charity work and in the planning of various special events.

All was right in my world, and I was basking in the glory of walking in the dust of my Rabbi.

*Chapter 15*

# UP THE LADDER

**L'dor V'dor**: Fullness of Generations

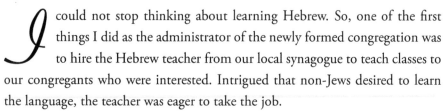

*"I am establishing my covenant between me and you, along with your descendants after you, generation after generation, as an everlasting covenant, to be God for you and for your descendants after you"*

Genesis 17:7 CJB

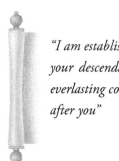

*I* could not stop thinking about learning Hebrew. So, one of the first things I did as the administrator of the newly formed congregation was to hire the Hebrew teacher from our local synagogue to teach classes to our congregants who were interested. Intrigued that non-Jews desired to learn the language, the teacher was eager to take the job.

I have now studied Hebrew for years, but I know I've only scratched the surface. I love this deep, beautiful language, and I'm fascinated by its multi-levels of meaning—deeper levels that can't even be translated into other languages.

Wanting to provide a biblically authentic and more Hebraic style of worship, Pastor Bron and I studied the first-century models of believers who assembled together. In the Book of Acts, believers met on *Motza'ei-Shabbat* (Hebrew for the evening *after* the Sabbath) which is considered the beginning of the first day in the biblical Hebrew reckoning of time. Based on this historical first century model, we established our services to be on Saturday evenings.

> On *Motza'ei-Shabbat*, when we were gathered to break bread, Sha'ul addressed them. Since he was going to leave the next day, he kept talking until midnight. Now there were many oil lamps burning in the upstairs room where we were meeting…Acts 20:7 (CJB).

## A Return to Tradition

Over the years, I discovered many churches have lost sight of the foundations of our faith by getting caught up in special programs, stained-glass windows, or concert quality sound and special effects. Although the component of modern worship is a valid focus, worship itself is not for entertainment.

In the first century, the Jewish fathers of the faith left us a simple model to follow. They defined their communities by three descriptions: *Beit Knesset* (House of Assembly), *Beit Tefilla* (House of Prayer) and *Beit Midrash* (House of Study).

We were modeling our Shalom Hebraic Christian Congregation on these three pillars, as God continued to prepare us to reach an even larger audience to help lift the spiritual fog that had descended over the Christian community since the 1st century.

~

Since we had an abundance of lush, private acreage, we organized a big Tabernacles celebration (called *Sukkot* in Hebrew) and invited other congregations to join us and camp out for the weekend. We all built our own *sukkah* or booth structure according to the biblical instructions, including the four species of represented plants.[56]

As the rich teachings of the first century filled our hearts, word spread we were a group of serious sojourners. Therefore, we began to attract many well-respected first century scholars, teachers, and musicians who desired to connect with us. In our passionate pursuit to learn the ways of Yeshua and the early believers, our fellowship already studied books written by many of these scholars, so for us, it was like being kids in a candy store.

During this time, our good friends Alice and Dr. Frank Lanza[57] introduced us to Barry and Batya Segal from Jerusalem, Israel. The Segals have since become some of our very best covenant friends. Over time, our home was blessed as we had privilege to host not only the Segals but many more wonderful people, including Jonathan Bernis,[58] Jonathan and Sharon Settel,[59] Maurice Sklar,[60] Hal Roning,[61] Dr. John and Pat Garr,[62] Paul Wilbur,[63] Dr. Brad and Gayle Young,[64] the late Dr. Dwight Pryor and his wife Karen,[65] and the late Dr. William Bean and his wife Trish,[66] We hosted Alyosha and Jody Ryabinov,[67] John McTurnan,[68] Joel Chernoff,[69] and Clarence Wagner with his team from Bridges for Peace,[70] and many, many other wonderful believers of our Jewish Lord.

~

Our congregation grew weekly, and we soon discovered there were Christians all over the city, nation, and even the world hearing this same clarion call and were returning to the first-century faith of Yeshua.

As our congregation developed, this new expression of worship emphasizing the Hebraic perspective occasionally experienced the pendulum swinging a little too far in rote Jewish tradition and then the other way in rote Greco-Roman tradition. As we learned how to implement this ancient (but new to us) expression of faith, we sometimes had to back up in order to go forward. With the Holy Spirit as our Captain, we eventually found a balance that expressed our hearts.

No matter what style of service, the message being imparted was always from the perspective of Hebrew eyes, not necessarily the way the early Greco-Roman pontiffs had interpreted it. Additionally, we always felt it important to remind those who attended our services that we were Christians—not Jews. We were, however, Jewish at heart.[71] And because we actually had Jewish believers in our congregation, we knew that all of us together were the fulfillment of this message written in the Book of Ephesians.

But now, you who were once far off have been brought near through the shedding of the Messiah's blood. For he himself is our *shalom* — he has made us both one and has broken down the *m'chitzah* (wall) which divided us by destroying in his own body the enmity occasioned by the *Torah*, with its commands set forth in the form of ordinances. He did this in order to create in union with himself from the two groups a single new humanity and thus make *shalom*,... (Ephesians 2:13-15 CJB).

When the Apostle Paul wrote this letter to the Ephesians, the Gentiles had been "far off" from the truth of Israel's God, worshiping pagan gods such as Tammuz, Astarte, Ba'al and the like.[72] However, now the Jewish Messiah, who came as a promise from the God of Israel, had opened the way that allowed *all men*, even Gentiles—to join into *His* faith, which was the perfecting of the faith of Abraham, Isaac, and Jacob.

Clearly, something changes within the mind of a progressive Christian when the hunger to understand the theology of our Jewish Lord begins to grow. As our fellowship addressed that hunger, our Hebraic congregation in fact grew.

So, too, did the overall scope of our ministry outreach as the Lord began to open our eyes to the incredible need that existed in the ministries of fellow brothers and sisters in Yeshua—kindred spirits who desperately wanted to further the calling God placed upon their lives.

The critical thing many of these ministries lacked was sufficient financial resources to keep them afloat.

We began to feel a tremendous burden to help as many of them as possible.

# Chapter 16

# THE ROOTS SUPPORT YOU

## ℕatan'el: Gift of God, Nathaniel

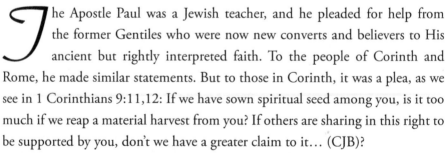

*They were pleased to do it, but the fact is that they owe it to them. For if the Gentiles have shared with the Jews in spiritual matters, then the Gentiles clearly have a duty to help the Jews in material matters*

Romans 15:27 CJB

he Apostle Paul was a Jewish teacher, and he pleaded for help from the former Gentiles who were now new converts and believers to His ancient but rightly interpreted faith. To the people of Corinth and Rome, he made similar statements. But to those in Corinth, it was a plea, as we see in 1 Corinthians 9:11,12: If we have sown spiritual seed among you, is it too much if we reap a material harvest from you? If others are sharing in this right to be supported by you, don't we have a greater claim to it... (CJB)?

The words of this apostle exploded in our hearts as we realized how far God had brought us on our journey—how intricately He had been weaving together the tapestry of an outreach that would provide desperately needed resources to His people. Because of the Jewish believers in Yeshua, the Good News of

Salvation had come to the nations, and we agreed with these scriptures that it was right to support our Jewish brothers and sisters—spiritually and financially.

When Administaff became a public company, we placed 10% of our shares into the Sarvadi Family Foundation. This amount equated to a hefty seven-figure balance—a balance that grew daily with interest. We marveled at what this foundation could achieve now, and we realized the time had come to restructure the organization. We were no longer talking about a few family projects—but millions of dollars in support to organizations around the world. We really needed a clearly defined mission statement and vision plan, a strong board of directors and, perhaps, even a different name.

Our kids were in favor of the changes. They could see the Sarvadi Family Foundation had become far more than a life lesson in tithing and charitable giving and could now be a major player in its ability to implement change throughout the world of ministry and philanthropy.

Dawn Rawson, one of our new board members, made several suggestions for the name change—and one, in particular, stood out in my mind.

"What about the Nathaniel Foundation?" she suggested.

In Hebrew *Natan'el* means "gift of God." There was no doubt God had showered gifts and blessings upon us. Yet, in a further study of this name, there were even more nuggets of intrigue...

The apostle Nathaniel was one of the original twelve disciples of Jesus. It was Nathaniel's friend Philip who introduced him to the Messiah—Yeshua, as written in the following Scripture.

Philip findeth Nathanael, and saith unto him, We have found him, of whom Moses in the law, and the prophets, did write, Jesus of Nazareth, the son of Joseph. And Nathanael said unto him, Can there any good thing come out of Nazareth? Philip saith unto him, Come and see. Jesus saw Nathanael coming to him, and saith of him, Behold an Israelite indeed, in whom is no guile! Nathanael saith unto him, Whence knowest thou me? Jesus answered and said unto him, Before that Philip called thee, when thou wast under the fig tree, I saw thee. Nathanael answered and saith unto him, Rabbi, thou art the Son of God; thou art the King of Israel. Jesus answered and said unto him, Because I said unto thee, I saw thee under the fig tree, believest thou? thou shalt see greater things than these. And he saith unto him, Verily, verily, I say unto you, Hereafter ye shall see heaven open, and the angels of God ascending and descending upon the Son of man. (John 1:45-51 KJV).

Nathaniel had sardonically said to Philip, "Can anything good come out of Nazareth?" At the time, there was little good to be said about the city.

When Jesus first lays eyes on Nathaniel, He seems (at least in my mind) to mimic Nathaniel's tone implying Nathaniel is "one who tells the truth and holds nothing back." His words actually speak to Nathaniel's candor and forthrightness—personality traits I related to.

In one of my early classes at the Institute for Hebraic Christian Studies, I passionately answered a question one might consider controversial. Dr. Booker smiled at me and said, "Victoria, one day you're gonna be a great teacher, but we really need to get those rough edges smoothed out."

I related to Nathaniel. He didn't pull punches—he had rough edges and said what was on his mind. I longingly imagined the Lord saying, "Behold my daughter Victoria, one who tells it like it is!"

I could also relate to the fig tree reference. As Yeshua told Nathaniel, He *saw* him long before they actually met when Nathaniel was under the fig tree.

I couldn't help but think back to the day in junior high school when I sat with Ricky under a tree and we talked about being born again as I tried to understand how God's Word had drastically changed my life in catechism class the night before. Apparently, the Lord saw me (like he did Nathaniel) when I was under my own "fig tree."

Then, *Yeshua* says a very curious thing to Nathaniel. He tells him he will see heaven open and the angels of God ascending and descending on the Son of Man. I related to this Scripture as well. When I lost my baby and almost my life so many years ago—God saw my distress, my need, and my heart. And He sent *Peretz*, an angel, to give me the resources I needed—resources that would carry me through decades of life lessons and spiritual seeking.

My life has been subject to many unseen messengers descending as they guide and minister to my family and me, and no doubt my prayers have ascended to the throne to receive such attention. I've always felt the prophetic visions He gives me are intended to grow His kingdom,[73] and this scripture intensified that conviction.

The story of Nathaniel touched me in a deeply personal and profound way, just as it did my husband and our newly formed board of directors. Hence, the name change decision was unanimous—and after submitting necessary legal paperwork, the Sarvadi Family Foundation became the Nathaniel Foundation.

~

Developing the Nathaniel Foundation was a humbling milestone for Paul and me.

Our God entrusted us with this storehouse of blessing and with it a call to help His people and support other ministries.

Our Jewish brothers and sisters have sown spiritual seeds among countless generations, and it was obvious to us many of them needed help. Therefore, our first goal was to bless these chosen people for the legacy they provided—by providing resources for some of their immediate needs. We wished to thank them for preserving the Word of God given to them and sharing it with the nations.

~

As word about the Nathaniel Foundation spread and funding requests escalated, we quickly began to grant funds to numerous qualified projects and programs in alignment with our mission and vision.

For some of our first projects, we bullet-proofed an ambulance, supplied blankets to an orphanage, installed a new roof on a synagogue, and bought medical machines and equipment for a hospital, all in Israel. We collected and shipped large containers of humanitarian aid from donors in our city to fulfill needs in this ancient land. Our grants began to make a difference, and Israel was becoming like a second home to us.

Clearly, God was turning our hearts to this sacred place of His Son's birth.

Through every stage of organization and development, God continually showed us "the way"—bringing us back full circle to ancient times.

However, at this point early in our ministry we had never physically been to the Holy Land.

As grant requests increased, we felt the Spirit calling us to see the needs with our own eyes. We planned our first trip for spring 1998 with Pastor Bron and Darlene, and my dad. Little did we know then that we would one day take our entire family.

There is a traditional saying after a Passover meal: "Next year in Jerusalem!" Our family had uttered those words of sacred tradition, but now the words would come to pass – at least for Paul and myself. Soon we would be celebrating Passover with our friends Barry and Batya in Jerusalem.

In preparation of our visit, we scheduled several meetings at various ministries, both Christian and Messianic in Jerusalem as well as in Judea, Samaria and Bethlehem.

## Going to Israel

Israel was everything I thought it would be and more. The life-changing memory started when the plane hit the runway as everyone on board our commercial flight cheered. We visited every holy site, even Bethlehem. Our highlight was having the Pesach Seder (known in English as Passover) with our Jewish friends, Barry and Batya, in their lovely home. It literally took my breath away to see the large full moon shining brilliantly above the ancient and holy city of Old Jerusalem from the large picture window in their dining room.

"What is it about this place?" I asked Batya as I stared out the window.

"You just love what God loves, Victoria," she said with her sparkling eyes and contagious smile.

The next day we took off to Haifa. We visited Mount Carmel where the challenge between the prophets of Baal, Elijah, and the one true God of Israel took place. It was hard to contain ourselves as we stood on the very mountain where God brought fire down from heaven and licked up the water that drenched the wood.[74]

It was there we found a new Christian and Messianic community called Kehilat Carmel. *Kehila* means "assembly" or "congregation" in Hebrew. After meeting the pastors, we caught their vision and felt this was a wonderful ministry we could help through our foundation.

We visited Bridges for Peace and were greatly impressed with the work BFP was doing to help destitute Jews assimilate into the country. They provided the basic essentials to help these struggling people get on their feet. Bridges for Peace also provided much-needed assistance to the soldiers in the IDF (Israeli Defense Force), and education to churches through publications and teaching material among many other humanitarian efforts.

We also met with an Arab Christian pastor in Bethlehem. We learned his brother was murdered by Muslims on the Mount of Olives because he was an outspoken Christian. This ministry to our Arab brothers and sisters in Christ, we felt, was another worthy cause for the Nathaniel Foundation.

However, the ministry outreach that made the greatest impression on us was that of Vision for Israel and the Joseph Storehouse, a non-profit humanitarian aid center located in the heart of Israel. Barry and Batya Segal became friends of ours early in our journey to explore the fascinating authentic teachings of our Jewish Lord, but seeing them in their home environment connected us on a new level. As Co-founders of VFI, they operate their ministry (established in 1994) with integrity and diligence.

Through the Joseph Storehouse—their humanitarian aid center—they provide assistance to countless organizations and individuals—from the widowed woman who needs some type of medical treatment to poor children who need back packs for school. From a destitute Ethiopian Jewish family who needs furniture to a hospital that needs an X-ray machine. The government clearly realized their value as well, as VFI is one of the first organizations called when there is a terror attack, or when some other disaster occurs in Israel. Vision for Israel has grown into a global organization with branches in the United States and Europe—being a great means for the nations to bless Israel.

Spending time with this anointed couple made us realize the Nathaniel Foundation needed to partner with this respected organization concerning the funding of grants for the overwhelming needs in Israel. We felt the Lord telling us that Barry and Batya Segal could be our eyes, ears, hands, and feet in the Holy Land. Fortunately, the Segals heard the same Spirit-filled call.

When our company went public, I had no idea God would use the growth of our business to help build His kingdom in such an amazing way. Although initially fearful of what might happen, going public was a tremendous blessing. It gave us the economic freedom to launch so many new endeavors that would have lasting impact on our family, community, and even on the world for generations to come.

Chapter 17

# EASTGATE

### 𝔅aruch and 𝔅erech: Bless and Kneel

*Blessed are those servants, whom the Lord when he cometh shall find watching: verily I say unto you, that he shall gird himself, and make them to sit down to meat, and will come forth and serve them.*

Luke 12:37 KJV

The number forty often symbolizes testing or judgment in the Bible. The Hebrews wandered forty years in the dessert.[75] Rain fell for the first time for forty days and nights during the great flood.[76] After Moses killed the Egyptian, he fled to Midian, where he spent forty years in the desert tending flocks.[77] Moses was on Mount Sinai for forty days and nights.[78] The Israelite spies took forty days to spy out the land of Canaan.[79]

I'll admit, this list of formidable forties contributed to the angst I already felt about turning forty. Although part of me felt my youth fleeing, I also knew God was taking me to a new level with every passing year. The Lord had prepared me for even greater responsibility.

The year I turned forty was the year Paul and I celebrated our twenty-fifth wedding anniversary, and Shannon gave birth to our precious and wonderful second grandson, Carter Matthew. Without doubt, 1999 was a significant year in my life, made even more so by the fact the world prepared to usher in a New Millennium. It was a historic time, and the uncertainty of what the year 2000 (Y2K) would bring was unsettling—there were so many possibilities—and conflicting predictions.

The number forty also holds spiritual significance as *Yeshua* ascended to the heavens forty days after His resurrection.[80] Ever since His departure from our earthly midst, countless generations have believed the biblical prophecy that *Yeshua* will soon return in their lifetime. "…so also the Messiah, having been offered once to bear the sins of many, will appear a second time, not to deal with sin, but to deliver those who are eagerly waiting for him."[81]

Generations of believers have eagerly awaited His return.

It appears to me that in our modern culture of believers, this promise of the Lord's return isn't taken seriously—at least not with the reverence it once was. Shouldn't we take the possibility seriously that *Yeshua* might return in our lifetime—especially since there are more signs now of His return than ever before in history?

Although it's impossible to accurately predict when that time will be, I think it's safe to say as believers we need to be physically, mentally, and especially spiritually prepared for the Lord's return as Judge and King.

The aspect of "eagerly waiting" for His return can be viewed and demonstrated from many perspectives. With that in mind, I have developed a teaching series specifically on revelation the Lord has given me on interpreting current events and biblical prophecy, and what it means for us to be eagerly waiting for the Lord's return to earth. [82]

When Y2K threatened to bring mass chaos, pandemonium, and an end to life as we knew it, many believers thought *Yeshua* must be coming back.

Although we didn't jump on the apocalyptic bandwagon declaring the world would come to an end at the stroke of midnight on the last day of that year, all the talk about Y2K did make us think we should cover our bases if our computerized world shut down for a while. Since we had the funds to invest, we decided this was an opportunity to be physically ready for any possible event.

That's when we decided to create a self-supporting haven, a place where we could live on back-up systems, sustainable resources, and even wood-burning stoves if we had to. If a Y2K disaster occurred, we would provide a place of refuge for our large family, as well as for those called to preach and teach the Word of God. If this became a catastrophic crisis, we wanted to be able to minister to the anointed ministers and lay teachers who God would use to speak hope, healing, and love to a hurting world. We desired to help as many people as possible who had no preparations.

But if nothing catastrophic happened, we would use the facility as a spiritual retreat center.

We developed a two-prong strategy to address both scenarios.

The prophetic Word declares when Messiah returns to Jerusalem, He will do so through the east gate of the city.

After this, he brought me to the gate facing east. There I saw the glory of the God of Isra'el approaching from the east. His voice was like the sound of rushing water, and the earth shone with his glory (Ezekiel 43:1-2 CJB).

In Jerusalem, the golden gate or east gate is a prophetic place. Thus we planned to name our retreat home *Eastgate*, in honor and anticipation of His coming—whenever that might be.

In 1998, we bought mountain property in Arkansas with our friends, Richard and Dawn. Two hundred and sixty five acres of beautiful wooded and rolling land with two stocked natural spring fed ponds. Then, Paul and I embarked on the ambitious task of overseeing the building of a 9,400 square-foot retreat center, positioned on the summit of the far east end of the property—complete with generators, a water well, eight propane tanks, and even our own gasoline tank and pump.

As the home was constructed, we wrote the promises of God's Word on the two-by-fours, sheet rock and concrete floors. We placed paperback Bibles inside the walls. At every stage, we prayed over the home, anointed it with oil and spoke words of peace, restoration, protection and blessing in every room. We prayed every person who ever walked through the doors would immediately experience God's shalom fall upon them.

Between juggling the responsibilities of parenting, ministry activities, my school studies, the building project, and countless other tasks, 1998 and 1999 flew by quickly.

Our goal was to have Eastgate completed by December 31, 1999.

Unfortunately, it was not.

On New Year's Eve, there was no carpet, no furniture, and no supplies to speak of in the house, but we planned to take some groceries and our sleeping bags and camp out on the concrete as a kind of initiation. Our family and several close friends joined us in Arkansas to pray and usher in the New Millennium— however it occurred. We knew many people around the world were fearful of the possibilities—yet we were peaceful that night—even in light of our unfinished surroundings.

We also knew we weren't the only people who had made provisions.

"As police throughout the world secured emergency bunkers for themselves, the TIME magazine and Time Inc. information-technology staff set up a generator-powered 'war room' in the basement of the Time & Life Building, filled with computers and equipment ready to produce the magazine in case of a catastrophic breakdown of electricity and communications."[83]

If Y2K had actually crashed our world, and taken us "back to the dark ages," we would have been hard-pressed to survive long-term in an "almost" finished Y2K house. Yet we trusted the Lord to take care of our needs. We were thankful a "catastrophic breakdown" never occurred, and the changing of the millennium was nothing more than a bleep on the radar. In fact, the day's most historic moment was actually the resignation of Russian President Boris Yeltsin.

$\sim$

With Y2K behind us, we knew immediately this retreat center would be used to bless others. God was calling us to be His servants, to care for His anointed and to bless His workers of the Kingdom.

How do you "bless" someone?

The word *baruch* means bless. All Jewish prayers start with *baruch*, as in "*Baruch atah Adonai, Elohenu Melech ha olam*" which means "Blessed, are you O Lord, our God, King of the universe."

*Baruch* is related to the Hebrew word *berech*, which means "to kneel." When one blesses the Lord or another person, they are, in essence, kneeling in humility in order to serve. When *Yeshua* washed the feet of his disciples, He knelt and blessed them, becoming a servant to them. If you bless another, you are offering yourself as a servant. I dare not ask the Lord to bless me, as that would be literally asking Him to humble Himself to serve me. Rather, I will bless the Lord because He has provided. I will bless the Lord because of His great favor. I will bless the Lord for all He has done for me. In essence, I am saying I humble myself before You, Lord, as your servant in response to the great things You have done for me.

In order for the Lord to bless (serve) us, we first need to humble ourselves and bless (serve) Him. As we bow down to Him and others, the Lord will exalt us.

We dedicated Eastgate to Messiah—to bless and serve Him.

~

We returned home to Houston a few days after New Year's Day, where we hit the ground running.

I was nearing completion of my studies to finish my associate degree with the Institute for Hebraic-Christian Studies. As I began to search for other schools that offered Hebraic classes, I discovered a staggering truth. Most universities and seminaries only offered traditional Greco-Roman perspectives in religious education, taught by Greco-Roman scholars. Where could a hungry student-seeker learn the Hebrew perspective of our faith? Where could I find professors that taught from a Hebraic perspective instead of the typical Greco-Roman point of view?[84] I prayed God would soon bring an answer to this heartfelt prayer.

I knew I wasn't alone in my desire and passion to learn more about how *Yeshua* viewed His faith and what the 1st century believers were "hanging His words on." In fact, one look at the activity on the grounds of "The Secret Place" proved it.

The small parking lot we built for members of the congregation overflowed with vehicles every day, and our backyard had people coming and going all hours during the day and night. Every square inch of office and storage space in the renovated barn was used to house the ministry operations, not only for the Shalom Hebraic Christian Congregation, but also for the Association of Jewish and Christian Believers (a network ministry we co-founded,) the Nathaniel Foundation, and for other various outreach projects as well.

We lacked more than just adequate office space. Our congregation was exploding, and we needed a bigger meeting room in which to worship. Our backyard barn was busting at the seams and frankly, as much as we loved being able to bless these thriving organizations, the time had come to reclaim our property as our home.

We had been talking randomly about the growing space challenges for a few months. With the oppressive threat of Y2K finally behind us, we had been home from Eastgate for only a few days when Paul and I began to seriously discuss alternative options for the congregation and agreed we should look for property.

In His infinite wisdom, our Messiah opened doors quickly to a new adventure of epic proportion.

# Chapter 18

# A GATHERING PLACE

**Kavanah**: Pureness of heart/zeal

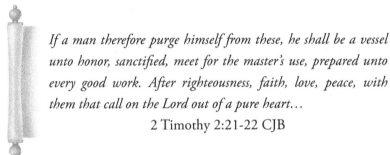

*If a man therefore purge himself from these, he shall be a vessel unto honor, sanctified, meet for the master's use, prepared unto every good work. After righteousness, faith, love, peace, with them that call on the Lord out of a pure heart...*

2 Timothy 2:21-22 CJB

When one prays with *kavanah* they are focused and are pure of heart in His Presence.

Twenty years before when our income level began to rise, we felt emboldened, proud, and anxious to buy status symbols to show our success. Back then, we had an agenda. However, that changed as Paul and I grew in faith and maturity in the Lord—as we learned to pray with *kavanah*.

The more we prayed, "What can we do for You, God? What 'project' is in Your heart?" the more He enabled us to help others.

In addition to blessing the "apple of His eye,"[85] Israel, He also burdened our hearts with the need to financially help ministries in our own country. Gratifying work that included reaching and saving souls, taking care of the sick, feeding and clothing the poor, helping victims of abuse and rape, providing for the widowed, orphaned, and homeless, and bringing hope to the broken hearted and imprisoned.

The Nathaniel Foundation funded numerous ministries here and abroad, and our outreach to restore the lost legacy of our Hebrew heritage grew. Finding a larger space to conduct business would enable us to continue the momentum.

However, I felt convicted that we needed to expand not only our *facility*, but our *visibility* as well. I felt the Lord calling us to plant a visible "tree" somewhere in our city, a tree with strong roots in a rich biblical foundation—roots that would sink deep in the community soil and produce abundant fruit for years to come.

When I found a former performing arts center in major disrepair in Kingwood, I felt certain we had found our new central hub—our own matrix from which to grow. There was potential for an auditorium that would hold more than six times our current occupancy. It had numerous offices, warehouse spaces, a good size parking lot, and loads of potential.

And while it was close to our country home, it wasn't literally in our back yard.

It was perfect.

When I shared my idea with the Nathaniel Foundation board of directors, they quickly joined me in capturing the vision of a facility that could be impactful in many ways.

"If we buy this building, our congregation will have a permanent home with a much bigger auditorium and plenty of office space," I said. "But wait, there's more. The building has enough square footage where we could have conferences and other ministry events, and even rent it out for receptions and parties to offset costs." Several board members jotted down figures and nodded.

"And…" I paused for a moment, wishing I had an actual drum roll for my next revelation and praying the board wouldn't think I was a lunatic, "… this building has the makings of a world-class stage, a place where we can offer quality family theatrical and musical events. It was once a performing arts center. Let's return it to its original roots—just as we're returning to ours."

An animated discussion followed and with endless possibilities, all bathed in fervent prayer, our decision was unanimous.

We were going to build a unique community center in Kingwood, Texas. We would call it the Nathaniel Center for Cultural and Biblical Education. And, it would be the home to our Foundation and house Shalom Hebraic Christian Congregation as well.

Within a few months, the Nathaniel Foundation bought and closed on the unique property in Kingwood and with our official groundbreaking ceremony on June 15, 2000, we embarked on a major renovation to make significant improvements.

We couldn't wait to see what God would do next.

~

We wrapped up final construction at Eastgate in Arkansas in February—it was now time for interior design and décor. I loved this part and Paul always gave me carte blanche to do whatever I thought was best. He trusted my ability and capability, and his support was empowering.

When all the interior embellishments were added, we started what became known as "Ministry Weekends at Eastgate." We would prayerfully choose and invite four couples in ministry to participate in a weekend of pampering, camaraderie, and shalom.

We insisted our guests stay in the plush robes we provided as we served them breakfast in bed. Massage therapists were available, and the spa was at their disposal. We fed them gourmet meals, prayed for them, and washed their feet in true servant fashion. Paul also provided personal and ministerial financial advice as well—a true blessing as full time ministry work and financial challenges often go hand-in-hand.

We have ministered to many of the Lord's faithful servants over the years at Eastgate, and we have been the recipients of such joy in doing so.

Dr. John Garr used Eastgate for a gathering of some of the most noted Hebraic scholars in the world. The meeting was a colloquium to discuss the cohesiveness of the growing Hebraic interest which had become an exploding grassroots movement. The symposium was established for these prominent theologians to meet and network. Along with host John Garr, our esteemed guests included the likes of Charles Abraham, William Bean, David Bivin, Richard Booker, Michael Brown, Carl Coke, JoAnn Magnuson, Dwight Pryor, Hal Ronning, Isaac Rottenburg, Clarence Wagner, Marvin Wilson, Brad Young, and at least twenty others. This was the first of many symposiums held at Eastgate for this distinguished community of international Hebraic scholars.

At the colloquium, I learned Dr. Bean had an accredited graduate program for ministers in Redlands, California called The Center for the Study of Biblical Research.

"How I wish there was a school like yours in Houston," I said to him.

His surprising response was such a blessing.

"If there are more ministers like you with this same interest, we could set up an extension program—a satellite school at the Nathaniel Center."

And that's exactly what we did.

It wasn't long before several scholars agreed to teach "biblical immersion classes" at the Center. We used Eastgate for these classes as well. People came from all over the country to audit these weeklong or weekend-long series of lectures at both locations. We had lectures streaming live online, as well as recorded classes available.

Being around these anointed men and women of faith—scholars and students alike—was surreal. I soaked up their knowledge and wisdom in direct proportion to how I thanked the Lord for giving me this treasure-chest of gifts.

~

My family responsibilities and growing ministry commitments kept me busy. The major remodel on the Nathaniel Center required increasing attention, and I had to learn how to efficiently multi-task and effectively delegate.

Although it certainly wasn't on his list of groundskeeper duties, we asked John Paul if we could expand his job description to include picking up Kristen and Brittany from school each afternoon and to do the weekly grocery shopping. With a true servant heart (just like his parents), John Paul was more than happy to help and his assistance with these two tasks made a considerable difference in my schedule. I was so thankful John Paul was such a responsible and respectful young man.

Then one day I got a frantic phone call from Kristen, now fifteen.

"John Paul is late picking me up from cheerleading practice, and I hear emergency sirens close by!"

I tried to calm her, but as it turned out, John Paul *had* been involved in a hit-and-run accident that caused his truck to flip three times. Bron and Darlene called me shortly after Kristen to inform me of the accident *and* of John Paul's insistence that Bron pick up Kristen from school and bring her with him to the hospital.

Bron said, "It's curious ... all John Paul was worried about as paramedics loaded him into the ambulance was Kristen."

Paul and I immediately left for the medical center hospital complex.

When we arrived, we were ecstatic to discover John Paul escaped the accident nearly without a scratch. However, Kristen was beside herself with emotion when she saw him. Bron, Darlene, Paul, and I watched as she ran to John Paul, and they hugged with great passion.

"I'm so glad you are okay," Kristen said repeatedly as tears cascaded down her cheeks, and she clung to him for dear life. Equally interesting, he was clearly clinging back.

John Paul lost his truck that day, it was completely totaled. But he and our daughter found something completely unexpected as a result of the accident. With the blink of an eye (or the rolling of a truck), their relationship forever changed.

After that day, there was no mistaking the sparks between John Paul and Kristen.

With a six-year age difference, we "strongly advised" them not to date until Kristen's sixteenth birthday. Actually, it was more than just "advice." We liked John Paul, trusted him, and approved of him—but our daughter was still *very* young.

However, John Paul lived in the back yard, so this wouldn't be easy—*oye vey*!

From then on, John Paul continued to work outside on the property during the day, but was showered and smelling good when he dropped by the house almost every night. While they were not permitted to go on "dates" by themselves we all dated as a family. We watched a whole lot of movies together at home and at the theatre. We ate out, shopped at the mall, and occasionally went to arcades and miniature golfing … together. We took chaperoning to a whole new level until Kristen (finally!) turned sweet sixteen.

~

At the same time, Cynthia and Diana attended college at Southern Methodist University (SMU) in Dallas. We were so proud of them and at how they made an impact for Christ on campus. Cynthia (who informed us, she was now too mature to be called "Cindy"), developed an all faith inclusive project at SMU called Fusion. The organization was founded to bring all the various campus Christian organizations together for special occasions of prayer and worship.

She also worked with special needs teens at the Capernaum Young Life ministry and absolutely adored all of them. There, she met a very amicable and quite humorous Dallas boy who also worked for the Young Life organization. And after a year of dating, David Heaton and Cynthia announced they were getting married.

In June of 2000, Cynthia and David married at the beautiful St. Paul's Methodist Church in West University, Houston. An elegant reception followed at the iconic Rice Hotel, a downtown landmark that would soon become known as the Rice Lofts, a luxury apartment complex.

The entire evening was enchanting, and she looked absolutely stunning.

Cynthia and David bought and remodeled a condominium conveniently located near SMU where they lived until they both graduated in May 2001. After graduation, they bought a lovely home in a gated North Dallas neighborhood. They both continued to work with special needs teens and David was hired as the director of the thriving and very popular Young Life chapter. Soon after, they took on the status of caretakers and guardians of three special needs teenage boys in their new home.

We all came to love these boys, and it was as if Lee, Antoine, and George had been with our growing Sarvadi family clan forever.

One time we were on a family getaway at Eastgate when I looked out the kitchen window and saw my dad walking hand-in-hand with George, a young man with Down Syndrome. My dad was tall—6'4" to George's 4'6" (if that)— and I couldn't help but smile as they walked together. My dad really did have a lot of compassion—I saw glimpses of it often. Unfortunately, for some reason, he couldn't show any of it to me.

Today, Cynthia and David serve on the board of directors of Cornerstone Ranch[86], a special needs community they founded in 2006 just north of Dallas.

~

That landmark millennium year was significant in many ways, especially concerning our family.

Wes still had issues at the private school he was now attending to the extent the principle was now "suggesting" that we remove him. We tried so many things: prayer, counselors, private tutors and schools, a move to the country, Christian camps, medicine, hospitals, metal chelation, herbs, whole food nutrition, naturopathy and yes, even "deliverance" sessions. We didn't know what was left.

Over the course of our rocky journey with our son, we discovered that it's during the first four years of a child's life that they develop trust in their parents, which produces virtues like honesty, and a respect for authority. As a little boy, Wes had never developed trust, and definitely lacked this basic life essential. It would take a lot of patience and love on our part (and a mountain of self-discipline on his) to turn this around.

We did some research and found a school in New Mexico specializing in a different approach to education and behavioral correction called "peer therapy." So, we decided to try something new and send Wes to New Mexico. Besides, Brittany really needed some one on one attention at home without the unpleasant competition and harassment of her outspoken brother. Parenting, at times, can be a huge challenge when it comes to finding balance.

~

The doors to the Nathaniel Center for Cultural and Biblical Education were finally and officially opened in late 2001, fourteen months after our groundbreaking.[87]

In addition to our satellite school and Shalom congregation, our initial tenants were the Nathaniel Foundation, AJCB, Vision for Israel, the Crossover Project show and studio, Call to Glory Christian dance school, and the A.D. Players day camp.

Over time, the Center became home to other organizations such as the Kingwood Chamber of Commerce, the Arthur Murray Ball Room Dancing

School, Rowland Ballard performances, and the Healing Room. Several marriage counselors set up offices at the Center. We also had Baptist, Methodist, and Assembly of God churches use the property for interim and long-term church services. Several Spanish churches and even a Romanian church have used our facility for interim services as well.

We conducted on-going beginner and advanced Hebrew classes, children's day camps, and various school activities. We've held hundreds if not thousands of weddings, receptions, parties, quincineras, and even funerals at the center.

We have hosted high-profile speakers such as journalist Bridget Gabriel and many government officials such as Ted Cruz and other senators and congressmen. Famous performers, authors, and scholars have appeared on our stage. One of the five original replicas of the Dead Sea Scrolls was on display during an international tour. We've held numerous art shows and hosted many other wonderful events. Currently, the Kingwood Pops, Center Stage Children's Theatre, Curtain Call Café Christian Theatre, and Opera Leggera all call the Nathaniel Center home, and present seasonal productions on our world-class stage.

Countless individuals have experienced the fruit of the Nathaniel Center tree—as our roots continue to grow deep into the Kingwood community. With a fantastic staff and gracious volunteers, the Nathaniel Center is a landmark hub for family and community. Thousands have crossed our threshold and experienced the love and favor of *Yeshua*, as He flows through the ministries who call this facility home.

Our intent is to continue our mission to partner with ministries of integrity, theatre, arts, and entertainment with equal integrity, portraying spiritual or at least wholesome family values in all we do.

~

After signing a contract with a commercial landscaping company to care for our personal estate grounds, I hired our property workers, Zack Alexander as our new IT tech and John Paul as our facilities manager. With the additional hiring of a personal assistant, a sound and lights director and an events coordinator, The Nathaniel Center was in business.

The new educational opportunity that the Center for the Study of Biblical Research offered credentialed ministers was a godsend. We were able to offer

Master and Doctorate programs by CSBR under the umbrella of the University system of California right in our community of Kingwood.

The late Dr. William Bean, founder and director of CSBR made frequent trips to the Nathaniel Center to teach. Other scholars also came to the Center and taught what we called "mini-mesters."

Our graduates received their accredited Masters and Doctorate degrees in divinity or theology in a matter of five years. What a blessing and a spiritual treasure trove this opportunity afforded us.

$\sim$

The end of November saw another milestone in our family as Kristen and John Paul "officially" got engaged on her seventeenth birthday. John Paul was doing a great job for the Nathaniel Center and going to school at Lone Star College. They planned to marry when Kristen finished high school.

$\sim$

When Administaff first went public in 1997, the stock opened at $23.00 a share. When it reached $40.00 a share, management determined it was time for the stock to split, a decision that increases trading activity as the stock is then offered at a lower price. By fall of the next year, Administaff reached a stock price of $66.62, and the management split the stock for a second time. There was no doubt the company was well on its way to lead its industry.

Earlier that year, the Administaff Amigos and Amigas took a memorable trip to Washington D.C. for the first of several presidential inaugurations we would attend. The Bush campaign was an Administaff client, and to attend the inauguration was truly an honor. We even attended the Inaugural balls.

Galas and banquets were now commonplace in our lives. In December of that year we were in another grand ballroom in Austin, Texas where Paul was about to receive a very prestigious honor. Seconds before he walked to the podium to accept the Ernst & Young Entrepreneur of the Year award, I kissed him on the cheek.

"Go get 'em, Paul Jason Perry Mason," I whispered my nonsensical nickname from our teenage dating years.

As he accepted the award and began to speak at the lectern, I glanced at Paul's image on one of the several huge Jumbotron screens and was aghast to see my kiss had left a perfect red imprint of my lips on his cheek. Receiving this award was a significant milestone in his career, and I was worried I might have made him look foolish.

Ah, but instead this particular "red badge of courage" endeared him to guests and reinforced his reputation as a man who loved his wife and family. He delivered his gracious speech with an infectious smile, glittering green eyes, and a bold red imprint of my true admiration on his cheek.

Six years later, he became the youngest man to ever be inducted into the Texas Business Hall of Fame. On that particular evening, I was careful not to wear red lipstick.

~

The recognition we received for our efforts was quite humbling and I couldn't help but think how surreal life had become, how blessed we were, and how hard we worked to get here. News articles and media blurbs concerning Administaff and the Nathaniel Foundation became more frequent. The Nathaniel Center also received a lot of press and attention. Kingwood was proud to have a performing arts and banquet center of our caliber. As we hoped and prayed, our programs and events made a positive impact on the community.

I was truly happy with our accomplishments and where we were in life. I always prayed God would keep my heart in check, but in retrospect, I was probably feeling a little more proud of myself than I should have been. My heart was sincerely on fire for *Yeshua*, but my purpose had become a little cloudy, and I had begun to feel tired and inadequate for the demands upon my time. My juggling act wasn't as easy as it once was.

Yet I pressed on.

I had been teaching some of Dr. Booker's classes at the Center. I added teaching a Yeshiva (an interactive Bible study similar to a Sunday school class) in addition to the ladies Bible study at Shalom. Not to mention, just running the Nathaniel Center was a full-time job in itself.

With little spare time, I ignored the signs I was nearing exhaustion.

~

After a whirlwind year, we thought it would be nice to take a break and treat all our kids, their spouses, and even dad to skiing at Red River, New Mexico during winter break. We invited Pastor Bron and Darlene to join us.

The snow at the higher altitudes was a fresh compacted powder, perfect for skiing. But I decided to play it safe and ski the bunny slopes at the base of the mountain. The snow we encountered there was called "dust on crust," a light covering of loose snow on top of snow that has a hard, icy outer layer.

Halfway down the slope, I hit a decidedly icy patch and was suddenly moving a little faster than I wanted to go. As I tried to slow down, my skis crossed, my right knee turned inward, and I heard two loud "pops."

The pain was instantaneous and excruciating. I screamed in agony as I knelt upon the ground and cried.

Paul encouraged me to get up, but I couldn't. My knee just wouldn't work.

The anterior cruciate ligament is one of the four main ligaments of the knee. Commonly known as the ACL, it provides 85% of the restraining force to stabilize the knee when turning or planting. It is essential to normal knee function and stability—and I had seriously damaged mine.

So there I was kneeling on the snow, unable to walk, and helplessly waiting for the ski patrol to strap me into a toboggan and tow me off the slope.

Looking back, I see God's plan to make me a humble servant had already gone into full effect.

*Chapter 19*

# A HECTIC HOT MESS

## Balagan: Turmoil (aka: a hot mess)

*Let us examine and test ways, and return to* Adonai.
Lamentations 3:40 CJB

There was no doubt in my mind God was doing a work in me I could not have accomplished on my own. However, that didn't make me invincible.

There was nothing natural about the pace I was running—it was only a matter of time before I hit a wall.

The month leading up to our ski trip vacation, I worked from 7:30 in the morning to sometimes 11:00 at night. Ministry and work at the Center were time consuming. There were often five or six people in the lobby at any given moment, waiting to talk to me. I received literally hundreds of emails a day. Plus, my class assignments often kept me up all night reading and preparing.

And somewhere along the way, I had lost my *joy* of ministry. I felt my goal each day was to cross off as many "things to do" from my list as possible. Where was the presence of God in *that*?

Now confined to bed and dealing with considerable pain, I pondered my current situation. I recalled that according to ancient biblical history, shepherds often needed to break the leg of a lamb that kept wandering off the path. That would be me, the wanderer—definitely off path. I'm not quite sure when it happened, but I had become a "human doing" instead of a "human being."

God knew I was headed for self-destruction, and it took a broken leg (or rather, a torn ACL) to slow me down.

When my surgery was scheduled for February 13, the date wasn't lost on me. This date marked the twenty-fourth anniversary of the day little George slipped away from us, and the very day I saw my guardian angel.

This time, fortunately, there were no major complications during the surgical procedure.

At the time I had my surgery, orthopedic surgeons used either a cadaver ACL or fashioned a piece of the patients hamstring tendon to create a makeshift ACL. I didn't like the idea of having a body part of someone else in my knee, so I opted for Door Number Two. However, over time, doctors eventually realized the hamstring tendon will stretch out, and it doesn't keep the knee in tight tension like the actual ACL does. Today, the patella is more often used instead of the hamstring.

As a result, my knee is weak. Like the Apostle Paul, it's the thorn in my side.[88] Like Jacob's limp from wrestling with God.[89] It's the weakness that reminds me daily that the Lord is God, not me.

An initial part of my recovery was to keep my knee flexible as it healed. A mechanical contraption was set up on my bed at home that exercised my knee for me, like I was riding a bicycle 24/7 from bed.

I hated lying there and doing little but sleep or look up at the ceiling, especially with so much to do. Kristen's wedding was only a few months away, and I needed to address wedding invitations.

I'd been home a few days when I asked Evelyn, our nanny, to help me. We laughed and talked during the process, reminiscing about how grown up the girls were, and marveling that Kristen and John Paul were actually getting married. Throughout the day, Dad stuck his head in the room and told us to "pipe down." I guess we sounded like a couple of teenage girls having way too much fun when we were supposed to be doing homework.

By this point, my dad had been living with us for about five years, and the tension between us hadn't gotten any better. I hoped seeing me as a parent and successful businesswoman would somehow open his eyes to the fact I was a capable adult, not just a little girl, and certainly not stupid. Unfortunately, that never happened.

In fact, life with dad got more stressful after my ACL surgery.

About a week post-op it was time to send out our foundation grant checks. Many of these ministries depended on these checks to pay their monthly expenses. As the executive director of the Nathaniel Foundation, this was one of my key priority responsibilities. Almost a dozen ministries depended on me to mail their monthly grant awards.

Everything I needed to conduct this critical task was on my desktop computer at the Nathaniel Center.

My doctor instructed me to limit my moving around, but if I had to be up, to keep my knee on ice. In order to do that, I was given a portable electric pump built in to a small ice cooler. The pump moved cold water through narrow hoses to an ice pad secured around my knee with Velcro. It was a cumbersome contraption, but it enabled me to get out of bed for brief periods.

Once again, I asked Evelyn for her help.

With carefully orchestrated precision, we put our plan into motion.

Evelyn drove me to the Nathaniel Center where Becky, my assistant, picked me up in a wheel chair at the porte-cochere in front of the building and then took me up the elevator to my office. Evelyn had to go back home to meet a service worker, but we agreed she would return in forty minutes. This would give me plenty of time to get the check process started for Becky to complete.

With the ice contraption plugged in and connected to my knee, I quickly got to work on the letters and grant checks. Becky helped to address envelopes she would later mail. We were operating like a well-oiled machine.

When Evelyn returned home, my dad inquired as to my whereabouts. When she told him where I was, he shouted a few expletives and stormed out of the house.

Becky and I were just about finished when I heard a familiar sound that brought old childhood fears to mind—the foot-stomping gait of an angry man fueled by adrenalin and purpose. I took a deep breath just as my father stormed into my office.

"You g-damn stupid kid!" he shouted, within audible distance of various ministry leaders, pastors and of course, my assistant, who all looked as shocked as me at the outburst. "What the hell do you think you're doing?" He marched across the room toward me.

I was appalled at his language.

"Dad, please don't swear," I said. "People can hear you..."

"I don't give a damn," he shouted, as he pulled my wheel chair away from the desk and began to roughly push me toward the door.

"Dad, stop!" I cried out. As he ignored my plea, I reached down and quickly grabbed the ice cooler that was plugged into the wall and screamed to Becky. "Unplug it!"

She rushed to pull the cord from the wall just in time, and it dragged behind the wheelchair like a lone tentacle as my dad pushed me with headstrong purpose toward the elevator. I was mortified as I tried to balance the small cooler on my lap and reel the cord in before the elevator door closed.

It was like being kidnapped in broad daylight, with paralyzed people standing nearby—the director and founder of this renowned center being whisked away in an angry fervor by her raving dad.

I was humiliated.

There was no talking to my father—especially when he was agitated. The irony was, he still saw me as an immature kid who needed discipline and parenting. I was an adult in my forties with two grandchildren, but to him, I was still a "stupid kid."

Some might say my dad was showing concern the only way he knew how.

In retrospect, I can see where that might be the case, no matter how off-base I thought he was at the time. Nonetheless, I was horribly embarrassed by his behavior that day. I felt like a little child being reprimanded in an abusive way, and the wedge between us grew wider.

However, at the end of the day, the growing problem wasn't just my dad screaming at me—it was my entire life screaming at me—the ever-increasing list of things to do, places to go, and people to please. My hectic life was challenging enough, and recuperating from an injury made it even more so—physical therapy added to my already full plate.

Additionally, the onset of peri-menopause had begun to affect my body, mind, and emotions. Yet for some reason, I remained in a state of denial, even when I started to have obvious hot flashes.

One morning I woke up drenched. Another time I was at the Center, and suddenly my sweat glands opened up without warning and, in record time, my hair was sopping wet and my clothes were completely saturated. There were definitely physiological changes going on in my body, something I had no control over. I started to fight some weight gain, too. I felt exhausted and unhappy.

Life for me became a *balagan*. In Israel, this is a commonly used term for a messy situation.

That pretty much explained my life—I was a real mess—a hectic *hot* mess.

I didn't have time for any of this, but there wasn't much I could do about it, so I just continued to plow on. I continued to push myself and refused to let anything—or anyone—stop me from fulfilling "*God's purpose.*"

~

I continued my physical therapy, and the months dragged on … and on … and on.

For the first time during my life, I felt my age. I also felt inadequate. I was nasty and short with Paul, who took the wise road of staying out of my path and wrath. Life had become a never-ending list of things "to do" without any creativity.

Yet, joy stopped in for a brief visit when our first granddaughter joined our family on the first day of April that year. Shannon did everything in her power not to have her baby on April Fool's Day, but shortly before midnight on April 1, 2002, Lauren Avery could wait no longer. She came into the world in her own time, as if to declare, "I'm no fool—look out world—here I come!"

One month later, Family Time presented me with their Women of Achievement Visionary award, which I was deeply honored to receive. On that beautiful spring evening in May my entire family, including my reluctant dad, attended the organization's signature event, the Hearts of Gold Gala. When I accepted the award, Paul and our girls stood and applauded. As I returned to our table, everyone made an effort to hug and congratulate me ... except my father—he simply turned his head away—as though he was embarrassed.

A week later, our little Kristen graduated as valedictorian from a private high school and just days later on May 11, 2002, true to her prophetic declaration as a young girl, Kristen and John Paul were married. It was a magical time as the virtuoso violinist, Dr. Maurice Sklar ministered to the 600 guests in attendance at the beautiful First Presbyterian Church of Kingwood. The elaborate wedding was followed by a lively reception at the Nathaniel Center complete with a live band and an exquisite plated dinner. They immediately bought a beautiful home in Kingwood, and both started attending the University of Houston.

Kristen had stepped effortlessly into adulthood.

After the wedding, I vowed to myself, I would take some time off.

Promises, promises.

In June of that year, Paul and I were chosen as co-honorees to receive The Defenders of Jerusalem award, along with Jeanne and the late Joe Samuels, the owners of the Jewish Herald Voice. The award was presented to us by Deputy Israeli ambassador, Moshe Fox, at a beautiful gala at the Westin Galleria in Houston. Truly a treasured memory.

~

As the year ended, I found myself resorting to popping a few more ibuprophen than usual. I don't like to take pain medicine, but it seemed as though my head always hurt and my knee often ached. My immune system also seemed to be down; frequent sinus infections, UTIs, and bouts with ovarian cysts and vertigo plagued me. I had way too much to do to take any time off. I tried to ignore these inconveniences because I simply did *not* have time to be sick.

Our family continued to grow. Cynthia gave birth to Tyler—our fourth grandchild—on April 8, 2003, an early birthday gift for me. In the midst of a whirlwind life, I had much to be thankful for, and I was never more alive and balanced than when I was around my babies.

My children—and their children—centered and balanced me.

Sometimes God allows us to feel pressure, so we will go in a different direction. Life was moving at warp speed, and I found it more and more difficult to keep up. However, I resolutely refused to give in to the mounting pressure.

I was still a hectic hot mess, but I did my best to maintain my juggling act.

This was particularly challenging as the friction between my dad and me increased and the dynamic of our roles began to shift.

*Chapter 20*

# DIFFICULT DECISIONS

**Kaddish**: Sanctification; A prayer recited at the death of a loved one

*One generation passeth away, and another generation cometh;*
*But the earth abideth forever.*

Ecclesiastes 1:4 KJV

After my ACL surgery, Dad did some increasingly strange things. When my mother died of cancer, he stopped smoking. He actually quit cold turkey and hadn't smoked for nine years—but now it was suddenly his new habit again. He also started meeting women on a well-known internet site and was actively "dating." And he began to discipline Wes and Brittany in ways that superseded my own authority. I didn't want my two youngest children to walk on eggshells like I had for so many years, so I tried to establish healthy boundaries with my dad, but it wasn't easy.

Communicating with him was never easy.

I was working on paperwork from home one day when Dad shuffled into the room.

He made nonsensical small talk before he put his hands in his pockets and, looking a little sheepish, blurted out, "I'm getting married."

I sat there stunned as an entire conversation ran through my mind:

*Oh my gosh, does this mean I'm going to have a stepmother? If it's the woman he's been seeing, this won't be easy; she seems grouchy. Where will they live? On the plus side, this means he'll move out...he will move out, right? I hope she's not planning to move in here. I hope he doesn't ask if she can. I'll definitely say no. Be ready to say no. What about him feeling so sick lately? Has he been to the doctor? Does she know he's been sick? Is she responsible for him smoking again? Does she know he has money? Should he get a prenup?*

My thoughts were like pick-up sticks falling over one another.

I got as much of my composure back as possible and asked, Wh-hen?"

"Probably in about a month."

"Oh my." I said. "So soon?"

"It's not that soon." he countered abruptly. Then, he changed his tone and asked if I could help him with the wedding.

I was stunned. *Was he actually asking for my help?*

"Of course, I'd be happy to help you. Weddings are one of my specialties," I responded confidently but, not sure what to say next.

My dad and I never had warm and fuzzy conversations, and I felt particularly awkward in this situation when he took a deep breath before asking another question.

"Could we, I mean could she..."

*Oh dear Lord! Was he going to ask if they could live here? If she could move into our home?*

I was about to shout, "No!" as he continued, "...could we have the ceremony in the front room where the guests could see her come down the spiral staircase?"

The request was completely unexpected.

Although it pained me to think of my dad marrying this disagreeable woman in the first place, and in my home no less, it was a far easier question to answer than the one I initially dreaded.

I heard myself say, "Yes." as my dad smiled meekly and began to cough.

I quickly changed the subject and asked if he had seen his doctor yet about this cough and the increasing lethargy he always complained about.

"I've got an appointment tomorrow." he said.

"That's good." I responded, as I tried not to think about "that woman" gliding down my staircase in all her sartorial splendor.

~

Dad's appointment didn't go well.

The doctor did blood work and scheduled an immediate biopsy on his lung. A few days later, we found out Dad had lung cancer.

The cancer was aggressive, and they recommended surgery right away.

One week later, the doctor ended up removing half of one of Dad's lungs. He made it through surgery okay, but due to his age and the seriousness of the surgery, they immediately sent him to the intensive care unit.

A few days after surgery, Dad developed a severe infection. They were administering massive doses of antibiotics, but nothing worked.

He slept a lot, and got visibly weaker every day.

One day, he said Mom came to him in a dream, and he felt like he might be joining her soon. He seemed very tender and told us all he loved us.

During one of our visits, he cast his eyes down. "I guess I was pretty hard on you, wasn't I, baby?"

"Yes." was all I could manage to say.

He looked up with tears in his eyes. "Well, that's how my daddy raised me."

I took a deep breath.

It wasn't really an apology, but it was an explanation. And with that explanation, I could have some kind of closure. Closure, finally realizing it wasn't me that was lacking all my life. It was how he had been raised—it was the only way he knew how to respond to me. I let out the breath I forgot I was holding and literally, for a moment, felt my entire body relax on a level I never felt before.

We all encouraged Dad to fight, but the infection was still raging and he had lost his will to live.

"Vicki," he whispered the next day, "I miss Momma."

I know. I do too. I whispered back.

His girlfriend, Betty, was there most all the time. I couldn't bring myself to call her Dad's "fiancée." She was constantly kissing his hand, forehead, and cheeks. I was unnerved by all the PDA (public display of affection.) I wasn't sure I could ever accept her, but it was obvious Dad cared for her.

One day, Paul and I arrived at the ICU to visit as a "Code Blue, ICU" announcement came over the intercom. As we approached my dad's room, we saw the medical team and crash cart at his bedside.

Betty had noticed Dad's blood pressure, heart rate, and blood oxygen saturation levels begin to drop. She yelled for a nurse, who arrived at the room just as Dad's heart flat-lined. The medical team was able to jump-start his heart, but as the nurse explained all this to us, I had a feeling of dread.

Paul and I stood outside the room until they took the crash cart out.

When I was finally able to approach his bedside, I could tell my dad wasn't there anymore. He was breathing with the help of a ventilator, and his heart was beating, but his spirit was gone.

Some days later, Dad slipped into a deep coma, and they needed to move him to a different hospital. He remained very ill, but couldn't stay in the ICU anymore. The treatment he needed was an aggressive, specialized interdisciplinary care for medically complex patients. They told us he needed to go to a transitional acute care hospital. Few options were left; his recovery would obviously extend beyond what was the norm.

I had a feeling he wasn't going to get any better. As his oldest, Dad had given me power of attorney, so I knew his health-treatment wishes. In addition to my dad's signed and notarized DNR (do not resuscitate) request, his Living Will paperwork also clearly stated if two doctors agreed he was legally brain dead, we were not to continue extraordinary life support measures.

However, even though the doctors all said he had very little brain activity, my sister Rhonda and Betty were staunchly against following his wishes. In fact, my sister told me if I turned off life support, she would never speak to me again.

Betty's response was worse.

"Why don't you just get a pillow and suffocate him!" she screamed. "If you turn off his life support, you are nothing more than a murderer!"

Then, she said something that sent me over the edge.

"*My* Bible says *my* God heals!" she yelled. Her emphasis being on the "my," as though we worshiped different gods.

I'm sure she was hurting and lashing out in any way she could. I had never been fond of this woman and to infer I worshiped a less-than-sovereign God, or followed a less-than-truthful Bible, made me angry.

And this is when I lost my temper.

"Well," I said, "the same Bible says: Precious in the sight of the Lord is the death of His saints. And; It is appointed unto men once to die, but after this the judgment."[90]

Then, I put my hands on my hips and leaned toward her. "Don't get into a Bible quoting match with me—you will lose!" I desperately tried to keep my composure.

She stared piercingly at me for a moment, then turned on her heels and stomped off.

Oh, was I ever mad at that woman! I was shocked at my sister, frustrated with the doctors, and regretful that my dad hadn't seen a doctor sooner. And I was angry at myself for losing my cool. In fact, I was upset with everyone and everything pretty much all the time.

And I was tired, so very tired.

After talking with the doctors and praying about it, Paul and I made the decision to take Dad off of life support to see if he would breathe on his own, but if he showed immediate signs of respiratory distress, we wanted them to reinsert the breathing tube.

When he began to breathe unassisted, everyone was surprised. I allowed a part of myself to think that maybe, just maybe, he would make it after all … maybe we'd have a second chance.

Unfortunately, every medical test thereafter revealed Dad's body had started to shut down. He had acute sepsis and his organs were systematically failing. Still he continued to hang on.

As the days rolled into weeks, every day was an emotional roller-coaster.

One month after his surgery, someone from the acute-care hospital called. They told me Dad's insurance had run out. They were going to have to remove his feeding tube and I would need to find another place for him to go.

The woman on the phone suggested I bring him home.

I tried to wrap my brain around all of this information when she said they were arranging for my dad's transport to take place that Friday—in just a few days.

*Whoa, whoa. What?*

I couldn't imagine getting everything ready in a few days, and we wouldn't even be in town that weekend as our entire family was going to Austin where two of our former youth group members were getting married. I convinced the hospital to keep Dad until the following Monday, and we would personally pay for the extra days the insurance didn't cover.

When I hung up the phone I went into hyper-drive.

Before we left for Austin on Saturday, I hired round-the-clock nurses to care for Dad and arranged for the delivery of a special hospital bed, medical equipment, and his liquid diet provisions. I arranged for a room on the lower level of our home to be converted with the same equipment as any hospital room would have. And finally, I lined up transport for Dad for Monday morning, June twenty-third.

We left Houston very early on Saturday and less than three hours later we checked into the hotel in Austin. We were getting ready for Nathan and Mindy's wedding when my cell phone rang, and an unfamiliar voice greeted me when I answered.

"Greeted" is actually an understatement, as the emotionless tone of voice was void of warmth. "Mrs. Sarvadi, your father has expired, and we need to know where you wish us to transport him?"

I sank onto the edge of a nearby bed and tried to compute the words I had just heard. "Uh, excuse me? Will you please repeat that?" I said, as I held up my hand to the noise being made by children in the background. Paul whispered loudly for them to be quiet.

"Your father has expired and we need to know where to transport his body." The voice repeated, in the same raw, insensitive way.

"Are you saying my dad has died?" I asked, as I put my hand on my forehead, bit my lip, and tried to hold back the emotions slamming against the dam I had, for so long, kept them securely behind.

"Yes ma'am, he has expired," she repeated again.

*Expired?* She spoke of my father like he was an old bottle of salad dressing in my refrigerator.

Although I had been expecting this phone call, the preparations over the past few days to bring my dad home had somehow made the possibility seem less likely. As strange as it sounded, I was hopeful about making him as comfortable as possible for whatever time he had left.

Now, I would never have that chance—I would never again see my father alive.

Despite our differences, I loved my dad, and this news crushed me far more than I ever expected.

I put my hands over my eyes and cried.

A twenty-one gun salute ended my father's full military funeral a few days later, and as an American flag was ceremonially folded and presented to me and my sister I couldn't help but think that Dad would have approved of this beautiful service. It was orderly and a bit formal—but very appropriate.

*Very nice, Vicki, very nice,* I could hear him say.

# Chapter 21
# MENOPAUSE MONSTER

**Livyatan**: Sea monster from the abyss

*On that day ADONAI, with his great, strong, relentless sword, will punish* Livyatan *the fleeing serpent, the twisting serpent* Livyatan; *he will slay the sea monster.*
Isaiah 27:1 CJB

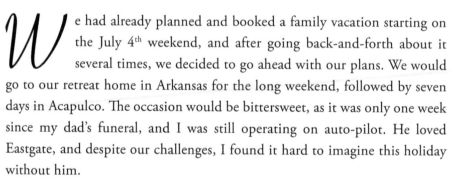

e had already planned and booked a family vacation starting on the July 4th weekend, and after going back-and-forth about it several times, we decided to go ahead with our plans. We would go to our retreat home in Arkansas for the long weekend, followed by seven days in Acapulco. The occasion would be bittersweet, as it was only one week since my dad's funeral, and I was still operating on auto-pilot. He loved Eastgate, and despite our challenges, I found it hard to imagine this holiday without him.

We celebrated the 4th of July twenty minutes from Eastgate at a beautiful nature park. We packed a picnic lunch, brought a football and Frisbee and enjoyed the shade and warm breezes.

I had a bit of a headache that day. It seemed like I was experiencing a lot of them lately. Between hot flashes, headaches, and the heartache over the loss of my dad, I was exhausted. So, I excused myself from all the activity and lay down on a blanket spread out on a soft patch of grass. The sun was warm and I tried to relax, but I was wound up tight—there was so much pressure bearing down on me.

I was behind in my "school" work, and I needed to finish a six-hundred page book on Constantine the Great before the end of the month. Plus, there was a ton of work to be done at the Nathaniel Center. I tried to enjoy the feeling of the warm sun, but my "to-do list" kept running through my mind with projected deadlines.

As I thought about everything on my plate, there were moments when I found it difficult to breathe.

That evening, when we returned to Eastgate from the park, I was hot, sweaty, and sticky from sunscreen and bug spray. Neither of which seemed to work; I felt slightly sunburned and picked a fat ugly bug off my belly as I jumped into the shower.

Later that night, I noticed my arms appeared quite red. Yep, I had clearly gotten way too much sun. The next day, my legs had the same red color, almost like a rash. I felt lethargic and listless, clear signs of over-exposure to the sun.

When I slept in the next day (something I seldom did,) I figured I had simply run out of steam. I blamed it on the combination of too much sun, the hectic pace I had been keeping, and the loss of my father. When I got out of bed at noon and stood up, I literally saw silver stars.

Clearly, all the stress finally caught up with me.

When we arrived in Mexico a few days later, the weather was perfect and the cove was gorgeous. We had been here back in the heyday of our Amway business—what seemed like a lifetime ago.

Our suite was huge and when I saw the luxurious bed, I couldn't wait to curl up and take a nap. I still felt like a deflated balloon, and in our travel to get here, I found walking and standing laborious. I constantly had to sit as I literally had no energy to stand.

On our first night in Mexico, I became emotional.

*What's going on with that?*

Some months before at Eastgate, Zack had met with Paul privately and asked for Diana's hand in marriage. Now he told us he was planning a surprise proposal on the Acapulco beach. Paul and I were ecstatic. We knew about the "walk along the beach" Zack was going to take with Diana that night, so I chalked up my emotional weepiness to that.

That evening, we all waited and anticipated their return. When Diana finally bounded into the room, she smiled from ear to ear, and her face glowed as she extended her left hand to reveal a beautiful engagement ring. Zack grinned like a little boy with his arm around her as we all jumped up and surrounded both of them, showering them with hugs and kisses.

It was a monumental occasion, and while I so wanted to stay up and listen to the details of the romantic story, I literally couldn't keep my head up or my eyes open. I turned in early.

The next morning, Paul got up at daybreak to play golf. I never heard him. When he came back around lunchtime and discovered I was still sleeping, he woke me up to ask if I was okay. I sighed and shrugged my shoulders, too tired to even talk.

I made myself get up and go down to the pool where most of the family was camped out. I found a chaise lounge under a lovely palm tree and proceeded to fall back into intermittent sleep, waking only to decline one of the tropical fruit drinks the waiters constantly offered.

When we returned home to Texas later that week, I had difficulty getting back into a routine. My appetite was gone, and I slept for almost three days straight. When I did wake up, I was often drenched and felt feverish, and when I tried to get up to go to the bathroom, the room spun. There were times I had to literally crawl to the toilet. A few times, I didn't have the energy to get back to my bed, so I just lay on the bathroom rug and fell back to sleep.

It was awful.

Paul was concerned these symptoms were more than just exhaustion or the flu, but my denial that it was anything "really serious," was convincing.

I had to force myself to get up periodically and get a little work done, but my body ached, and I couldn't shake the feelings of lethargy and lightheadedness. All attempts to return to my usual schedule (or even some semblance of a schedule) were short lived. I slept every day until one or two in the afternoon, took a nap around five, and then feel asleep again by nine.

I lived like this for several weeks.

I thought I was dying.

But there was far too much to accomplish, so I mustered up all the strength I could and forged on…if it was a good day.

~

Diana and Zack decided their wedding would be held in Dallas in the month of December. Time was critical as we interviewed wedding coordinators, bands, and florists. We looked at bridal gowns, bridesmaid dresses, tuxes, wedding invitations, and locations for the reception and the bridal luncheon.

I forced myself to help Diana make a million decisions in a very short time period, and she helped me see that I had an important decision of my own to make. I had to do something pro-active about my health. I couldn't continue to pretend I was getting better—because I wasn't.

I called my naturopathic health-care practitioner friend to come visit me and try to figure out what was wrong. Jody flew to Houston from Florida and began her series of unconventional tests.

"There's something wrong with your teeth." she finally said, after one of her tests. "I want you to see a biological dentist."

*My teeth?* That made absolutely no sense to me, but neither did this illness I couldn't shake, so I did what she suggested and began to look for a "biological dentist."

Holistic dentistry, also known as biological dentistry, takes into account a person's entire state of physical and emotional health. Holistic dentists use natural therapies (often in combination with conventional ones) to prevent, diagnose, and treat diseases of the oral cavity.

The naturopathic dentist I saw used a relatively new diagnostic tool and conducted a "resonance frequency analysis" (RFA) on my teeth. Apparently, there are different frequencies associated with oral conditions. Who knew?

"Victoria," she said, "all of my frequency tests point to a bacterial infection—specifically, Lyme disease. Do you recall being bitten by a tick?"

I searched my foggy brain and suddenly remembered the fat disgusting bug I'd plucked off my belly in the shower after the 4th of July picnic.

"Yes!" I said, wondering why I hadn't made the connection sooner.

"I want you to see your D.O. immediately and get a Western Blot test." She went on to explain more about her diagnosis and the test.

The Western Blot is a laboratory test specifically developed for Lyme disease testing. It detects antibodies that identify the bacterial infection associated with this disease.

I made an emergency appointment with my osteopathic doctor, and the immunoblot test came back positive—I definitely had Lyme disease.

*No wonder I have been so sick.*

My D.O. recommended a six-week antibiotic regimen, which Jody strongly advised me against. I understood her preference for a more natural approach, but I couldn't live with these symptoms another day—I truly thought I was dying. So, I opted for an aggressive course of antibiotics.

The medication began to work quickly. I felt somewhat better physically, and I could return to work. More important, I could continue to help with wedding plans. But unfortunately, my memory and concentration fell short. I hoped those symptoms would eventually disappear in time.

~

However, my season of recovery was short-lived. By the holidays, many of my initial symptoms had begun to resurface.

I remembered what Jody told me when I started taking the antibiotics.

"Only about 85% of the Lyme bacteria will die." She said. "The other 15% will go dormant as the bacteria encloses and protects itself from the fighting antibodies. Then, the entire culture will pleomorphesize into a different bacteria form that will be resistant to the antibiotic. Sometime later it will show up again and begin to colonize and grow, and you will get sick again."

When my D.O. suggested a second round of antibiotics, I called Jody instead.

"Victoria, this cycle will continue repeatedly, until you use up the entire spectrum of antibiotics," she said. "And while all those antibiotics are trying to kill the bad bacteria, they are also killing all the good bacteria, and you're going to have to address a laundry list of things that are going to start failing in your body. Antibiotics are *not* the answer."

What she said now made sense—so I decided to listen to my natural health practitioner and abandon the conventional protocol for the natural one.

Jody took me off all sugar. I mean *all* sugar, no fruit, dairy, or root vegetables. The reason is two-fold. First, you must starve the Lyme bacteria of the sugar it thrives on. Second, the immune system must be strengthened in order to fight, and this is best achieved through the absence of sugar, coupled with various herbs, enzymes and a clean diet.

This new way of eating was very difficult at first—especially during the holidays—but the better I felt, the easier it got.

I could stay awake a little longer each week, although I still required more sleep than most people, but I began to see definite improvement.

I wasn't a hundred percent yet but one by one, I began to pick up and juggle some of the plates I had been neglecting.

The year ended with Diana and Zack's stunning wedding—an absolutely perfect event featured in the book, *Spectacular Weddings of Texas, 2004.*

The ceremony took place amongst hundred's of vibrant red poinsettias at the historic and iconic Highland Park Methodist Church located on the SMU campus.

The winter wonderland reception was held at the beautiful Fairmont Hotel in downtown Dallas. We had a Duke Ellington-type big band, hundreds more red poinsettias and candles and scores of leafless trees strung with white lights all over the ballroom. A horse-drawn carriage took them away as the fairytale night came to a close.

After the wedding, I folded up like a battered accordion in a suitcase and retreated to my bedroom where I slept for days. I couldn't push myself any further. I was weary of fighting the two alien life forces inside me. The Menopause Monster and the Lyme Disease Demon were like parasitic twins with a purpose of devouring me alive. I wondered if this demonic duo had partnered together to take up residence in my life.

Although I had begun to get a little control of the cunning and untimely attacks of the Lyme Livyatan, the other monster was not as easy to anticipate—or control.

I never lost my faith in God, I knew He was more than able to slay these creatures completely and keep my shipwrecked life afloat, but I did lose faith in myself. I blamed myself for not being able to handle everything—as though I was an omnipotent being with such power to begin with.

As the year came to an end, I resigned myself to a strange half-life where energy eluded me, and fatigue reigned. A mercurial life punctuated by periodic bouts of semi-normalcy where I could power my way through a few tasks before I reverted back to a lethargic haze. A fractured life where I couldn't do it all anymore and void of emotional equilibrium.

## My Own Tsunami

The entire next year was almost a blur.

By May 2004, I finally fulfilled all the credits to receive my Masters of Theology (THM) from the Center for the Study of Biblical Research. But the pressure didn't let up as I entered into the doctorate program.

With four of our six children married and starting their own families, one would think my active mom role would slow down a bit, enabling me to have a little more free time to study.

However, that wasn't the case.

Growing up in a large family, all our girls longed to continue the legacy, and starting their own families was important to them and Zack and Diana wanted to start right away.

But when both Diana and Cynthia suffered miscarriages just a few months apart, we were all devastated. My heart ached for them—literally and figuratively, as there were times when it seemed my heart beat out of my chest.

Such irony occurred. In the midst of losing babies, healthy ones were also being born.

Shannon and Mark's fourth baby (our fifth grandchild,) was born November 6, 2004. Jake Ryan, was healthy and absolutely perfect.

Unfortunately, I couldn't say the same about me.

I will never forget that year. I turned forty-five, celebrated my 30th wedding anniversary, and cried with my precious daughters as two of them suffered miscarriages within months of each other. Through it all, the physical and emotional symptoms of fighting Lyme disease and perimenopause kept me on a constant roller-coaster. My health was precarious and the pressure and stress of my responsibilities—of my entire life for that matter—reached critical mass.

This was also the year when the world's deadliest tsunami and earthquake hit the Indian Ocean and devastated parts of Sri Lanka, India, and Thailand. Over 230,000 people were killed, and a half million injured by the giant tidal wave that swept across Southeast Asia on December 26, 2004.

Resetting my perspective, I ended one of the worst years of my life thanking God for the gifts of love and life He had given me and my family, and praying for everyone who had tragically lost those fragile gifts in the devastating disaster.

# Chapter 22
# PRESSURE COOKER PERIL

### 𝕃ev: Heart

*The troubles of my heart are growing and growing; bring me out of my distress.*

Psalm 25:17 CJB

The Menopause Monster continued to thrive. I developed erratic monthly cycles, and my cramps often felt like labor pains, especially in my lower back. There were days I could barely stand and I was exceptionally crabby. My emotions and temperament were all over the chart. New symptoms showed up every week, and I never knew which malady to blame, perimenopause, Lyme disease, or just my crazy life in general.

Jody gave me some new herbs to help me stay calm, but life continued to be challenging.

There was also mounting pressure for Paul to get involved in politics, but with all the other stress factors in my life, I couldn't imagine taking on the gravity and drama of being a politician's wife. Paul seemed to romance the idea, but I was steadfast and emphatic with my, "No thank you."

In this country, it's not just the person seeking office who is subject to public exposure. By default, their entire family is subject to living under the same public microscope, equally vulnerable to attacks, truth distortions, and even lies. I didn't want that life for me or my family—not then—not ever.

~

My dissertation began to take on a life of its own. The entire process involved more books, more papers, and more homework. More history, more Hebrew, and more exegesis. More teaching and more learning.

I decided my dissertation would be the writing of a Bible study with a Hebraic perspective for young girls, ages thirteen to nineteen. I was motivated to help teen girls as I saw the struggle my own daughter Brittany was going through. My heart broke for my young teenager who always seemed so sad and so determined to grow up too fast.

The study would be written for adolescent teen girls to prepare them for situations and circumstances they may face during this stressful and confusing time. Transitioning from childhood to womanhood takes guidance. So many young girls take their cues and lessons from Hollywood or each other. This Bible study, entitled *Immersed in Myrrh*, would use Hebraic insight to teach girls biblical truth and include a teacher's manual component.

Kristen helped me teach the prototype class that we promoted through the Nathaniel Center. We had over twenty girls sign up with zero attrition for the twelve-week course.

~

Within a short time, both Diana and Cynthia were expecting again, followed several months later by Kristen and Shannon's pregnancy announcements. The year 2005 was rather monumental, as our new grandbabies now came in pairs. Clearly, fertility was not an issue in our family.

Bron and Darlene were so excited at the prospect of their first grandchild and we were happy at the thought of welcoming our sixth, seventh, eighth and ninth grandbabies.

With a growing family, I couldn't believe I was still being called "just a little girl," but even more so as my shape shifted.

It turned out the no sugar diet had a serendipitous side to it. I lost twenty-two pounds and went from a size ten to a size two. It felt good to clean out my closet and buy some cute clothes. I was done wearing jackets to hide my bloated tummy. I've always loved shoes, but I developed a new affinity for them, despite my bum knee that occasionally acted up. I even let my hair grow a little longer.

I only wished I felt half as good as I thought I'd started to look—unfortunately, that wasn't the case—not by a long shot.

I didn't think of Lyme disease as my biggest problem anymore, that issue seemed to be at least under control with my diet. But this menopause thing? That was another story and I didn't like being trapped in its plot. The hot flashes got worse and sleep didn't come easy. I woke up every night unable to drift off again.

And I was *tired*—so very tired.

*Why can't I sleep, Lord? Why do I feel so unsettled?*

I prayed that once I finished my dissertation, life would return to normal.

∽

It was a September morning, and I was sitting on my sofa opening mail when I heard car doors slamming and wailing at my front door. When Kristen and John Paul appeared in the living room my heart sank. I knew Kristen was seeing her obstetrician that morning. Something was obviously and terribly wrong.

"Our baby died, Momma!" Kristen fell in my arms, John Paul behind her with his head down, openly and unashamedly grieving. A familiar emptiness flooded my body as I held my daughter in my arms. I shook my head at the idea of a third grandchild being presented before the presence of the Lord.

It was only five days later Diana had a scheduled Cesarean section and our little Emily Kate Alexander was born. It pained me to watch Kristen and John Paul, so fresh from their traumatic loss, try to muster a smile though eyes swollen by tears.

∽

## October 10, 2005

My dissertation was officially due on October fifteenth, but I was aiming for five days sooner—the date of Cynthia's scheduled Cesarean delivery. Rylie Jane Heaton would be joining our family on the tenth, and Paul and I planned to fly from Houston to Dallas to be there for the delivery of our third granddaughter. I worked day and night to complete the final references and glossary information.

I finished almost everything on my monumental project the night of the ninth.

When I woke up early on the morning of October tenth, a familiar ache greeted me. There was no mistaking the intense abdominal pain, as I scoured my medicine cabinet for an 800 mg Motrin left over from the last ovarian cyst I had the previous year.

*Please, Lord, help me get through this day.*

I printed the final copy of my dissertation and gingerly held it like a priceless treasure before I left the house to make the required copies and put them in overnight mail. I sweated and grimaced as I drove to the nearby copy center. Once there, I had five copies made, collated, and bound with spiral combs. Each one had a shiny cover.

It was like giving birth to quintuplets.

On our way to the airport, I mailed copies of my dissertation via overnight delivery to the head chancellor, Dr. William Bean at CSBR, Dr. John Garr, and Dr. Brad Young. The fourth copy was for me and the fifth was just in case I needed an extra. I clutched my copy like a life preserver as we flew from Houston to Dallas to be there for Rylie's birth.

The pain in my abdomen was excruciating.

I slept in the waiting room of the hospital on a bench until they announced Rylie was here. After we saw this beautiful and perfect baby girl—a spitting image of Cynthia—Paul took me back to the hotel where I tried to get comfortable and catch up on some much needed sleep.

## October 22, 2005 - Arkansas

Fortunately, the pain in my abdomen finally ceased, but much to my dismay, it would soon find another place in my body to hijack and consume.

Paul was hosting a business retreat at Eastgate and asked me to help. I asked Evelyn to go with us, since I never knew if I was going to feel good or not these days. She helped cook for the attendees and ended up taking care of me.

The first night at Eastgate, my ear started to hurt. In a frighteningly short time, it escalated from a nagging ache to an excruciating pain. I took some pain medication, but it did absolutely nothing to stop the intense anguish.

Evelyn stayed with me and prayed over me, and after about an hour of constant off-the-chart pain, my cries turned into screams.

When he rushed into our bedroom, Paul took one look at me and helped me to my feet.

"We're taking you to the emergency room. Now."

The ER doctor quickly diagnosed my problem, or at least *one* of them. I had a severe ear infection that had caused an ulcer (perforation) on my eardrum, which was most likely caused by strep. He gave me morphine for the pain and an antibiotic, and instructed me to see an ENT specialist as soon as I got back home to Houston.

## October 25, 2005 - Houston, TX

By the time I got home, my ear wasn't the only problem plaguing me.

With my dissertation behind me, my body had given itself permission to shut down—I was in full system crash.

In addition to battling extreme hormonal fluctuations and fighting the last vestiges of Lyme disease, I had an ovarian cyst, a severe sinus infection, strep throat, an ear infection, and a chest cold.

I was very, very sick.

My D.O. put me on more antibiotics and strict bed rest.

A hearing test by an ENT doctor revealed I had lost 85% of my hearing in my left ear. He thought I would most likely get my hearing back, but this wasn't something he could determine for sure.

I spent the next two weeks nursing my ear and all of my various maladies—I felt like death warmed over.

Evelyn, our longtime nanny, was a wonderful nurse. Through a merciful God who hears prayer, and a relentless determination to get up and do something, I somehow rallied and began to feel a little better.

## Mid-November, 2005

It was the week before Thanksgiving and I was in my home office studying for my ladies Bible study and talking to Evelyn when I began to feel very strange.

I put down the pen and massaged my temples.

"What's the matter?" Evelyn asked.

"I don't know… I think maybe I'm getting a migraine."

I'd never had a migraine before, but I'd often heard them described and it was the only explanation I had for the sudden intense throbbing in my head, followed by a wave of nausea that took my breath away and made my heart jump.

Within a millisecond, I felt horrible.

"I'm not sure what it is…" I tried to stand up but felt woozy and sat back down. Evelyn stopped what she was doing and came closer.

I took a deep breath, but the intense pain in my head made it hard to breathe and it felt like my heart was skipping beats in order to keep up … like I was swallowing air instead of breathing it. Then, my left arm felt tingly, like it was going to sleep.

When I explained the sensations to Evelyn, it was almost like an out-of-body experience as I watched her crisis intervention skills immediately commence.

"We're going to the hospital now, Victoria," she said firmly as she helped me stand and practically dragged me toward the door. Her voice (and grip) said it all, and I didn't argue as she led me to the car with one hand and grabbed our purses with the other.

Things happened quickly as soon as we entered the Emergency Room where I was immediately seen by a cardiologist.

Dr. Li and her team acted fast, and when it was clear I wasn't in an immediate life-threatening crisis, she began a more thorough examination and ordered a series of cardiac tests.

At my request, Evelyn had called my D.O. and he arrived as Dr. Li conducted her assessment.

When Dr. Li discovered I had been fighting Lyme disease for over two years, she called in an infectious disease doctor who looked a lot like Luciano Pavarotti, the opera singer.

Then, this trio of exceptional professionals began to question me like a crime victim—taking copious notes of all my responses to their inquiries about my physical condition. It seemed they were jockeying for position—each determined to get to the bottom of whatever it was that caused this incident—and my systematic health decline over the past few years.

For the next five days I was poked, prodded, and strung up by my toes (figuratively, if not literally.)

Pavarotti couldn't believe I was trying to fight Lyme disease naturally.

My D.O. couldn't believe Pavarotti was unaware of how successful natural treatment had become, particularly in the realm of diet and nutrition.

And Dr. Li was frustrated with both of these men as she listened to their differing opinions on preventative medicine while they virtually ignored the symptoms that brought me here.

~

I met with Dr. Li some days later in her office to discuss the results of the tests she ordered during my recent hospitalization.

After a warm and sincere greeting, she didn't waste time getting to my results.

"You don't have a mitral-valve prolapse," she said. "You don't have any evidence of congenital heart defects, or any type of cardiovascular disease. In fact, except for throwing PVCs, nothing is majorly wrong with you."

She explained PVC's to me, "premature ventricular contractions," and said this irregular heartbeat issue is more common than most people think. She described reasons and symptoms, and said she wanted me to wear a heart monitor to determine how often this was happening.

Only then could we get to the bottom of the puzzle.

"Why do *you* think this is happening?" I asked.

She looked at me thoughtfully before responding.

"I'm sure you know that stress in life is inevitable—and in proper proportion it is good, helpful, and even necessary for survival. However, stress *overload* puts our body and brain into negative distress, and this often results in wear and tear on both our physical and emotional health."

She let her words sink in before continuing.

"Mrs. Sarvadi, have you been under any unusual stress?"

*Have I been under any unusual stress? Ha!*

I wasn't certain how to answer that question, but it was like an emotional dam burst when she asked, and I think my combination of hysterical laughter and tears scared her.

When I couldn't seem to stop, it scared me.

When I was finally able to contain myself, she got up from behind her desk and sat in the chair next to me.

"Okay, Victoria … may I call you that?" I nodded yes as she continued. "Why don't we take a quick little inventory and see what we're dealing with, okay?" She reached into her pocket for a pen and turned one of the pages over on her clipboard.

"How about if you tell me some of the stressors you've had over the last two years or so, and I'll jot them down. Okay? Can you do that?"

*Could I do that? Sure I could. But where should I start?*

"Okay," I said. "Let's see, in the last two years…

Three of my daughters have had miscarriages, and one of them is still mourning because it just happened. She wants a baby so bad, it breaks my heart…

Another daughter just gave birth to a little girl whose breach entrance into the world created the need for a Cesarean.

I guess you could say those two things were stressful."

I took a deep breath and continued.

"I also have a son who has behavioral problems . He's been kicked out of three schools and is now enrolled in a military school in Kansas City, but we're already getting bad reports from them, so that might be short-lived.

And I have a daughter who's in some kind of Goth subculture—they call her an emu or is it an emo? I can never remember which one it is. She thought we were horrible parents and moved out of our house and in with her older sister for three months. She's back home now, but she's distant. I don't know how to reach her—and I'm really afraid for her...."

I looked over at Dr. Li's list to see that she is numbering my items.

"My dad, who always had a big problem with me, was dating this really mean lady and he started smoking, developed lung cancer, had surgery, coded, went into a coma for two months and then he died. Actually, he *expired*, which is what some insensitive nurse said when she called to let me know..."

"Oh my ..." Dr. Li said quietly. "I'm so sorry..."

"You're very kind ... it was a pretty awful time. My sister threatened to never talk to me again if I enforced the DNR that Dad trusted me to enforce. Oh, and his really mean girlfriend called me a murderer."

I refused to get emotional about this, so I forced down a sip of water as I glanced again at the list the doctor was keeping.

"So, do we count those last two things separately as five and six? Or lump them both under number five?" I didn't wait for her to answer. "I say lump them together, since it's all one big mess any way."

Dr. Li writes the number six on a new line and waits for me to talk.

"Okay, let's see, what else ... well, a few years ago I helped start a Hebrew church in my back yard, today I'm the minister of education for the same congregation at the beautiful Nathaniel Center, and I'm in charge of all the teachers, education, and curriculum for all age groups. I love my position there, but I guess it can be stressful at times.

I'm also the executive director of a charitable foundation. I write the monthly grant checks, execute all the orders of the board of directors, and communicate with all our grantees. I love this work, too, but there are times...

Oh, and I'm also on three very active non-profit boards. One of which is dissolving and there are very different opinions on what to do and I'm kind of in the middle of a couple very good friends and that's challenging...

That's six, seven, and eight, right?"

I didn't wait for Dr. Li to answer as I forged on.

"We were on a family vacation in December of 2001 when I tore my ACL while skiing on the bunny slope. You've probably got that listed somewhere in my chart. Anyway, I had surgery, months of really painful rehabilitation, and my knee still bothers me. But I refuse to stop wearing high heels even if it's killing me."

I look at my strappy cream-colored four-inch Christian Louboutin heels and at Dr. Li's classic black pumps and muster a smile.

"Nice shoes," I say, as she nods appreciatively and I continue.

"Okay, number ten has to be the 4th of July picnic in Arkansas in 2003 when I got bit by the blood-thirsty tick that gave me Lyme disease, but you know all about that stressor, right?"

She nods as I continue.

"I really thought I was dying and it took a while before anyone could diagnose the problem. Did I tell you part of the natural approach to combating the disease is that I've been on a very strict diet for a year? I haven't had any sugar in twelve months, and I would really like a piece of chocolate cake. That definitely counts as stressor number eleven—no cake."

Dr. Li smiles and I notice she is now using a form of shorthand chicken-scratches as she jots down my responses.

"Speaking of cake," I say, "we had a wedding at our Kingwood event center a few days ago where we served five-hundred slices of cake for dessert. I can't remember if I ever told you that I founded and oversee a performing arts center in Kingwood? It's officially called The Nathaniel Center for Cultural and Biblical Education, but I usually just call it the Nathaniel Center...any way, it's a very popular venue for parties and receptions. The staff is great but I still take a personal stake in every event we have there. Stressful. Right?"

She raises her eyebrows as if to say, "I don't know, you tell me..." and I see her jot down the number thirteen.

"Wow, thirteen? And I'm just getting started." I nervously laughed.

"Okay, this next one is a biggie, it probably shouldn't be so far down on the list—but we're not numbering these in priority order, are we?"

Dr. Li shook her head.

"Good," I said. "I'm married to a really successful businessman who is being courted by party officials to run for political office. If he decides to do that, I told him he would do it alone, I don't want any part of that lifestyle. I doubt it will come to that, but I hate to even think about the pressure that would cause...

Oh, and my oldest daughter moved her family to Colorado, including my five grand kids. And by the way, she's pregnant again." I had to fight back the tears after thinking of my children and precious grandchildren. "Gosh," I added, and sighed. "I really miss them." I took a breath.

"Let's see, what else? Oh, I currently teach two classes, a ladies Bible study and a Yeshiva class which is equivalent to a Sunday school class. I just finished up a young girl's class, which was a prototype for my dissertation. That's actually a relief.

I suppose we should count that as a huge stressor—my dissertation. I just finished my doctorate in theology. I turned in my dissertation a few weeks ago, on the same day my daughter gave birth to our seventh grandchild. I was in a lot of pain then from an ovarian cyst, but thank God that pain is much better. Anyway, next month I'm going to walk the stage in Redlands, California and get both of my graduate degrees."

I was on a roll by then and I heard my voice take on a more high-pitched timbre.

"Did I mention my husband is CEO of a big company in Houston that went public a few years ago? Between company events, travel, and spending so much time in Dallas with my kids and grandkids, I'm living out of suitcases and in hotels most of the time.

And you know I had a really bad ear infection a week ago and now I have only 15% hearing in my left ear, right? Oh yeah, that should be added to my medical history.

Plus, I'm definitely in menopause and if harboring an alien life force inside you isn't stressful, I don't know what is!

And last but not least, we can't forget about my heart that has been throwing PDQ's or PFC's or whatever the heck they are. I know you said it's a somewhat common problem, but I have to say, it still stresses me out a little."

By this time, I'm almost hysterical. I've nearly hyperventilated and fought back tears—certain if I started to cry I would never be able to stop. I leaned back in my chair and tried to look relaxed, but my hands gripped the armrests for dear life as I blurted out my final declaration.

"So, I think that about does it for my inventory, at least for now. How many is that?" I glanced over at her list. "Only twenty? I'm sure I'm forgetting something, do you want me to think about this a little longer and go on?"

She slowly put down her clipboard, took off her glasses, and leaned toward me as she took a deep breath and looked me straight in the eyes. "Do you want to live, Victoria?"

"What do you mean?" I answered in an insouciant tone of voice that surprised even me and was accompanied by a dismissive shoulder shrug and a roll of my eyes at the absurdity of the question.

"I mean, Victoria, do you really want to live? Are you serious about staying alive?" Her stern voice brought immediate contrition to my heart as I realized she wasn't joking.

"Well, of course I do." I blinked through tears I could no longer control.

She holds up the list and waves it in front of me. "Then, you must let go of all of this. *Now*. Any *one* of these things are enough to cause added stress in life, Victoria, and you've got twenty stress issues on your list. *Twenty*. Think of these stress points as individual fractures—one on top of the other. Then, picture them all merging together...Victoria, these individual fractures are going to break you!"

Dr. Li reached out and placed her hand on my arm. "You need to take a sabbatical and get away for a few months. Let go of the responsibilities that can be handled by others. And I suspect many of them *can* be handled by others."

I knew she was right. There were things I could let go of.

I did my best to appear stoic and resilient, but Dr. Li saw through all of my posturing as she handed me the tissue box from her desk. "Victoria, stop trying to do it all. Go spend time with your grandchildren and take care of yourself—those are the responsibilities no one else *but* you can handle." Then, she asked me something I should have been asking myself all along.

"Victoria, what are the most important things in your life?"

Once I stopped to think about it, it didn't take long to respond. "My relationship with God and my family."

"Well then," she said matter-of-factly, "you can't very well be a testimony for God if you die, can you? And you won't get to spend any time with your family if you are in a grave. It's time to ask yourself why you have put so many other things in front of what is really important to you."

*Wow. When you put it like that...*

We talked about my motivations, intentions, and the serious nature of the roadblock I'd hit when she quietly asked, "Is there somewhere you can go to get away for a while? Somewhere you can go for a retreat?"

*It just so happens...*

## Thanksgiving Day in Arkansas

That Thanksgiving we all escaped as a family and went to Arkansas—to Eastgate for a nice relaxing vacation—my mini-retreat. The heart monitor I wore that week was a powerful reminder of how serious the situation had become.

I had some serious choices to make.

## December 2, 2005

A week later, I crossed the stage with sixty-two other graduates in California, as I received my Masters and Doctorate in Theology.

Paul loves to quote lines from movies. The day I graduated, almost every time a comment was made or a question posed, he would lean over to quietly ask me the same question. "So, doctor, do you concur?"

These few words are from a scene we both knew well. In the movie *Catch Me If You Can*, Leonardo DiCaprio plays a man who pretends to be a doctor. When confronted with an actual medical emergency, he is clearly out of his league and overwhelmed as an intern rattles off a quick diagnosis. Thinking fast, Leonardo the "fake" turns to the "real" emergency-room resident doctor, and asks of his colleague, "So, doctor, do you concur?"

Paul's witticism wasn't lost on me, and he made me smile.

It had taken a long time to get here, but *that day*, I became that "real" doctor. I was now "officially" Dr. Victoria Sarvadi.

It felt good.

Really good.

I smiled at Paul and said the line he wanted to hear.

"Yes, I concur."

When I received my degree, I hugged and thanked all of my professors. They'd changed my life, brought me to a new place in God, and gave me mountain-size gems of knowledge and understanding.

With school behind me, I feel certain things would settle down and balance out.

Little did I know the tapestry of my life hadn't finished unraveling.

# Chapter 23
# INTERNAL COMBUSTION

### 𝔈sh: Fire

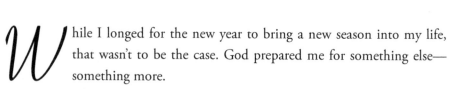

*Now if any man build upon this foundation with gold, silver, precious stones, wood, hay, stubble; Every man's work shall be manifest; for the day shall declare it because it shall be revealed by fire, and the fire shall try every man's work of what it is.*
1 Corinthians 3:12-13 KJV

While I longed for the new year to bring a new season into my life, that wasn't to be the case. God prepared me for something else—something more.

Without fire, we cannot be purified.

Just as fire and extreme heat are the methods used to bring out dross in gold, God will purposely take His children to a place in the wilderness to bring out their impurities. He will continue to stoke the fire we need to become the people He wants us to be.

Apparently, I needed a lot more heat.

God guides us by His Spirit, not by the flesh. The things of the Spirit are higher than our mortal flesh. He does not want us to operate in the flesh alone (or even in a combination of flesh and spirit), and that's exactly what I had been doing.

As Dr. Li's words, "Victoria, do you want to live?" forced me to look at my life, I wondered how I got to this place. There were people all around me, yet I felt lonely. I had so much to do, yet I wasn't doing the things I wanted to do—or the things I felt God had called me to do. How could I be doing great works for God when I didn't feel as close to Him as I once did? How could I love His Word, but be too tired to study it?

I began to ask myself serious questions. *What is the actual 'quality' of my work—my life—at this point? Am I walking in God's plan and purpose? Fulfilling the calling He placed on my life? Why am I not happy?*

Then it finally dawned on me – it has never been about what makes me happy. I will never be totally at peace or happy until the One who lives inside of me is happy. And He won't be happy until I stop trying to do things in my own power.

I knew I had some of my own hay and straw mixed in with the Spirit's gold and silver.

"Fire" in Hebrew is the word *esh*. *Esh* is spelled with two Hebrew letters -*aleph* and *shen*. The letter *aleph* means father or ruler and the deepest meaning of the letter *shen* means to return to God. So the Holy Fire of God becomes our teacher and disciplinarian—the Headmaster who causes us to turn away from error and return to Him in truth. The process is often painful. Although it can feel brutal at times, this is actually an act of mercy on God's part.

This holy fire had smoldered inside me for twenty years before it combusted.

I didn't completely understand what I was supposed to learn through all of this—the death of my father, Lyme disease, and now perimenopause—but I did know the answers were in the Lord.

*God, I want out of this fire ... please.*

I needed new direction and clear instructions. I needed to know God's will for me.

I wanted to pray, but I was exhausted. I needed true *kavanah* prayer—the kind of pure and focused prayer we talked about in Chapter Eighteen, *A*

*Gathering Place.* I called a few of my friends and asked them to pray for me because I just couldn't do it anymore.

God often puts a mirror in front of us during rough times and asks, "Why did you do this?" God *will* confront and redirect us. But we need to welcome the Spirit to lead us *to* a place in the desert, without a million distractions, and actually listen to Him. We need to retreat to a private place of confrontation and growth. Only then can we leave behind the unpleasant choices and consequences of our flesh.

I needed to make some serious changes.

The Lord showed me I often did "things" for God as an obligation—that I was checking things off as a mere "to do" list. He showed me I had begun to hold myself in too high a regard as being the "one" many came to for advice and spiritual direction. Perhaps the most valuable lesson, however, was when He showed me how many "things" had become idols to me.

I had put *things* and *people* before God.

And it pained me to know I had broken His heart.

There is an established order for all things, and in my desire to do it all, I fell short.

I wasn't living the blessings of the appointed times in my life as much as I was hurtling through them at warp speed—almost like years before when my earthly life ceased on a hospital bed in the ICU, and I was given a glimpse of God's miraculous gifts.

This time God led me to a season of complete surrender where death once again had to occur. However, this time it was a far more difficult death I needed to experience—death to my own will.

In many ways, I was still just a little girl fighting against an earthly father whose words and actions often left me aching and vulnerable. The desire to succeed at all cost and prove him wrong bubbled beneath the surface of my choices for decades.

God is not an angry "Big Daddy" in the sky who wants to strike us down and put us in our place. He wants to lead us gently and lovingly so we long to run to His side and willingly take our place in His Kingdom. His vision and purpose for us are already in place—I had to learn to stop fighting it—to stop going my own way.

God isn't pleased when we get caught up in "doing" instead of "being," when we get so full of ourselves and our abilities that we forget who is at the core. He tells us, "where your treasure is, so too is your heart."[91] My heart's true desire was to introduce others to the Jewish Messiah and help them see Him in His authentic and organic context.

Somehow, I doubted the crazy-busy life I led was anything my angel wanted me to have. The day I experienced the heart-wrenching pain of losing a child, I had also been given a tremendous gift. An ability to see the treasures of my heart as God distributed them on the timeline grid of my life. I painfully realized that once perfect vision had faded over time, as I added things on the timeline of my own free will.

While my intentions may have been honorable, the things I added were not always in keeping with God's ultimate plan—with *Yeshua's* calling on my life.

I suddenly knew with complete understanding that all the spiritual revelation poured into my life and the prophetic wisdom God wanted me to share (as per *Peretz*) would all be for naught if I continued on this course.

As I realized this, my prayer soon became "God, help me die to my own stubborn flesh."

I wondered how long I was going to have to stay in the wilderness when I remembered several examples of wilderness experiences recorded in the Bible. I was among great company. Besides *Yeshua* himself, John the Baptist cried out in the wilderness and carried the burden of reconciliation.[92] After his revelation on the way to Damascus, the Apostle Paul was blinded and spent three years in the wilderness, a place where he often saw visions and, no doubt, grew accustomed to conversing with angels and the Spirit of the Lord.[93] He emerged with power and with a newfound understanding of great mysteries in life.

The fire of God changed these men, and now it was my turn.

God had been giving me prophetic visions for many years, but now they were flooding my spirit. God gave the Apostle Paul marching orders, and He was now giving me mine.

When *Yeshua* was baptized at Bethany, a voice from the Father in Heaven proclaimed that *Yeshua* was his Son.[94] This reference is indicative of the "Prince" of Daniel 9:25.[95] The Holy Spirit lighted upon Him as a dove, and thus began the powerful and spiritually dynamic ministry of *Yeshua*, complete with miracles. In the next chapter of Luke, *Yeshua*, now filled with the Holy Spirit, is led by the Holy Spirit into the wilderness to be tempted by the adversary.[96]

It had taken me a long time, but I had begun to see the correlation of testing in my own life. There was definitely a discernible pattern. The bigger and stronger our outreach grew, the more of a threat I became to the enemy.

Now that my ministry was being confirmed by the power of the Holy Spirit, I was being led into my own wilderness to be tested.

I knew the enemy used physical challenges to put roadblocks in the way of anyone trying to make a difference for God. Yet for some reason, I overlooked that truth in my case. I was being hit with one medical problem after another, but why was I letting this obvious tactic of the enemy overwhelm me?

I was also floored by the realization that the adversary will often uses Scripture to convince man of their position in God. I knew I had to be able to discern the voice of the evil one when he uses God's Word and His covenant promises to cause me to succumb to counterfeit power, which leads to pride and error.

The realization hit me that my entire life is "God's thing," and there is no use arguing with God and His plan.

And so…

I became far more selective in accepting invitations to attend local community and social events.

I phased out my ladies Bible study and Yeshiva classes.

I handed over the executive position of the Nathaniel Foundation to my capable son-in-law, John Paul.

I turned in my resignation to Shalom's board of directors, although Paul would continue to serve on our behalf.

And, I divided the Nathaniel Center workload between my newly promoted general manager, Jackie, and my newly appointed chairman of operations, John Paul. In fact, they both willingly stepped up to the plate and welcomed the challenge.

Philip was a new seminary graduate and eager to jump into the ministry. After a thorough discussion, Bron and I agreed we should offer him my position as Minister of Education of Shalom. Philip was absolutely elated. In fact, the offer was an answer to prayer for him. How like God to have someone waiting in the wings—to call someone into a new place of service, just as He calls someone else out.

As Dr. Li had predicted, the world still turned without my help to spin it—and turn it did.

## My Crazy Shades of Gray

Although I cut back on my workload, there were still some crazy things going on with my body—things I should have been prepared for but for some reason, couldn't (or wouldn't) comprehend. I had all the classic symptoms of menopause: headaches, irritability, forgetfulness, hot flashes, insomnia, and lack of libido. But I told myself I was too young for menopause—I was *just a little girl.*

Perhaps all the additional emotional stress of the last few years exacerbated the natural change-of-life experience I was going through. I didn't know how much more my body could take, but I trusted God would get me through it. As I hoped and prayed for these horrible symptoms from hell to stop, I developed a new set of mind-boggling symptoms almost overnight.

Gone was the coy, hard to get, and physically reserved wife. In her place was an adventurous woman. Suddenly, I wanted to try all the sensuous things I never had the nerve to try. I was completely fearless and unabashedly unreserved. I even bought fancy lingerie. Feeling this amorous was totally unlike me, and this strange anomaly didn't line up with the typical menopausal profile I had read about. I didn't know what to think about how I was feeling—and acting.

Paul, on the other hand, thought he'd hit the jackpot.

This period of sexual euphoria lasted a total of one week, and I came to learn it wasn't a strange anomaly at all—but a very real symptom of menopause called "ecstasy phenomenon."

My D.O. explained it succinctly: "When women ovulate they become more amorous in order to conceive—a natural physiological process. But because you are on the brink of full-blown menopause, you most likely had a huge release of estrogen, which caused your ovaries to "dump" all of your eggs at once. Your body was suddenly flooded with the FSH hormone, and that is why it was an epic week."

I had no idea this was a hormonal change that sometimes happens to women. I was relieved with this information as I was beginning to feel like I had multiple personalities and needed deliverance—or something.

However, after the surreal and unusual week was over, I suddenly took on yet another personality. This one wasn't nearly as fun, and unfortunately, she stayed around longer than a week.

I became easily angry with violent mood swings, frequently frustrated, and totally uninterested in my new lingerie. In fact, I found intimacy very painful. It was a complete flip. I became depressed and often felt paralyzed. Poor Paul didn't know what to say—or do. Suddenly, it was "talk to the hand" all over again, just as it had been years ago when I struggled with facing the loss of our baby.

My physical body didn't feel like my own. My emotional and mental capacities were diminished and entirely undependable.

I wondered why I wasn't more prepared for the changes my body was experiencing? Why didn't someone warn me this might happen?

I gave birth to five children and had been to countless doctor appointments over the years. I had yearly check-ups, all the typical "well-woman" tests. Yet at no time did anyone tell me about the possibility of overt changes that could make me feel like a stranger even to myself. No one ever cautioned me to beware of the Menopause Monster who lurked within.

## A Weekly Commute to Healing

Paul's love language is (giving) gifts. He tried to help me get through these drastic physical and emotional changes, but gifts alone couldn't snap me out of this deep hole. I needed more than flowers, jewelry, or even a new car. I needed a miracle.

Dr. Li thought I should start an exercise regimen and find some kind of therapeutic hobby. I could embrace the exercise prescription, but I really didn't want a "hobby"—I wanted some semblance of normalcy and familiarity in my life—I wanted the kind of feelings I had when I was nurturing and loving children.

It was around this time we made our way to Colorado to welcome our eighth grandbaby. Shannon delivered the biggest baby of the clan on May 9, 2006. Ten pound, Julia Clare came into the world with exquisite maturity and passion. I'll never forget how I felt when I experienced for the first time in my life, a newborn look me straight in the eye and smile.

When we returned to Texas, we began to visit our new grand babies in Dallas almost every weekend. It was there I found abundant joy. The babies just made me so happy.

We didn't want to burden our girls with trying to accommodate us every weekend, so we usually stayed in a hotel. Spending hours in transit every week and living out of a suitcase wasn't all that conducive to stress-free living. After eight weekends of doing this, we had spent literally thousands of dollars at the same hotel. That's when we both thought it would be more prudent to buy a home centrally located to our daughters where we could stay (crash) whenever we drove or flew from Houston to Dallas.

Our basically unfurnished home-away-from-home was on a beautiful wooded creek in a suburb of Dallas. At first, we weren't too interested in decorating or furnishing the house, so we slept on air mattresses, bought a few plastic lawn chairs and ate cereal out of Chinette bowls before heading out to spend the daytime hours with the kids.

Every Friday we arrived in the Big D (Dallas) to see our grand babies and every Sunday evening we headed back home to H-Town (Houston).

Despite the travel, it was just the therapy I needed.

As time progressed, we brought more and more of our personal belongings to our Dallas home. A few pots and pans, a set of dishes, more clothes.

Shoes.

Yeah, it was starting to feel like home.

During this time, God was getting a lot of spiritual sludge off of me. I began to see when one receives the Holy Spirit, he opens himself up to the spirit world. The deceiver will begin to sound like God as he uses Scripture to justify blessing or prosperity in one's life. He will cause one to validate his own "holiness or consecration" instead of giving God the glory for the manifestation of miracles and power. If I'm not truly consecrated, then I am double minded. I must be consecrated and not rationalizing. Praying with true *kavenah* is an absolute necessity. My life must reflect the character of God. Not anger, deception, strife, or dysfunction; confusion, frustration or hatefulness. None of those are the fruit of the Spirit.

I desired a new character to emerge—one of complete honesty, purity, and encouragement, one of exhortation, peace, joy and humility.

Ironically, I found that reflecting the character of Christ became more possible with fewer ministry responsibilities in Houston, and with increasing quality time with my children and grandchildren in Dallas. Go figure.

One week Paul had to go to Boston on Monday and would be gone all week.

"I really don't want to stay by myself in Houston for the whole week," I said.

So, after that particular weekend with our family, I stayed in Dallas while Paul was out of town and enjoyed the babies all week. I felt completely happy when I was with them. They were such a joy. And they loved me. I could feel it. I had an epiphany when I realized this is what I needed. I could actually feel myself walking out of the wilderness.

These babies were healing me.

From that day, I opted to stay in our "crash home" as much as possible. It wasn't long before John Paul and Kristen moved to the DFW area and this home would be situated conveniently between three of my daughters and their growing families.

~

With this healing came new revelation. I now understood the time had come to stop trying to "do everything," and do only what He called me to do. It was time to intentionally focus. I also understood that everything happens for a reason, and now that my children were grown and my "formal" education was complete, God knew I was ready to handle the truth He was imparting. He knew I was almost ready to completely embrace the mother lode mission for my life. He had given me knowledge, truth, wisdom, a supportive and successful husband, financial resources, a healthy growing family, and access to spiritual teachers and Hebrew scholars who were ready, willing and able to pour into my life. And He was giving me prophetic instructions.

His word was so clear in my spirit; I could almost hear God speak to me in an audible voice. "Victoria, you know the Greco-Roman God is *not* who I am. And I've always wanted you to tell others who I really am."

I suddenly felt like I could breathe deep again. My roots began to settle into the fertile soil of North Texas. God had a powerful plan for me here—I could feel it. Like Abraham it was time to get up and leave my old life behind.

# Chapter 24
## SEASON OF SURRENDER

### ᴛefillah: Prayer

*Trust in the Lord with all thine heart; and lean not unto thine own understanding. In all thy ways acknowledge him, and he shall direct thy paths.*

Proverbs 3:5-6 KJV

By mid-summer 2006, we officially had two primary residences. Paul split his time between Houston and Dallas, and I went to Houston once or twice a month for a few days, sometimes for a week. But as soon as possible, I made my way back to Dallas. At first, it was a logistical nightmare, but we made it work for us.

In many ways, it works far better than we ever imagined.

Brittany didn't want to move to Dallas, but it wasn't her choice to make. She was only sixteen and already starting her senior year in high school, and because of Paul's schedule, she would have been unsupervised a great deal of the time without me in Houston. I knew she wanted to stay there, but I could not go back to the pressure cooker of that lifestyle, and she needed to be with me.

Life was not easy for Brittany in Dallas.

Not only did she have to acclimate to new surroundings and her own natural teenage hormonal changes, but to an ever-changing mother who struggled with her own physiological changes as well.

I continued to often feel dizzy, forgetful, and I seemed to have a constant headache. Hot flashes remained frequent companions. At times, it felt like I was on fire. Although the intense pain in my ear had subsided, my hearing had not completely returned—it was as though I had water or cotton in my ear. I couldn't sleep, and I frequently became frustrated for really no reason. I had no control over these crazy symptoms.

One day, I found myself driving somewhere with no idea where I was going. I knew I had some place I needed to be, so I drove around hoping it would eventually come to me. I never remembered so I went home and cried. I truly thought I could be losing my mind. About a week later, I went to Home Depot. I walked up and down the aisles trying to remember why I was there. I returned home empty handed. A few days later, I remembered the reason for my trip: to get a copy of my house key.

I seriously worried that I'd had a stroke … or maybe a brain tumor?

As the year 2006 came to an end, I tried my best to deal with my health issues and focus on my family as we prepared to welcome two more babies into our growing brood.

When she delivered her first child, Diana had a Cesarean section, but this time she wanted to try to deliver her second baby through natural measures. Her doctor was supportive, although prepared for any last-minute changes. After being in labor most of the day, Diana was having a difficult time. When the baby showed sudden and definite signs of distress, alternative measures were initiated. On December 16, 2006, after an emergency forceps delivery, our little eight-pound Sarah Grace was born blue; she was quickly revived and sent to the neonatal intensive care unit (NICU). She was so beautiful and twice as big as the other babies there. This little beauty was strong and determined and by fervent prayer and God's loving mercy and unrelenting grace, our little Gracie pulled through.

However, I worried about Diana. Doctors were concerned about a possible hemorrhage. I vividly remembered the same had happened when I delivered Kristen twenty-two years before, when I'd almost bled to death. As a mother, you never stop worrying about your children, no matter how old they are. Thankfully, Diana recovered.

Only ten days after Diana's special delivery, Kristen almost effortlessly (relatively speaking, of course) delivered our little seven-pound Joshua Preston the day after Christmas. He was our holiday blessing, a wonderful and perfect gift.

## Homeopathic Hope and Healing

Even though everything went smooth with Joshua's birth, by the time he arrived, I still struggled to find stability.

Something had to change. Menopause was driving me crazy.

I searched for a naturopath and found Dr. David Brown, a highly trained professional in several areas of alternative medicine. In 2004, he founded the North Dallas Alternative Medicine Center,[97] and had been in full-time clinical practice since 2001.

After his own personal experience with symptoms that baffled medical doctors, he became frustrated with the lack of results and turned to natural medicine. From that point on, natural medicine became his passion, and he went on to complete a three-year internship in Naturopathic Medicine. With a B.S. in medical biology from Oklahoma Christian University as well as a Doctor of Chiropractic degree from Parker College of Chiropractic, he also had extensive training in classical homeopathy, certification in Chiropractic Acupuncture, and was a Diplomate in Applied Kinesiology.

He has had quite a respected reputation.

Some years later he and my daughter, Kristen would launch Marpe,[98] a company that provides immune building health products.

But back then, I had to wait about two months to see him for my initial (and extensive) visit. After I explained my symptoms, he gave me a homeopathic remedy called Sepia. I couldn't believe it, but my ear miraculously popped open by about fifty percent, right there in his office, after an entire year of being closed. I began to see Dr. Brown every four weeks.

Over time, my ear wasn't the only thing miraculously healed.

Within six months, I had no symptoms or indication of ever having Lyme disease and all Lyme tests proved negative for the first time. And after a series of hormone tests, it was determined my testosterone was on the high range of normal, my estrogen was on the low range of normal, but my progesterone was extremely low. This combination is considered "estrogen dominant" in relation to progesterone. This hormonal imbalance explained my emotional, mental, and even physical problems. I learned that estrogen dominance can cause many health issues, one of them being cancer. I thought of my mom and remembered all of her similar symptoms. Hmm…. I wonder…

Dr. Brown found the right homeopathic bio-identical hormone therapy for me, and I started taking natural hormones. This course of action proved to be life changing insofar as regulating my menopause symptoms.

A few other symptoms, however, weren't so quick to go away.

Although Dr. Brown commended me for the changes I told him I had made since my graduation, he emphasized I still needed to work pro-actively to find balance in my life. He also agreed with Dr. Li that I should start working out. A regular exercise program was critical to my healing. I eventually found a trainer who became my first close friend in Dallas. I started training with Debbie four days a week, and I loved how I felt afterward. I started getting therapeutic massages every week and regular manicures and pedicures. I started to breathe and smile with more ease. As I began to return to the land of the living, I spent more time reading God's Word.

For the first time in a long time, I was hopeful.

I had been experiencing a difference in my physical body, and it paralleled a change in my spiritual life. It became evident to me that God desired to reveal to me another level in Him.

God's Word says, "But then I will win her back once again. I will lead her into the desert and speak tenderly to her there" (Hosea 2:14 NLT).

The word for "to speak" in Hebrew is *m'deber*. A Hebrew word for desert is *midbar*. Both words have the same root (or *shoresh*). So it is in our lonely and desperate times that God speaks loudest. It took reaching the end of my rope to completely and utterly depend on God.

Although I remained ministry weary, I have to admit I really wanted to hear God's new directives for me. My hopes were up. Help and healing were very, very close. I still had no idea what God wanted me to do next. But one thing I knew for certain—I was not going back to where I had been. I was changing—God impressed that I was to leave where I once was to go to a new place in Him - but the first place He led me was into the wilderness. He was there with me and He was talking but I wondered if this was going to be an extended visit to the desert.

## Another Retreat a Different Life

It was time for our family vacation and this year we chose Hawaii. We enjoyed the spectacular weather and the lovely accommodations and activities. We went sailing and snorkeling. A few times the men played golf while the women and children enjoyed swimming. It was almost non-stop activity, and for the first time in a very long time, I felt good, I felt healthy.

After we returned from our activity one day, five month old baby Josh ran a fever. He seemed lifeless and limp, and a strange bruise-like rash developed all over the lower parts of his body. We called a local doctor who suggested we get him to his regular doctor as soon as possible. As we flew back to the mainland on the corporate jet, little Josh cried for the entire nine-hour trip. In fact, we all cried. It was agonizing. I can't imagine how we would have faired on a packed commercial flight. The emergency room doctor diagnosed him with pneumonia and said an antibiotic should help him.

Five days later, he wasn't any better.

Josh was admitted into the hospital and soon diagnosed with Kawasaki disease.

Kawasaki is an autoimmune disease in which the medium-sized blood vessels throughout the body become inflamed. He was treated with intravenous immunoglobulin and it was determined he had some damage to his heart. Doctors didn't think he would ever be able to be active or participate in sports. They said running would be difficult for him and would jeopardize the health of his heart.

This was devastating news.

Our family and many friends went to prayer for our tiny baby boy.

God is so good—an ultrasound six months later concluded his heart was completely healed. The doctor couldn't believe it. He ordered a second ultrasound to confirm the first.

God had healed Josh's momma's heart when she was a baby, and now He had extended the heart-healing blessing to her baby as well. What a gracious God!

And, He was doing the same for me ... He was healing my heart.

God wanted me to understand the critical need to "go rest" (ie: *Shabbat*).[99] He wanted me to understand my blessings, and calling—in relation to the ministry outreach He gave me. These concepts work together. When one is out of balance, they all are.

By the end of the year, I began to laugh more and relax a little more. There was definitely a light at the end of what had been a very long, very dark tunnel.

Fortunately, Paul was able to adapt to this strange phenomenon called menopause. I deeply appreciated his amazing sense of humor and great wisdom. Not only as we traveled back and forth between Houston and Dallas, but also between the obstacles the enemy placed in our path over the years. To have a husband willing to stand beside me during this season of intense transition enabled me to once again appreciate the gifts of the grid *Peretz* had revealed to me so long ago.

All of the amazing gifts I had seen passing before my eyes as my body laid lifeless on the ICU bed so many decades before were now sitting at my feet, and coming alive in my spirit. Many had already been opened—some were awaiting a future time when the Holy Spirit would give me permission—and encouragement—to tear off the wrappings and bows like a wide-eyed child ready to accept their contents with wonder and faith.

# Chapter 25
## GIFTS OF THE GRID

### M'shiah: Messiah

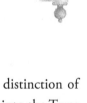

*"Before I formed you in the womb, I knew you; before you were born, I separated you for myself. I have appointed you to be a prophet to the nations."*

Jeremiah 1:5 CJB

As 2007 came to an end, Paul received the honored distinction of being named the youngest man to ever be inducted into the Texas Business Hall of Fame.

My husband has been walking in his gifting and calling for years, and God uses him in mighty ways to further His kingdom work. It's been such a blessing to support him throughout our amazing journey together.

He has come so far—we have *both* come so far.

As I settle in to a quieter and calmer existence, I feel almost euphoric that I've come through the wilderness with the wisdom and knowledge that I already possess the ability to use the gifts God gave me. Like Dorothy and her red shoes,

I possessed the ability all the time but had to walk through the wilderness before realizing it.

Confident that the Lord is preparing me to go to the next level in Him, I am content to let things unfold naturally.

After months of traveling back and forth from Houston to North Texas, in the early part of 2008, Paul and I thought we might want to build our primary home in Dallas. That's when I met Sharon, a wonderful liaison among the world of home design and boutique builders in the Dallas area.

Sharon became a good friend as we spent countless hours looking at ideas for roofs, cast stone, lighting, and appliances. However, after our home in Houston had been on the market for a while and we hadn't received any viable offers, we had to rethink our strategy. We decided instead to upgrade the place we stayed at in Dallas when we visited our children and grandchildren—the comfy place we called our "crash home."

With this new shift in focus, Sharon continued to give me advice and direction on ideas, improvements and even on beautiful furniture. This woman had connections. She knew the best designers and the most renowned vendors in Dallas.

In retrospect, it's impossible for me to deny that Sharon was a messenger—a conduit if you will—sent by God to direct me on the path He always planned for me to walk.

As we traveled all over the city, our conversations would often go to the Bible and the Jewish theology of *Yeshua*. There's no mistaking that I am passionate about the topic—and Sharon was genuinely interested—not just being polite. Clearly, she was hungry to know more.

Later, I discovered that Sharon would often drive around aimlessly, taking her time getting to our destinations in order to prolong our conversations. In fact, she began to strongly encourage me to have a home Bible study.

"Please, Victoria. You have to share this with others…"

"I hardly know anyone in the area." I said.

"I will get people there if you agree to teach." she replied.

I told her I would pray about it.

Part of me feared that if I cracked open the door, I'd once again bite off more than I could chew and get in over my head in ministry responsibilities.

Although I spent many years as a respected businesswoman and ministry leader in my work with the Nathaniel Foundation and the Nathaniel Center, I can't deny I frequently felt the sting of outside judgment because I challenged the traditional roles of a woman in ministry leadership. I can't deny the frustration of not being taken seriously—of being thought of as "just a little girl." And I can't deny being affected by that little-girl voice deep inside my brain that often echoed my father's words, "Just who do you think you are, Victoria?"

All this "negative noise" acted like constant low-level static in my spirit for years—noise that interrupted my ability to operate at full frequency. Noise that kept me from clearly hearing the voice of God.

I had finally reached a glorious peace in my walk when I learned to block out the noise. I wasn't certain I was ready to jump back in to the fray.

However, Sharon's innocent request to start a home Bible study reignited my passion. Her searing questions, undeniable hunger and open heart drove me to keep an open mind and explore the possibilities.

I thought back to April of 1973 when I was truly saved, and how far I traveled to get to this place.

In the 1970s, the Jesus Movement spread among the hippies, the youth, and many Jewish people through music and the arts. I was not left out of the outpouring of this movement. The believers in this movement, which included me, found the gem of heart-felt worship and joy in the Lord. I remembered wearing my Jesus Freak button to school with great pride as I sang with great passion *I Don't' Know How to Love Him*, the song Helen Reddy recorded from the rock musical, *Jesus Christ Superstar*.

This is the movement that was sweeping our nation when I met Jesus—when I was born again as a new creation and meshed my doctrine of Lutheranism with my own personal revelation and conviction of being saved by grace through faith.

Decades later, a new movement was in the air and I couldn't deny the feeling that I was destined to be a part of it, as I took my concerns to the Lord in prayer, and searched the Word for direction.

Searching His Word, analyzing the state of the church, and considering my own journey, I began to see what I already knew in a different light.

Soon, I found it impossible to deny the personal revelation and conviction calling me to return to the biblical model of church restoration.

## In the Beginning

One day, Sharon asked me how non-Jews first learned about the Torah.[100]

It was a simple question that opened Pandora's Box, and I did my best to explain.

"When 'The Way of *Yeshua*' began in the first century, Gentiles, who were also called pagans at the time, were invited into the faith by the original followers. These followers were the Jewish people that believed *Yeshua* was their promised Messiah, spoken about in their Holy Scriptures by their prophets.

The Gentiles were introduced to the God of the Jews (aka: the God of Israel,) grafted into their covenant, and began to learn the ways of their Bible—the Torah. They soon discarded their own pagan ways, as they received salvation through trust in the Jewish Messiah.

Unfortunately, as the new believers from the nations grew in this new faith, they ventured out in boastfulness and turned the pure faith into something almost unrecognizable.

Over the centuries, they began to infuse pagan traditions and idolatry into "their" newfound religion. They incorporated Greco-Roman and eventually Western mindsets and customs into the ancient faith of *Yeshua*. They ignored the original customs, tradition, language, and idioms that *Yeshua* was accustomed to. Eventually, three centuries later, the original first century faith and instructions of "*Yeshua's* Way" became a corrupt, dark, controlling institution completely void of its original spiritual emphasis and power. This period was called the Dark Ages.

It was during this time the process of reformation began."

Sharon was enthralled. When I stopped speaking, she began to ask questions and the discussion that followed was enlightening and empowering—for both of us.

I personally knew that reformation was not the total answer. Man reforms but God restores. As I look at the multitude of "Christian denominations" I often see a web of back-biting, finger pointing and unrelenting hostility as each one demands "they are right" and everyone else is wrong.

Now I ask you, how can that stubborn mindset possibly be right?

The only way Christians (and Jews – for that matter) can totally agree is to embark on restoration. We don't need to *reform* all the countless permutations Christianity has experienced over the centuries—we need to *restore* the faith *of* Christ—the faith *Yeshua* passionately taught to Jews and subsequently the Gentiles when He walked among us. We need to go back to the beginning—the genesis. The genesis of God walking with man, talking with man and revealing mysteries by His Spirit.

The Messiah was slain from the foundation of the World.[101] He has been in the plan of redemption from the beginning. He was the Ark that saved Noah and his family. He was the Burning Bush that spoke to Moses. He was the Rock that followed the Israelites in the dessert providing them with Living Water.[102] He was the Serpent on the staff that healed them of their diseases. He was a Cloud by day, Fire by night, and the Smoke in the Temple. He was the Angel of the Lord that came to Abraham and Sarah, the Angel that wrestled with Jacob, *the perfect Passover Lamb* that was slain. The Holy One has shown up countless times as one agent of God or another.

And, rest assured, He is coming again.

This time, however, in the most terrifying form of all: The Righteous Judge, Conqueror, and King yet at the same time the long awaited *M'shiah* and Bridegroom.

As children of God, we all have our place. Our traditional "ideas" (the things we may have learned as children) may not be so accurate—we must learn to listen to the Voice of the Spirit and study what God's Word of Truth (Torah) really says.

The more I visited with Sharon, the more she wanted to know.

And the more I studied and prayed, the more convicted I became.

I sense I'm being called to share the Jewish Jesus—*Yeshua*—in a new way—a fresh way, to teach others about our Jewish roots unlike that of traditional teachers and scholars. Not in the package of an institutional church with man made traditions and government that differs from the time of Christ. All this may sound new to the Church but really it's an ancient path. I believe my unique perspective and entire life journey has prepared me for this time!

As *Peretz's* words take on new meaning and new revelation, I feel my own spiritual amnesia lifted. I reel from prophetic flowing and impartation, and the revelation the Lord is flooding into my spirit is mind-boggling.

The healing, truth, and wisdom I am now experiencing is overwhelming.

I feel as though I've been reborn- again. What was once skewed in my life is now clarified. His Word explodes and I begin to see everything with more focus than I ever have. We are all in different places of revelation at any given time. We can never assume we know everything about God. I know I don't.

We can be in humble service in the Body of Christ yet still have big ambitions and big dreams—especially if God lays those callings on our heart. To ignore and downplay a calling is just as wrong as it is to be prideful and haughty about it.

At last, I feel I have reached a healthy balance between the two.

The prophet Daniel had a glimpse of the End Times before *Yeshua* was to come back with His Kingdom. The prophet was perplexed by what he saw and heard and so he asked the angel to explain it further. The angel however, informed Daniel that it wasn't for him to know, but in that time and to that generation who was seeking Him, God would reveal the meaning.[103] That time is now. God is opening the eyes of those who are purified to His Truths. He wants to reveal the secret things that have been sealed and known as mysteries in centuries past.

The more questions Sharon asked, the more I found myself on my knees crying out to the Lord…

*God, are You leading me out of the Greco-Roman model of the institutionalized church and into a home fellowship?*

## Let's Start at the Very Beginning

One of my favorite movies as a young girl was the *Sound of Music*. When Maria sings *Do-Re-Mi* she is teaching the Von Trapp children the very essence of creating music. They learn the critical rudimentary components that are the foundation of every song they will ever hear or sing.

So it is when we talk about learning and applying *Torah* truth.

We must start at the very beginning—a very good place to start.

It's not about getting bigger to get better. The growing phenomena of mega church worship cannot possibly connect members together on an intimate level to develop the kind of personal relationship God wants us to have with our brothers and sisters of the faith, church leaders and with His Son.

I feel completely convicted that it's time to embrace the biblical model of house-to-house ministry that existed during the first century theology of *Yeshua*. A new type of Bible study using the old Hebraic model—a place of accountability and close friendships. A place focused on restoring the community of *Yeshua*. It would serve mega churches well to encourage small home groups in order to provide intimate times of fellowship, worship and accountability to their congregants.

As I prayed for further direction, I started to think about the timeline of the church, while transposing it with my own life experience. I've included this Church History Timeline as an article on my website at VictoriaSarvadi.com, and encourage you to read it and perhaps even discuss it in your own small group setting..

Through all of these prayers, studies, and one-on-one time with Sharon—a true seeker—I began to realize that by ignoring God's calling I had been doing a disservice to Him in not being who He called me to be.

And He called me to seek Him, receive His truth, and teach it.

It's as simple as that.

## Chapter 26
# FOLLOWING THE RABBI

### 𝐻𝑎𝑙𝑙𝑎𝑘𝑎ℎ: Walking with God

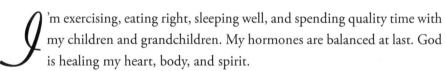

*Many Gentiles will go and say, "Come, let's go up to the mountain of Adonai, to the house of the God of Ya'akov! He will teach us about his ways, and we will walk in his paths." For out of Tziyon will go forth Torah, the word of Adonai from Yerushalayim.*
Micah 4:2 CJB

*I*'m exercising, eating right, sleeping well, and spending quality time with my children and grandchildren. My hormones are balanced at last. God is healing my heart, body, and spirit.

We are all critical links in God's chain—and He has called all of us to share where He has brought us, whether that sharing takes place over the backyard fence, in a carpool, in a corporate board room, in a home-based Bible study, or on the pages of a book. We are all in this world to accomplish His Plan, to advance His Kingdom, and be obedient to His Will. None of this can be done in our own power.

Whatever I accomplish, I just want to hear God say, "Well done my good and faithful servant."

I couldn't shake Sharon's hunger for knowing more about the Jewish Jesus, and how I could best facilitate her growth. One evening as I read a passage of Scripture I'm almost certain I heard God whisper.

"Victoria, are you ready to start that Bible study now?" I literally looked up because it felt He was right in front of me.

Yes. I was ready. In fact, it was aching in me. I was so full of revelations I thought I would explode. God had shown me so much over the past few years, and I felt healed. Healed from the emotional onslaught in my mind, the physical menaces in my body, and the spiritual turmoil that demanded clarity for so long.

Yet, in order to give *Yeshua* true honor and glory, I had to fully recognize and embrace the part I played in the tapestry God was creating. I had to unlearn the "exclusive" modern church model, and relearn the "inclusive" Hebrew model. I had to realize that in God's plan, there is a final scene, and I wanted to be in it, lock, stock, and barrel.

I knew it was critical for me that I completely adopt the first century model and not try and retrofit the model into our Greco-Church institution. Back then, believers met house-to-house. The groups were small. The teaching was Hebraic. This is why it's sometimes difficult to understand the writings of the Apostle Paul. If you don't look at his teachings through the lens of a first century Jewish believer, you will invariably miss it.

I decided to really implement the *"What Jesus Would Do"* philosophy in my life and teach the unadulterated theology of our Messiah, far away from the permutations of all the centuries that came after it. Restoration to the first century was my answer. The model for this type of worship is in the book of Acts.

Sharon's request was granted in the spring of 2008 when our weekly fellowship was founded.

I initially invited some of my adult children, and Sharon invited her friend, Les, and we had a wonderful study.

We started with one of Richard Booker's books *The End of All Things is at Hand, Are You Ready?*[104]

Les came back the next week with his friends, Tracy and Michael. We eventually finished that book and started another. Michael invited his wife, Tawana and her best friend Eunsil. Then, everyone started inviting friends and on and on it went. I couldn't believe it. They kept coming back and bringing more friends. I loved these people. They were truly hungry to embrace the ancient ways of our Lord.

This was the most organic Bible study group I had ever seen.

In a relatively short time, we grew into a sizeable fellowship. These faithful lovers of the Word and servants of God were good, solid, and dedicated people. They were doctors, lawyers, business owners, salespeople, home builders, ministers, clerks and stay-at-home moms. They were male, female, single, married couples, black, white, Hispanic, Asian, Eastern Indian, Filipino, Lebanese, Persian, African, Arab and Jewish. They all had different religious affiliations and came from various denominational backgrounds but they all had one thing in common - they all had a true hunger to understand the teachings of our Jewish Jesus. You see, their identity was no longer attached to a denomination or an ethnicity, but rather to Christ. We are a Holy nation, a peculiar people, all brothers and sisters in the Lord *Yeshua*.

I felt convicted from the start not to take money from anyone in our home fellowship. If someone wants to present a love offering, or anyone in the group wants to give a tithe, it goes straight into the Nathaniel Foundation and then on to the ministries we support. The same goes for all profits from this book— everything goes to the Foundation.

Our home group took on an identity as a true fellowship. Without any of my own planning, without a mission or vision statement, a business plan, or man-made goals, God created His own fellowship of believers, just as He did in the first-century. We became a congregation that does not seek profit or sheer numbers but is simply motivated to press in, to know Him in Spirit and in truth, and to support and encourage one another. We are an assembly that refuses to model itself after Greco-Roman hierarchy or pontification, and everyone contributes along with the teacher as we share a Scripture, testimony or revelation.

## Going Backwards to Move Forward

In a relatively short time, I realized this is what God has been preparing me for all my life. He wants to re-build His temple – stone by stone and person-by-person.

I personally experienced the whole gamut of reformations only to come to a new crossroad. A road that led me all the way *back* to the first-century model of the followers of *Yeshua.*

I realized it really wasn't about reformation at all but rather *restoration.*

It dawned on me that there is no final reformation -because as soon as one reforms, one divides. Going back to a universal church as Constantine the Great enforced is not the answer either. Creating a one-world global religion even if it is based on an aspect of Christianity as Constantine did in the 4th century is the goal of the evil one. Scripture tells us there will be a false prophet that will herald in a religious institution that will ride on a political beast.[105] The great falling away of Christians will happen as a result of this one world effort to unite everyone in religion. There will never be a perfect government until the Messiah comes and sets up His Kingdom and Government. There will never be true peace until He puts away those who challenge Him and His ways. He doesn't need man to take dominion before He comes. He is completely capable of taking dominion and bestowing to His true followers their inheritance. He will restore all things. In fact all creation is groaning and waiting for this time of promise.[106]

And He will remain in Heaven until an appointed time already known and determined by the Father.[107] I realized that I just need to be obedient to the tasks and mission field He has called me to (whether it's big or small). It's His world and His creation and if He wants to He is more than able to even send His angels to witness to those who are seeking no matter how misguided they may be. I don't need to be militant or arrogant. I just need to have faith and get out of the way and let Him build this thing.

And build, He has. Before long, the group wanted to "officially" name our growing fellowship.

"We want to be a part of what Nathaniel has been doing in your life and ministry," they said one evening.

And thus, the Nathaniel Fellowship was born.

We have the Nathaniel Foundation to support the ministries that have answered the call and mandate to bless Israel. We have the Nathaniel Center, a local performing arts and biblical educational facility in Kingwood, TX that houses several churches and ministries, and provides wholesome and often biblically based entertainment to the community. And now, we have the Nathaniel Fellowship, a home Bible study and community of believers that has created in me the true heart of a shepherd.

As a shepherd, I pray God will forever stay my source of power and direction. I heed His warning that a major sign of the End Times will be many false prophets will arise and that deception will be rampant through out the church. I need Him more now than ever as this phenomenon is happening before our eyes.

How we walk daily is important; life is not a parody. Our identity in Christ brings us peace—we don't have to be afraid of whatever comes. I realized that we are all living out God's kingdom plan whether we know it or not. The question then becomes, "What side of prophecy are you on"?

As the Nathaniel Fellowship grew, it was apparent the Lord was crystallizing and spiritually strengthening this small body of believers. The group bonded and grew in so many ways. I reached out to three of my professors, friends, and mentors and asked Dr. Brad Young, Dr. Richard Booker and Dr. John Garr to be adjunct professors to this dedicated assembly. They all agreed to come to our fellowship to teach several times a year. Having ministry partners is imperative.

We follow the same ways and traditions of Yeshua. We meet on the Sabbath and celebrate the feasts. This includes Passover, a *Shavu'ot* (Pentecost) all night prayer watch, Yom Kippor, eight nights of teaching in a *sukka* in my backyard during Tabernacles and *Chanukah* and *Purim* parties.

The *Chanukah* party is a major highlight as Paul and I offer a catered meal with live entertainment and the telling of the "*Chanukah* story" and our miracle working God. We invite neighbors, family, and friends from outside and inside the fellowship. Between eighty and ninety people attend each year in our home.

Our growing group of "Jesus Freaks" are learning to hear the true Master's voice. Yeshua is the only One who restores, and He has gathered us. The Word says *He* will gather, and believe me, it will happen organically even supernaturally.

～

Our Nathaniel Fellowship isn't the only thing growing.

Love is unfolding in miraculous ways in my life, through my blessed and beautiful children and their babies.

August 2008 brought us another wonderful blessing, little Miss Ashtyn Mae Barkley.

Just a week later we fervently prayed and relished thanks upon the Lord for bringing our struggling little Miles Mather Heaton back to health after experiencing a very difficult delivery and week in the NICU.

In April of 2009, Shannon's sixth baby was born. Cute little Ava Michelle Breuer bounded into the world and hasn't stopped since.

My 50th birthday and our 35th wedding anniversary came and went as time flew by.

August 2010 brought us Everett Nicolas Barkley. He is a mini John Paul. So much so that we now call John Paul "Big Everett."

February 2011 brought us grandchild number fifteen, as our Shirley Temple-haired, Eliana Rose Alexander miraculously joined the family and proved to us all once again that even in the most dangerous and scary situations God hears our prayers concerning the safety and healing of difficult deliveries.

Over the years, our company experienced new and positive changes as we added more Human Resources (HR) services and administrative relief options. On the company's 25th anniversary, management decided it was time to change our name from Administaff to Insperity. Continuing to provide access to better benefits and reduced liabilities, Insperity offers a significant range of HR services, including Workforce Optimization®, a system developed by my husband.

Insperity is more successful than we ever dreamed.

God imparted His wisdom and calling so strongly to my husband, and because we listened (and continue to listen,) Paul has become a leader in his industry.

Now, God has been calling me into a season where I feel it's my time to bloom where He has planted me.

And as our family continues to grow, that's exactly what I'm doing. Blooming. And it feels so good.

*Thank you, Jesus- Todah, Yeshua.*[108]

Our beloved children.
Brittany, Shannon, Diana, Wes, Kristen, and Cynthia.
2016

## Chapter 27

# AN AGENDA OF LOVE — WHAT I LEARNED FROM MY CHILDREN

### Mishpochah: Family

*Train a child in the way he should go: and when old, he will not depart from it.*

Proverbs 22:6 KJV

*L*arge families, tribes, and clans were a sign of blessing to the ancient Israelites.

In that tradition, we felt equally blessed.

January 2013 brought us the handsome Brooks Remington Barkley, Kristen and John Paul's fourth child.

Not long after the tragic miscarriage that sent another precious child to heaven, our Diana gave birth in the summer of 2013 to another miracle named Olivia June. We know no child is lost in Christ. And we're thankful for the little ones He entrusts to us.

It was in December 2013 that our youngest and very bright daughter, Brittany graduated from the University of Colorado with a degree in Criminal Justice.

In April 2014 Ariya Jordon Elizabeth Sarvadi, our son's beautiful daughter came bouncing into the world.

It's with great joy I announce that Diana and Zack are finally adding a son to their brood - our number nineteen.

The current score at this time;

Boys = 9

Girls = 10

The word for family is *mishpochah* in Hebrew.

In the Bible, the word *mishpochah* connotes to a strong and dedicated familial connection. The word is also used to describe a household, or a group of people joined together by common ancestry, marriage or contractual agreement. Parents, children, grandchildren and extended relatives all share a responsibility of care and support for one another and are simply connected, whether by genetics or by law.

To "train up a child" isn't just about teaching and disciplining our children in their formative years. It's also about the traditions we build with our children that will become the traditions they pass on to future generations.

As the Lord brought me out of my wilderness, I began to see the legacy of faith we had instilled in our children—and what they, in turn, were instilling in their own children. Family is sacred. My family is my legacy and a continuation of myself. One day when Yeshua comes back as King with His Kingdom, He will join us all together in Him.

The season that God took me out of all my ministry business (and busyness), and placed me firmly back into the lives of my children, and grandchildren saved my life. In that dark season, my children were giving me new life—God was using them to give new blood to a new mama and nana.

I realized that each of my precious children were like guardian angels in my life, placed here by God not only to show me the path to take, but to guide the next generation into a knowledge of *Yeshua* and His love for them. I see wonderful things in all of them. I pray they find their God-given strengths, their own special spiritual gifts to use for His glory, and the peace that passes understanding in their lives.

My children and grandchildren have helped to shape me into the person I have become. Each one represents a feast to my heart and soul.

### Shannon Michelle - My Sacrifice and My Maturity

Having a baby so young, I had to step up to the plate and learn whatever it took to assume the responsible and proper role as a parent. I came to realize that Michelle (later called Shannon) needed me to be everything to her and yet she was also my teacher. The first time she said "Momma" it touched my heart. I happily and willingly said goodbye to my childhood and found that I really loved being a mommy. She has always been so bright and confident. What a beautiful young woman and a fantastic mom she has become. Shannon was the foundation on which I built my role as a mother.

### Little Rodney George - My Grief and My Gift

This child was bittersweet and the turning point of my life. I never knew I could feel so much pain yet feel so close to God. Deciding not to name him Christopher Paul as planned but to instead honor our fathers, Little George made me aware of a whole other dimension to myself. Because of this little one I started my quest for God's truth and purpose for my life. My husband changed too as he realized his need for the Lord in his life which, in turn, helped our strained marriage. Such a short life to accomplish so much! Little George actually opened a spiritual gate for us. I'm so thankful to know that *no child is lost in God*. I look forward to our being together again someday.

### Cynthia Pauline - My Healing and My Trust

This child amazed me. She was a child of promise and prophecy. God is so good to deliver. I have always wanted to develop in myself what came naturally to her. I witnessed her deep spiritual awareness and compassion from the start. She seemed to be entertained by angels, smiling and responding to something I was unable to see as an adult. I admired her care and concern for others, her selflessness and desire to please God. Sweet, tender hearted, soft-spoken yet with a spirit of a powerful warrior, Cynthia remains faithful and dedicated to the Lord and an iconic inspiration to me.

## Diana André - My Surprise and My Laughter

We weren't expecting this child to show up so soon. I looked at my nine month old Cindy and the "positive" in-home pregnancy test with wide-eyed shock. From the very beginning, Diana taught me to laugh and sing. I often watched her shake off rejection and embrace affirmation. Unabashed and loving the limelight, she was our entertainer and our joy. When he returned from a trip, Paul often whispered to her, "You are the one I miss the most." (It was actually the joy she brought us all that he missed). I really appreciated her comic relief to help me erase the stress and disappointments of the day. She is still a burst of sunshine and her beautiful spirit warms my heart.

## Paula Kristen - My Resolution and My Dedication

When Paul finally allowed himself to feel his grief five years after our baby's death, he visited Little George's grave. When he told me this, I suggested the idea of having another child. Kristen was the answer to our prayers. It was during this pregnancy I experienced the power of the Holy Spirit and another level of His Glory. This child has taught me how to press through to the goal. She shines with vision and determination. She received the female version of the name we originally thought Little George was to have. Paula Kristen is the epitome of confidence and drive. She's willing and able, resourceful, capable and always ready to pursue challenges. My little Kristen never quits.

## Paul Westin - My Testing and My Hope

Adopted at four years old, Wes was a faith challenge for me. He kept me on my knees and made me aware of my own weaknesses hidden inside me. He showed me without doubt that perseverance, patience, and trust were my challenged virtues. The pride of a perfect family was replaced by the humbling of a struggling one. I've always believed that Wes would be healed of the issues that challenged his life—and ours. I felt like I entered an intense time of testing myself and I needed God more than ever. Wes has taught me humility and now I rejoice as I see God has blessed him with his own "little family" for the healing of his soul.

## Brittany Elise - My Mercy and My Grace

Adopted as a newborn, Brittany blessed us with wonder and awe. Very independent and absolutely brilliant, as she got older she began to keep many of her thoughts and concerns to herself. Her reserved communication style and desire to be different challenged me. God reminded me that it is His grace that guides us back to Him and it's His mercy that pursues us. I know Brittany fights her own demons and I have learned to give her space. I refused to believe she would venture too far and I trust that God would surely keep her. She has responded to our unconditional love and has taught me the faithful love of the Father. Family is very important to her and I am so thankful for our Brittany.

## A Legacy

We have been chosen by God to be stewards over our children. There is a great responsibility in raising children up in the admonition of the Lord.

The Bible says, Whoever spares the rod hates their children, but the one who loves their children is careful to discipline them (Proverbs 13:24 NIV).

This scripture is often misunderstood by those with a Greco-Roman mindset. We have inappropriately thought that as parents, it means we must "spank our children if we truly love them." This is not what this Word is necessarily instructing us to do.

When shepherds herded their sheep, they used a goad. When a lamb got away from the herd or off the path, the shepherd would use the goad to gently prod the lamb back on the path. At times, the goad may be used a little harder depending on how determined the lamb was to go his own way. The goad was not used to beat the sheep.

Many children who stray away from the biblical family values they were taught when they were young, deal with inner conflict as they live outside the common family identity. My prayer is if my children stray, they will hear the Word of the Lord that has been planted deep in their souls and come back to the truth we taught them. The memory of the Word of God and the power of the Holy Spirit is much more effective than my badgering.

God's Word tells us: Grandchildren are the crown of the aged, while the glory of children is their ancestors (Proverbs 17:6 CJB).

In biblical times, it was common to name children later in life after their personalities were formed. I have studied my nineteen grandchildren, identified their individual character traits, and have given them new names. I've shared these names, along with revelations about ancestry in a *Precious Gems* teaching.[109] If you are a grandparent, I encourage you to read this article and try this exercise yourself.

As I ponder the tribe God has given us, and the legacy that will continue long after I'm gone, I'm overwhelmed with thankfulness. Our wonderful children and grandchildren have witnessed the importance of God, the loyalty of family, and the joy of giving throughout the years.

I long for them to feel secure in their God-given identities, be thankful of their gifts and blessings, and mindful to walk without pride or prejudice. My heart's desire for all my babies is that they walk in humility and selflessness, and to know that true happiness comes from blessing others.

**Jake, Christian, Carter, Tyler, Lauren, Riley**
**Everett, Ashtyn, Grace, Brooks, Victoria, Ava, Paul, Olivia, Eliana, Kate, Julia**
**Joshua and Miles (not shown-Ariya)**

## *Epilogue*
# HOME IS WHERE THE HEART IS

### $\mathcal{S}$halom: God's peace

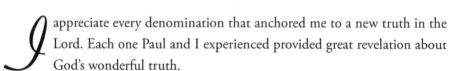

*Don't worry about anything; on the contrary, make your requests
known to God by prayer and petition, with thanksgiving. Then
God's* shalom, *passing all understanding, will keep your hearts
and minds safe in union with the Messiah Yeshua.*
Philippians 4:6,7 CJB

*I* appreciate every denomination that anchored me to a new truth in the
Lord. Each one Paul and I experienced provided great revelation about
God's wonderful truth.

As I passed through various denominations over the years—adding new
revelations to my treasure chest—I often witnessed how denominational
dogma had replaced love and temperance. There were many times I experienced
judgment and boasting from Christians instead of kindness and godliness. God's
Word calls us all to a higher purpose. Not to judge others who don't see God
exactly like we do—as if we have Him all figured out.

The most profound realization I have had in my spiritual journey through the
churches is that I do not *belong* to a denomination—I *belong* to Jesus Christ—to

261

*Yeshua.* We can easily leave a place of worship, but *Yeshua* has built His temple *in* His people, He lives inside of us, never leaving us or forsaking us.

When I began this book, Allison Bottke encouraged me to ask myself some tough questions, and to answer them with as much honesty and transparency as possible. It has been through this journey of asking and answering that I've come to know myself in an unexpected way.

God's gifts and callings for our life are irrevocable. Acquiring and implementing spiritual wisdom and knowledge is the "race" we need to run and *Yeshua*—the Crown of Life—is the trophy achieved at the end of the race.

At first, I really didn't understand the magnitude of my death experience. Throughout the years, as I read and re-read my journal from that moment in time when I hovered over my body and conversed with *Peretz*, I slowly began to fill in the blanks concerning the surreal experience, and even more so the words spoken by this powerful entity. However, the greatest revelation did not come to me until the fall of 2014, shortly before I first sat down with Allison to begin this book.

By that time, I had come to know Messianic Rabbi Y'tzak Shapira, the author of *The Return of the Kosher Pig*.[110] Rabbi Shapira was born into a traditional Sephardic Jewish home in Israel, and found the Messiah after searching the *Hebrew* Scriptures. He has a great deal of respect for Jewish literature, but focuses his argument on where Jesus is revealed as the Messiah within Hebrew Scriptures. His wisdom and insight into the Jewish meanings of Scripture is profound and his enthusiasm about *Yeshua* is electric.

It was such a blessing when Rabbi Shapira accepted an invitation to speak at a Nathaniel Fellowship gathering. After an intense teaching, we were all standing in the kitchen enjoying food and fellowship when he asked me a question. "Victoria, how did you get started in teaching the Jewish roots of our covenant faith in your home?"

"Well, it actually started a long time ago in 1978 when I died and talked to an angel," I said.

The Rabbi, who I had come to know as Itzhak, immediately raised his eyebrows and said, "Really? What did he look like?"

I could tell he was sincerely interested as I smiled at the recollection.

"I will never forget how this angel looked." I said. "His face was like shimmering bronze and so full of light that his features were somewhat skewed—but I recognized him immediately."

"You recognized him?" he asked.

"Yes." I replied. "I saw him when I was a little girl. But I surprised myself when I called him by name. I don't recall ever knowing his name until that moment."

Itzhak leaned in closer and asked, "What was his name?"

The way in which the Rabbi asked made me believe something big was about to be revealed. Maybe there was a Jewish Talmudic story of angels that he was going to relate to my story, or perhaps he knew of an ancient book with the names of various angels.

"His name was *Peretz*."

What happened next still sends chills down my spine as I remember Itzhak's startling reaction.

*"You saw Peretz?!"* he shouted, as he slammed his hand down on the kitchen granite in obvious excitement.

Then, the Rabbi began to quote Scripture from Micah 2:12 (CJB), and my knees literally buckled as he used the Hebrew word *Peretz* instead of the English translation "one breaking through" from the prophet Micah.

"*I* will assemble all of you, Ya'akov;
*I* will gather the remnant of Isra'el,
*I* will put them together like sheep in a pen,
like a herd in its pasture —
it will hum with the sounds of people."
*PERETZ* [The one breaking through] went up before them;
they broke through, passed the gate and went out.
Their king passed on before them;
Adonai was leading them.

Even though I had studied this scripture in great detail in one of Dr. Brad Young's classes, it never occurred to me that the Angel of the Lord, (*Peretz*) would have a function of gathering people out of the evil system of man, including "the political business of *church*" in order to preserve them from the coming apostasy of the church and the evil deception coming on the whole world.[111] I know Scripture proclaims that at the end of the present age, the angels will go out and separate the evil people from the righteous people.

For some reason, I never equated *my Peretz* with *the Peretz*. I was stunned by the connection the Rabbi was making.

My hands began to shake, and I could only stutter at first.

"Wh—wh—what are you saying?" I stammered. "You think I actually spoke to Messiah?"

"I *know* you spoke to Messiah! It all makes perfect sense now. You—this group—what *Yeshua* is doing here…" He waved his arm at our group as he beamed from ear-to-ear. "Perfect sense!"

However, the heaviness of this revelation made me weep in the days to come.

I thought of Abraham and Sarah, who were visited by three angels and one of them was the Angel of the Lord, who informed them they were going to have a child. A child of promise. *I related to that.* I thought of the Angel of the Lord that wrestled with Jacob all night and the angels ascending and descending on a heavenly ladder. *Just like Nathaniel,* I thought. I recalled Gideon, who as the youngest in his family conversed with the Angel of the Lord under the pistachio tree. The Angel informed him that the Lord was going to give him victory over the whole Midian army. I recalled myself as a little girl who learned about Jesus from my friend Ricky under a shade tree.

It was overwhelming—and humbling.

Later that evening, the Voice of the Lord rang in my ears as He spoke plainly in my spirit a rather curious version of the Scripture Rabbi Shapira had quoted earlier that evening. A text that mirrored the message but in a new and personal way. It was confirmation to my spirit when I looked at my version side-by-side to the actual Scripture.

**Micah 2:12 (CJB)**

"I will assemble all of you, Ya'akov;

I will gather the remnant of Isra'el,

I will put them together like sheep in a pen,

like a herd in its pasture —

it will hum with the sounds of people."

*PERETZ* [the one breaking through] went up before them;

they broke through, passed the gate and went out.

Their king passed on before them;

Adonai was leading them.

**The version given to me by the Lord**

I am assembling Abraham's descendants.

I have gathered a remnant of them. Do you not see them before you?

I have placed those that are in right standing in pens of safety from wolves.

I fence them in a place where they will be taken care of through times of testing.

Those places will sound with the praises of those who have chosen Me and have called out to Me. Do you not hear them in your own ears?

I will break through the barriers of spiritual fog, Greco-Roman thought and practices.

It is then, they will see and be able to leave the beast system as you did.

Have no fear. I will help you lead them.

*Had I really seen the Messiah on the day I died? Had He really told me I was to seek knowledge to share with His sheep for this appointed time? Could He really be using me (as He is using others who are being called in this new season) to help Him pasture His sheep for a greater cause?* As these questions flooded my spirit, I said to the Lord once again, "But God, who am I that you would appear to me? I'm just a little girl."

He immediately led me to the prophet Jeremiah, where I read the words in awe.[112]

In the first chapter of Jeremiah, the Lord came to the prophet and told him, "Before I formed you in the womb, I knew you; before you were born, I separated you for myself. I have appointed you to be a prophet to the nations." Upon hearing this, Jeremiah exclaimed, "… Lord, I don't even know how to speak! I'm just a child!"

Wow…I could surely relate to Jeremiah's confusion. However, the Lord's response shook me.

"Don't say, 'I'm just a child.' For you will go to whomever I send you, and you will speak whatever I order you. Do not be afraid of them, for I am with you and I will rescue you." At that point, the Lord put out his hand and touched Jeremiah's mouth and said, "There! I have put my words in your mouth. Today I have placed you over nations and kingdoms to uproot and to tear down, to destroy and to demolish, to build and to plant."

The questions that previously flooded my spirit were answered in a miraculous way by this Scripture. I couldn't argue with the fact that in my own life, He truly has put His Words in my mouth—many times.

When I died in 1978, God placed a calling on my life. God saw me for who I really was, not for who my earthly father said I was. God gave me a mandate for what He wanted me to do and my ongoing life-purpose has been to carry out that mandate—that calling.

My desire is to instill a hunger in my brothers and sisters to be more informed about denominational beliefs and choices, which in the big picture may seem unimportant. However, the truth is, we need to know Him in His true context, before man changed the perception of His culture, traditions, and *hallachah (ways)*. We can only find true peace in life when we lift the fog—the filter—of spiritual amnesia that keeps us from knowing God's truth.

As the Lord swings wide the door to share this intimate story of my life, my ultimate desire is to encourage others to grow closer to Jesus/*Yeshua*—the Messiah. To boldly *walk* in God's will and purpose for their lives.

Over the year it's taken to write this book, I've learned the underlying foundation of memoir is not a lecture, a lesson, or a rich and bubbly stew of information and facts.

It's about personal truth, vulnerability, and transparency.

It's not by my power or understanding that I function from day to day but rather by yielding to His Spirit in me to give me discernment, divine health, knowledge, counsel, and the strength to overcome the daily weakness of my flesh.

Happiness is achieved when a person is doing what they are called to do. Finding my peace came in finding my purpose. I've learned I must give of myself as *Yeshua* gave Himself. Every believer has their own personal spiritual story. Thank you for allowing me to share mine.

Looking back, Paul didn't marry a Hebrew scholar, and I didn't marry a corporate CEO, but we have supported and loved each other as we have walked into our respective places of destiny and calling.

My husband has always been behind me as I took risks and made choices. And I have applauded and supported him in turn, as he reached for the stars in skies filled with opportunities. Together, we have built a solid legacy with God as our foundation.

As this manuscript was in its editing stages, we made another pilgrimage to Israel. Once again, we visited for Sukkot, and I was given an opportunity to speak at the Segal's Sukkot conference.

Although I was in Israel to speak at the conference, my main desire was to declare to the Jewish people that I have good news—and that is, "Your King is coming!"

Tens of thousands of Israeli Jews were on the sidelines of the Parade of Nations that day when I (along with 15,000 other Christians from all over the world) proclaimed, *"Your King is coming and His salvation is with Him!"* Many nodded and acknowledged me.

There was a time when I worried about not being taken seriously. A time when being just a little girl meant being seen and not heard.

That time has passed.

Today, there is nothing but thankfulness to prove.

Adonai said to Jeremiah, "Do not say I'm just a child." Those words touch me in a special way in this season of my life. And I know in one sense I am definitely not a child, but strong and capable to do all things through Christ, who lives through me. But I also know that to my Heavenly Father, I will always be His daughter, just a little girl who loves Him with a profound passion and purpose. Just a little girl whose mouth He has touched and whose heart He controls. Just a little girl who goes wherever He tells me to go, and speaks whatever He orders me to speak—and you know what? At long last, I'm good with that.

Home really is where the heart is, and my heart belongs to my Father—my Abba—my *Yeshua*. And it doesn't get any better than that.

Shalom to you, dear reader, and to God be all the glory!

**Paul and Victoria Sarvadi**     *Photo by Paul Lester*

# AFTERWORD

By: Brad H. Young, Ph.D.

Dr. Victoria Sarvadi's riveting life's story is a page turner that one would want to read in one sitting because it's hard to put the book down. As a little girl, her (what many would call a male chauvinist) father, belittled her often and discouraged her from achieving goals that he perceived as too lofty. Victoria, however, took opportunities and made the best of them. The book details a spiritual journey that has followed a path to immense joy, educational achievement, personal success, and esteemed community service to others. Today, Victoria is not only an accomplished scholar but also a generous philanthropist. Without a doubt Victoria and her husband Paul have achieved considerable material wealth. But Victoria's true wealth is discovered in her spiritual awakening, the love within her family, her relationships with friends, and her selfless service to others. The book challenges the readers to follow her spiritual journey to life transformation as she shares her life's wisdom. Her personal experience gives insightful perspective that enables and empowers her readers. What a reader learns from studying this book will open doors of opportunity that may have seemed locked and securely closed.

The death of a child causes intense personal grief and suffering. Probably no pain surpasses the hurt of losing a child. When a parent dies, an individual loses the past but when a child dies, a person loses the future. Any mother who loses a baby is overcome with a great sense of loss, as was Victoria when she lost her baby boy in death. On top of this tragedy, she went through her own near death experience, which changed the trajectory of her life. As a Lutheran, she was grounded in a historic spiritual heritage. But, as meaningful as that heritage was for one stage of Victoria's spiritual journey, it was not sufficient to help her deal with the grief she experienced when she lost her child. Lutheran doctrine taught that a baby who dies without baptism is forever separated from God in Hell. This doctrine seemed right when it was taught in the church setting, but seemed so wrong in real life experience and then later when it was studied in Scripture. When Victoria died she experienced a revelation of incredible hope. Her death experience showed her that her son lives forever in the joy of God's presence. Often the death of a child fractures the fragile nature of marriage but this new path placed value on family, friends, and relationships and Paul and Victoria discovered a way through their intense pain to strengthen their relationship with one another. A new direction for her life would lead to meaning and fulfillment. Her encounter with death makes every reader aware of his or her life's mission. Each day counts and every day of life is a gift. Everyone needs wisdom to find and to fulfill that calling.

Coming out of the Lutheran stage of her spiritual walk brought her into the Baptist Church. The Baptist denomination placed value on biblical teachings and provided a strong evangelical perspective. But it stopped short of fulfilling the longing of her heart. She wanted a personal relationship with God that would give strength, wisdom, and guidance in the struggles of everyday living. She entered a new stage by discovering the Spirit-filled renewal movement. Lutherans mention the Holy Spirit in the prayers of the liturgy or in reciting the Apostle's Creed. But the Lutherans do not always seek a deeper awareness of the Holy Spirit in daily life. Baptists speak about the Holy Spirit in accepting Christ but typically do not acknowledge a deeper experience of the Holy Spirit for daily discipleship and the equipping of ministry. The Holy Spirit creates awareness of the divine presence and the manifestation of the supernatural. Victoria experienced the power of the Holy Spirit directly as a wife, a mother, and a highly respected leader in the community. She discovered that God hears and answers prayers. Her experience with the Holy Spirit not only brought inner joy and serenity but also made her aware of a calling to help other people. The presence of the Holy Spirit brings healing for the body and the soul. She could pray and believe for the healing of the heart of her newborn baby girl and no surgery was necessary. James Martin had it right when he observed, "So joy is not a selfish thing to seek but a selfless thing to find."

Even though Victoria's life with Paul became filled with fun, laughter, travel, and meaningful relationships with family and friends; something was still missing. The eminent Jewish teacher from the time of Jesus, Hillel the Elder taught, "The one who does not learn forfeits his or her life." The esteemed rabbi Louis Finkelstein observed that when you pray you talk to God, but when you study God talks to you As a serious disciple of Bible and theology Victoria discovered the indisputable fact that Jesus was not a Christian! Jesus was Jewish. Christians often misunderstand Jesus because they do not understand Judaism. The authentic context for Jesus's life is Israel and the Jewish family. Pope John Paul II said it well, "Whoever meets Jesus meets Judaism." Jesus was a Jew. Jesus never changed religions. Victoria immersed herself in the study of Jewish wisdom and the authentic foundation of her sincere faith experience.

This kind of wisdom flows from a spiritual impartation. This characteristic of prophetic insight flows from a rich inner life of study and personal commitment. Not only has she been able to study the words of Jesus in the authentic Jewish context with prophetic awareness, but also she has been able to travel to Israel numerous times to discover the original biblical setting through archaeology, history, and culture. Israel makes the Bible come alive. She spends time in the land of the Bible, learning Hebrew, and discovering fresh perspectives. Victoria's openness to learning and her willingness to share her discoveries has made her a natural leader. Many benefit from learning her insightful teachings. Her spiritual gifts flow naturally from a sincere heart and a sound mind. She is not satisfied with easy answers that impede true scholarly reflection. She is a scholar of Bible and theology. Her impeccable scholarship challenges the politically correct demands that obscure multifaceted issues. She sees the larger problems from a spiritual vantage point with wisdom and precision. She is grounded in the teachings of Jesus and the Jewish roots of Christian faith experience.

The revered Jewish scholar Abraham Joshua Heschel declared, "The world is not a vacuum. Either we make it an altar for God or it is invaded by demons. There can be no neutrality." In today's world of sound bites, social media, wise crack tweets, internet downloads, and constant advertising for endless lines of new and wonderful products - it is difficult to imagine a vacuum anywhere in the world. Many, however, intuitively know that something very important is missing in their lives. This empty void is a spiritual vacuum in the human soul that can become completely devoid of joy and meaning. As the media and educators celebrate neutrality and freedom from religion the human condition worsens. Lives without spiritual learning and discipline as well as active involvement in helping others are soon invaded by demons of indifference and self-gratification. Many celebrities idolized in today's society are public successes troubled by private failures and personal agony. Victoria's spiritual journey offers an alternative. She changed her world by following the path of Jesus in Jewish discipleship and in returning to the model of the early church in the book of Acts. She is leading others in the way of spiritual transformation for a meaningful life well lived. Victoria leads by example and her story is filled with hope.

If just a little girl can achieve a meaningful life with public success and personal happiness maybe there is genuine possibility for anyone else who is willing to learn from her experiences. This book is a must read that will be widely distributed. Every time someone reads this book new insights and fresh ideas for spiritual growth and personal success jump off the page. Friends will share this book with friends. Many will read Victoria's story again and again. The timeless message has immediate practical application. A reader can discover a path to the realization of a dream. A career aspiration is attainable. A relationship can be healed and restored. True applied wisdom will lead to financial sustainability and success. Jesus taught, "All things are possible to the one who believes." Victoria's exciting story challenges the reader to believe.

# ABOUT THE AUTHOR

Dr. Victoria Sarvadi received her Th.M. and Th.D. in 2005 from the former Center for the Study of Biblical Research in Glendora, California, accredited at the time by the University of the State of California. A certified minister in the Hebraic Christian Global Community since 2000, she is a frequent contributor to *Restore!* Magazine, a publication of the HCGC. She has been a speaker for conferences, congregations, women's ministry groups, Bible studies, and at the *Vision for Israel Sukkot Conferences* in Jerusalem, Israel. As a featured guest on national and international radio and television programs, her appearances on both the Crossover Program and Brad TV have been seen worldwide. Her *Precious Gems* teachings on the Jewish roots of Christianity have appeared in numerous publications and will soon be available online at VictoriaSarvadi.com. She has six children, nineteen grandchildren, and is married to Paul Sarvadi, Chairman, CEO, and Co-Founder of Insperity, Inc., a world leader in business and human resources services based in Kingwood, Texas. As co-founders of the Nathaniel Foundation, the Sarvadis philanthropic contributions support numerous charities in the U.S. and abroad. All proceeds from *Just a Little Girl* will fund the Nathaniel Foundation.

## About the Editor

Allison Bottke is the bestselling author of 30+ books, including the *God Allows U-Turns* anthology and the award winning *Setting Boundaries* book series from Harvest House Publishers. A self-proclaimed, "Memoir Midwife," she works with a limited number of private clients every year to help give birth to compelling works of inspirational narrative non-fiction. For more information visit AllisonBottke.com or SettingBoundariesBooks.com.

# ENDNOTES

## Prologue

1

2    See *What Happened to Judah's Brothers?* at VictoriaSarvadi.com

3    1 Kings 11:31-36

4    https://en.wikipedia.org/wiki/Aliyah

5    See *Connecting to the Land* at VictoriaSarvadi.com

6    Visit NathanielCenter.com

7    Isaiah 42:6,7, also see *The Light to the Nations* at VictoriaSarvadi.com

8    Visit VisionForIsrael.com

## Chapter 2

9    See *The Bible in Dynamic Tension* at VictoriaSarvadi.com

## Chapter 3

10    Ephesians 2:8-9 (NIV)

## Chapter 7

11    Daniel 9:25-26, Matthew 3:13-17

12    Matthew 7:7

13    See *What is Grace* at VictoriaSarvadi.com

14    See *The Mikveh* at VictoriaSarvadi.com

15    Luke 24:44-49

16    1 Corinthians 12: 7, Galatians 5:22-23

17    See *Intercession and Prayer* and *Fasting* at VictoriaSarvadi.com

18    https://www.Aglow.org

## Chapter 8

19    See *Filled With The Spirit-A Burnt Offering* at VictoriaSarvadi.com

20    Matthew 3:1-13

21    James 2:19

22    Numbers 6:24-27, Revelations 3:12, Revelations 14:1, Revelations 22:4

23    Gifts of the Spirit – 1 Corinthians 12:7-11 and Fruit of the Spirit – Galatians 5:22

24    Philippians 4:13

25    https://en.wikipedia.org/wiki/Dispensationalism

26    Acts 2:1-4

## Chapter 9

27    Romans 2:13-15

28    Acts 17:4

29    Joel 2:28,29, Acts 2:17-18, John 7:38-39

30    John 16:7

31    John 14:12

32    2 Corinthians 1:21-22

33    See *Tithing* at VictoriaSarvadi.com

34    See article -*PARDS, The Four Levels of Meaning in Scripture* at VictoriaSarvadi.com

## Chapter 10

35    Joel 2:25

36    2 Timothy 3:16-17

37   Hebrews 13:8

38   Luke 22:15

39   1 Corinthians 11:23-26

40   See article *The Birth of the Greco-Roman Church* at VictoriaSarvadi.com

41   Jeremiah 6:16 (NIV)

## Chapter 11

42   http://www.Depelchin.org

43   Deuteronomy 8:18

44   *What Would Jesus Do* was originally published in 1896 by Chicago Advance publishing house as *In His Steps.* The novel has sold over 30,000,000 copies and is considered one of the best-selling books of all time.

## Chapter 12

45   See article *Christianity's Hidden Foundation at* VictoriaSarvadi.com

46   Visit RBooker.com

47   See *Learning His Ways* at VictoriaSarvadi.com

48   *Jesus the Jewish Theologian was published in 1995 by Hendrickson Publishers*

49   Hebrew idioms - taking away your bow means taking away your strength; One who has a good eye means one is generous.

50   Deuteronomy 22:12

51   Matthew 9:20 (CJB)

52   Ephesians 5:18

53   https://www.youtube.com/watch?v=2X1HC-3s3uI

54   Mark 10:25

## Chapter 14

55   http://shop.SoundsoftheTrumpet.com/?page_id=435

## Chapter 15

56   Leviticus 23:33-43

57   http://www.HineniMinistries.org/

58  http://www.JewishVoice.org

59  http://www.Settel.org

60  http://www.MauriceSklar.com

61  https://www.youtube.com/watch?v=5ddaOz9F6u0

62  https://www.HebraicCommunity.org

63  https://www.WilburMinistries.com

64  http://www.JerusalemPerspective.com/author/brad-young/

65  http://JCstudies.com

66  http://www.csbr.net

67  http://www.SongofIsrael.com

68  http://DefendProclaimtheFaith.org/blog/

69  http://www.TheJosephExperience.com

70  http://www.BridgesForPeace.com/us/

71  Romans 2:29

72  See article *The Unholy Trinity* at VictoriaSarvadi.com

## Chapter 16

73  See article, *The Kingdom of God at* VictoriaSarvadi.com

74  1 Kings 18

## Chapter 17

75  Joshua 5:6

76  Genesis 7:12

77  Acts 7:30

78  Exodus 24:18

79  Numbers 13:25

80  Acts 1:2,3

81  Hebrews 9:28

82  See *Watching and Waiting for His Return at* VictoriaSarvadi.com

83  http://time.com/3645828/y2k-look-back/

84  http://www.hebraiccenter.org/portal/web/guest/home; http://shuvu.tv

## Chapter 18

85   Zechariah 2:8

86   http://www.cornerstone-ranch.com

87   http://www.NathanielCenter.com

## Chapter 19

88   2 Corinthians 12:7

89   Genesis 32

## Chapter 20

90   Psalms 116:15 KJV, Hebrews 9:27 KJV

## Chapter 23

91   Matthew. 6:21

92   Matthew. 3:1, Mark 1:3

93   Galatians 1:11-12, 17-18

94   Luke 3:21-22

95   … from the issuing of a decree to restore and rebuild Jerusalem until Messiah the Prince…

96   Luke 4:1-2

## Chapter 24

97   http://www.dallasalternativemedicine.com

98   https://www.marpewellness.com

99   See *What is Shabbat?* at VictoriaSarvadi.com

## Chapter 25

100  See *How the Torah relates to Christianity* at VictoriaSarvadi.com

101  Revelations 13:8

102  1 Corinthians 10:4

103  Daniel 12:8-10

## Chapter 26

104 RBooker.com

105 Revelation 13, 17

106 Romans 8:21,22

107 Acts 3:19-21

108 Thank you (In Hebrew)

## Chapter 27

109 See *The Jewels in My Crown* at VictoriaSarvadi.com

## Chapter 28

110 http://www.kosherpig.org/

111 2 Thessalonians 2:3 and Revelation 12:9

112 Jeremiah 1:4-10 (CJB) paraphrased by author

Printed in the USA
CPSIA information can be obtained
at www.ICGtesting.com
JSHW022212140824
68134JS00018B/1005